THE
INVISIBLE
WOUND

THE INVISIBLE WOUND

A New Approach to
Healing Childhood
Sexual Abuse

WAYNE KRITSBERG

BANTAM BOOKS
NEW YORK   TORONTO   LONDON   SYDNEY   AUCKLAND

THE INVISIBLE WOUND
A Bantam Book / January 1993

The examples used in this book are based upon actual case histories of survivors of childhood sexual trauma. In order to insure privacy and confidentiality, I have either changed the names of the persons in the examples or have created composites of case histories.

Book design by Irving Perkins Associates, Inc.
Illustrations by Aher/Donnell Studios.
Technical illustrations by Patrice Fodero.

Library of Congress Cataloging-in-Publication Data

Kritsberg, Wayne, 1942–
    The invisible wound : a new approach to healing child-
hood sexual abuse / Wayne Kritsberg.
        p.   cm.
    Includes bibliographical references (p.   ) and index.
    ISBN 0-553-08984-6
    1. Adult child sexual abuse victims—Counseling of.
2. Adult child sexual abuse victims—United States—Case
studies.   I. Title.
HV6570.K75   1992
362.7′64—dc20   92-20158
                                                              CIP

Published simultaneously in the United States and Canada

Bantam Books are published by Bantam Books, a division of Bantam Doubleday Dell Publishing Group, Inc. Its trademark, consisting of the words "Bantam Books" and the portrayal of a rooster, is Registered in U.S. Patent and Trademark Office and in other countries. Marca Registrada. Bantam Books, 666 Fifth Avenue, New York, New York 10103.

PRINTED IN THE UNITED STATES OF AMERICA

BVG   0 9 8 7 6 5 4 3 2 1

*This book is dedicated
to the survivors of childhood sexual abuse:
women, men, and children—both those who are healing
and those who are waiting to heal.*

The sexual instincts are the most malleable of any instincts. Let them be repressed, let their direct aim be denied them, and they will soon assume unrecognizable forms, from the depth of vice to the highest exaltation of art and religion.

—ROBERT BRIFFAULT
The Mothers

Contents

Acknowledgments   xv

Introduction   xvii

PART ONE:
THE WOUNDED HEART

1 What Is Child Sexual Abuse?   3
"Not Guilty"   4
Myths and Realities   8
Who Commits Child Sexual Abuse?   9
    Family Members   10
        Kate's Story
        John's Story
        Gloria's Story
    Acquaintances   16
        Carol's Story
        Jean's Story
    Strangers   19
        Don's Story
    The Accomplice   21

2 Categories of Child Sexual Abuse   23
This is a memory-jogging chapter for adult survivors.
        Brenda's Story

Physical Sexual Abuse   25
    Common Physical Sexual Abuses   25
    Violent Physical Sexual Abuse   29
        Brad's Story
    Seductive Physical Sexual Abuse   34
        Paula's Story
Emotional Sexual Abuse   38
    Violent Emotional Sexual Abuse   39
        Carla's Story
    Seductive Emotional Sexual Abuse   40
Combined Physical and Emotional Sexual Abuse   42

3   Living with Secrets: The Effects of Childhood
    Sexual Trauma   43
        Alan's Story
    The Traumatization Process   44
        The Child   45
        Sexual Trauma   46
        Shock State   46
        Inability to Resolve the Trauma   47
        The Core Defenses   48
    Survival Living   54
        The Tensions of Survival Living   54
        Secondary Consequences   56

PART TWO:
HEALING AND RECOVERY

4   Recovery: An Unfolding Process   75
    The Three Stages of Recovery   75
        Stage One: Discovery   77
        Stage Two: Active Healing   79
        Stage Three: Integration   80
            Laura's Story
    The Whole Person   84
        Windows to the Past   84
        The Body   85
            How the body "remembers" trauma

The Emotions   86
    Although fragmentary, "emotional memories" shed
    light for survivors trying to piece together a history.
The Mind   88
    Cognitive memories: With or without them, survivors
    can heal.
The Spirit   90
    Untouched by trauma, the spirit stands free.

5   **The Experience of Healing**   92
The Healing Cycle   92
    Recovery is nonlinear, occurring in a series of
    cycles. Each healing cycle involves:
    1. Exposing the Wound   93
    2. Reexperiencing the Trauma   95
    3. Externalizing the Pain   95
    4. Healing the Wound   96
    Jenny's Story
Working with Healing Cycles   102

6   **Healing Your Inner Child**   104
By meeting this small one within, a survivor
encounters compassion, close to home.
The Wounded Child   104
The Magical Child   107
Finding Your Inner Child   110
    "The Gift of the Star"   110
Parenting Your Inner Child   113

7   **Healing Energy**   116
By using healing energy, survivors are empowered
to become active participants in their own recovery.
Releasing the Energy of Held Pain   117
Healing Energy Meditations   125
    Earth Healing   126
        Women's Meditation   126
        Men's Meditation   128
    The Blue Sphere   130
Directing Healing Energy to Other Parts of Your Body   132
    The Energy Chalice   133

Healing Touch   134
    Healing Touch and Your Boundaries   134
    Healing Touch and Energy in a Group Setting   136
A Healing Circle   138

8   **A Safe Place**   139
Finding a Therapist   140
    Some suggestions for interviewing and choosing
    someone who can guide you through recovery.
Treatment Options   144
    Individual Therapy   144
    Group Therapy   145
    Treatment Programs   145
    Treatment Intensives   146
    Psychiatric Drugs   147
    Support Groups   148
Your Sexual Relationship   148
Parenting   151
Your Family of Origin   154
    Confrontation   155
Your Family of Choice   157
The Temple of the Heart   158

PART THREE:
THE HEALING JOURNAL
Writing your way to wholeness

9   **Keeping a Healing Journal**   163
Setting Up the Journal   166

10 **Daily Expressions**   168
A log of your day-to-day experience in recovery.

11 **Family History**   170
The Family Tree   170
Family Environment   173

12 **Family Members**   175
Letter Writing   178
Dialoguing   179

13 Personal History 182
Milestones 183
Your Sexual History 186
Writing About the Sexual Abuse Incidents 187

14 My Body 191
Dialoguing with Your Body 192
Creative Coloring and Artwork 195

15 Self-discovery 197
Self-description 197
Through the Eyes of Others . . . 199
Feelings Responses 199
Feelings Statements 201

16 Welcoming the Inner Child 205
Letter Writing 206
Dialoguing with the Inner Child 208

17 Dreams 212

18 The Abuser(s) 216
Letter Writing 217

19 Affirmations for Healing 219
Creating and Using Affirmations 220

20 Spiritual Reflections 223
Letter Writing 224
Spiritual Exploration 224
Forgiveness 225

21 Integration 227
Experiencing Healing and Moving On

22 Some Questions and Thoughts 231
In Closing . . . 237
Bibliography and Resources 238
Index 247

Acknowledgments

I would like to thank all the survivors whose courage allowed them to confide in me, and all those who generously provided the journal material, personal stories, poetry, and artwork contained in this book. Their determination to return to themselves, to experience the whole of life, has been nothing short of inspirational. This book is only one part of their legacy to the many who still seek to recover from childhood sexual abuse.

Many colleagues offered invaluable professional input and loving support during the writing of this manuscript. To them a heartfelt thanks, especially to Carl Kirsch, M.D., of Austin, Texas, and David Reynolds, Ph.D., of Olympia, Washington.

Thanks to my mother, who has always supported my work and my recovery.

Thanks also to Toni Burbank, my editor at Bantam Books, whose ideas and insights were integral to the shaping of the final book.

A special thanks and appreciation must go to my wife Ceci Miller-Kritsberg, a poet and writer. She spent long hours editing the manuscript and offered valuable thoughts and ideas. Ceci's contribution, however, goes beyond the writing. Her loving support and personal spiritual commitment gave me strength when I was discouraged. It took over five years to write *The Invisible Wound*, and Ceci was in on it from the beginning. Without her this book might not have been written at all. Thank you, Ceci, from my heart.

I thank my Higher Power for the gift of my healing, and for the unconditional love and guidance I have received throughout my life.

Introduction

It was never my intention to work with survivors of childhood sexual trauma. When I began my professional career as a therapist in the midseventies I, like many other therapists, had little knowledge of the extent of childhood sexual abuse in our society. That began to change as I worked in a variety of public mental health programs and medical settings, where I received intensive training for work with survivors of rape and other kinds of sexual assault. During this time I had begun to identify Adult Children of Alcoholics (ACOA's) as a special population with special needs, and I focused my clinical work in that direction. Working with ACOA's, I began to discover that some of my clients had been sexually abused as children.

When I searched around the professional community where I lived, I found there were very few services available to meet the specific needs of survivors of childhood sexual abuse. So I continued to work with these clients, focusing on their sexual abuse issues in the context of the ACOA group experience. As I began to work with one or two identified sexual abuse survivors in these six-person ACOA groups, an odd thing happened. Other group members began to remember their own childhood experiences of sexual abuse. Within a short time, my groups became dominated by sexual trauma survivors. I was amazed, and I wondered if my experience was unique.

In the early 1980s I began traveling around the country quite a bit, lecturing and giving workshops on ACOA issues. Participants would often share with me their sexual abuse history. I soon realized that there were vast numbers of people who had survived sexual molestation as children. The more I heard from people at the workshops and the more I learned from clients in my practice, the more convinced I became that I was seeing only the tip of an enormous iceberg. This indeed has been the case. Over the years I have watched as researchers raised the estimated population of sexual abuse survivors to greater and greater numbers.

How is it possible that such deep wounding of human beings was overlooked for so long? The answer is simple: The wound is invisible. Most survivors carry no outward signs that they have been sexually traumatized, other than "blank spots" in their memory to cover the painful event. Add to that the survivor's denial and repressed emotions and our society's collective denial of a taboo subject, and the wound of childhood sexual abuse recedes quickly into the shadows. When I studied psychology in the early sixties, I was given the impression that child sexual abuse was almost nonexistent. Since that time our aware-ness has grown, and along with it our sense of a human problem far out of control. We now know that more than "just a few" children are sexually abused, and that survivors are men as well as women. I believe that in the 1990s, child sexual abuse will emerge as a primary issue of concern for both men and women, with far-reaching implications for our society as a whole.

This book is written for the survivor of childhood sexual abuse. Although friends of survivors, family members, and therapists may also find this material useful, I want to speak directly to you, the survivor. You are the one who is in pain. You are the one seeking a way out of your suffering. It is my hope that the information and ideas presented here will offer you a pathway out of your difficult past, introducing you to the abused child you once were and to the magical child who waits to show you the mystery of your own great inner beauty.

This book is for you if you know you have been sexually abused as a child, if you have ever wondered whether you were sexually abused in childhood, if you have a family member who was sexually abused as a child, or if you are the friend or lover of a survivor of childhood sexual abuse. This book is also for teachers, therapists, clergy, social workers, and community health professionals. It is for anyone likely to come into contact with someone who suffered sexual abuse as a child—in this respect, it is for everyone. If you think you may be a survivor of child sexual abuse but you have few or no specific memories of having been molested, this book will be useful to you in sorting out your experience and retrieving any memories you may have repressed.

This book is for both men and women. While our society tends to view male and female survivors of sexual abuse differently, any child who is sexually molested has been traumatized. The healing of this childhood trauma is essentially the same for both sexes. Throughout this book are the stories of both women and men survivors recovering from childhood sexual trauma. While the details of their abuse may vary, in every case the courage of these survivors is remarkable. Man or woman, rich, poor, or middle-class, mainstream or minority, each one of them has gone back to the frightening past, sifted its contents, and found their inner gold: a new strength and a new experience of wholeness.

Some people advocate same-sex support groups for healing, while others feel that coed support groups are more effective. I believe that each individual survivor will find exactly what is needed for healing to take place. You will make the choice as to where your healing can best occur. Some of my clients started out in same-sex therapy and support groups and remained there, some moved to coed groups, and some started in a coed group and stayed there. Each of them discovered what worked best. My role here is simply to offer options and support.

The information presented in this book is based on my clinical experience, my direct involvement with my clients. This is not a research document. The techniques described here have all been used successfully in the therapy groups I facilitate for survivors of childhood sexual trauma. I have also used many of these techniques myself as part of my own ongoing recovery from childhood trauma. I know both the pain and the joy of deep healing.

In recent years it has become common for many survivors of childhood sexual abuse to be diagnosed with a condition called post traumatic stress disorder (PTSD). Although I do not take issue with this term, I chose not to delve into the subject of PTSD here. Because this book is written for the survivor, not the clinician, I felt that the less labeling and generalization, the better. However, in support groups and elsewhere, you may hear references to PTSD in the context of clinical treatment for childhood sexual abuse. For further information about PTSD, it is probably best to refer to a qualified therapist (see Chapter 8, Finding a Therapist).

The book is divided into three parts.

Part One, The Wounded Heart, describes the nature of child sexual abuse and some of the effects it may have had on your life. This part is designed to trigger repressed memories, so as you read it you may experience "new" or additional memories of the sexual abuse, as well as intense emotions. If this happens, stop reading for a moment (or longer) and take a few deep breaths. This is strong stuff. Don't push yourself to finish the book in one sitting. If you find you are becoming overwhelmed and panicky, and if you don't belong to a support group, I would strongly suggest turning to the "Bibliography and Resources" at the end of the book and calling one of the crisis numbers listed there. This way, you will be able to speak directly to someone who understands your difficulty. Then, when you are able to collect your thoughts, you can begin taking action to join a survivors' support group or therapy group. If you already belong to a group, remain in close contact with these people. They can help you cross the bridge from the unfolding darkness of your past to the strong survivor you are becoming. Reading this book alone cannot accomplish the intricate process of your recovery from sexual trauma. Breaking your silence, telling your experience to others, is absolutely necessary.

Part Two, Healing and Recovery, gives an account of each stage of the healing process and of the elements essential to real and lasting recovery from childhood sexual abuse. Here you will be introduced to the active part of the process, as you observe the progress of recovering survivors through their personal stories. (All survivors are referred to by pseudonyms.) This part of the book explains how the physical body is affected by denial and introduces techniques you can use to become an active participant in your own recovery. Exercises given in Part Two include guided imagery and the use of focused awareness and energy in healing your invisible wounds. Recovery from abuse is an "inside job"—the more you learn about how your body and personal energy have been affected by the abuse, the better you will be able to cooperate with the natural process of healing.

Part Three, The Healing Journal, guides you through a step-by-step journal-writing process designed specifically for survivors of child sexual abuse. The journal creates a place for you to explore and discover your history and your feelings about it. As you read excerpts from the journals of other recovering survivors, you'll learn a variety of writing techniques you can use to fuel your own recovery. If you like, you can begin the experiential part of our work right away by reading Part Three, The Healing Journal, before you begin Part One. Once you have set up your journal based on the directions given, you will have a place to record your feelings and reactions as you read the rest of this book.

The Invisible Wound is written from my point of view as an involved counselor, and is addressed to you, the survivor. I hope that what I have presented here will shed light on your path to healing and will ease the release of your childhood pain. Mine is the less difficult job—to guide and facilitate the mystery of healing that is already taking place within you now. You will do the work, you will experience the pain, you will reap the joy of fully knowing and feeling your life. It is your own courage and persistence, your own need to make the "invisible" visible again, that brings about your recovery. And as you heal, your inner light will begin to illuminate the way for others who, like yourself, are looking for the door that leads upward, out of the pain.

PART ONE

THE WOUNDED HEART

But such is the irresistible nature of truth, that all it asks, and all it wants, is the liberty of appearing.

—THOMAS PAINE

CHAPTER 1

What Is Child Sexual Abuse?

Your sexuality is intricately interwoven into the fabric of your humanity. Moments after conception, your sex was determined. During the nine months of development in your mother's womb, your body became either male or female. You came into the world naked, already a sexual being with a particular gender. In our culture, if you were born a girl, you probably received pink clothes and toys. If you were born a boy, you probably received blue things. From the moment of birth—and sometimes before—you were identified by your gender.

Throughout childhood your gender determined your identity; in American culture, gender largely determines how children are disciplined, what they are told about themselves, and what kinds of play they will be encouraged to try. Through observing the attitudes of parents, teachers, peers, television, movies, and countless other influences, your sexual identity becomes clearer and more refined.

Your sex is a core element of who you are. When you were sexually abused, you were wounded to the very core of your being. Sexual energy is one of the most vital and creative forces in human existence. Without sexual energy we human beings would literally cease to exist as a species. Because your sex and sexuality is such a powerful force, when you were sexually wounded, it deeply affected you. The wound of childhood sexual abuse has continued to affect you from the time you were abused through every subsequent stage of your life: as a child, as a young adult, as a middle-aged adult, and as an older adult. The wound of sexual abuse has also touched each one of your relationships, whether sexual or nonsexual.

3

Acknowledging the depth of your emotional pain and the far-reaching consequences of your abuse is a giant step in the recovery process. You must recognize that you will always be a survivor of your past abuse. That fact about yourself can never be changed. Healing the invisible wound of child sexual abuse is painful and difficult. But you can heal. To heal means to accept that you were abused, to integrate that knowledge into your life, and to return to your natural state of spontaneity and joy. Your past will then cease to control your choices, and the pain you feel because of the abuse will lessen in both intensity and duration. Remember this during your healing process: Accepting that you were abused does not mean that you in any way condone what was done to you. Acceptance simply means that you acknowledge that the abuse happened, that you could not have prevented it, and that you have survived it.

"NOT GUILTY"

The first important thing you need to know about being sexually abused is that you were not at fault. The child is never responsible for the abuse. It is always adults who are responsible to care for and protect children, not the other way around. Children who are sexually abused are victims. Children are powerless to protect themselves, and they are not mature enough to make decisions that will ensure their safety. It was not your job, as a child, to protect yourself from abusers either within your family or outside your family. This includes other children who may have been sexually abusive to you. In families and in society generally, protecting children is an adult responsibility. You were not in any way to blame for what happened to you. Although you may feel that the sexual abuse was your fault (which is quite common), it was not.

Sexual abuse is a betrayal that crushes a child's innocence and trust. When you were forced, coerced, or seduced into engaging in sexual behavior as a child, you became a victim of sexual abuse. By surviving that trauma, you also became a survivor. You learned to adapt, to do whatever you had to do in order to continue functioning in your world as well as you could. In spite of a painful betrayal, you have made it this far. Having survived such a deep wound, you can know without doubt that you are strong and capable.

The second important thing you need to know is that you are not alone in having been sexually abused. An increasing number of women and men who were sexually abused as children are now coming forward to tell their stories. These survivors tell of their abuse, how it affected them, and what they are doing to heal themselves. That great numbers of people are seeking to heal their childhood sexual trauma is both encouraging and shocking. To heal from your own trauma, you will need the support of these other survivors who are engaged in the recovery process. You can be encouraged to know that, because there are so many of you, you will have a lot of company on your way back to health.

We are only beginning to realize how many people have carried this deep pain and for how long it has been kept secret. During the time period when most of my clients were being sexually traumatized and exploited, the accepted myth was that childhood sexual abuse was very rare. But recent statistics indicate that one out of four women and one out of seven men were sexually abused as children. It is my belief that these numbers will continue to grow as more survivors speak out about their experience.

In a culture in which sexual abuse has been covered up and denied to such an alarming extent, arriving at an accurate definition of child sexual abuse can become a complex task. Here I will use the definition below:

> Child sexual abuse exists when a child is used by an adult or more powerful child for the purpose of sexual gratification. Child sexual abuse also occurs when an adult or more powerful child unconsciously violates a child's sexual boundaries, either physical or emotional.

When an adult (or another child) uses a child for sexual gratification, the child is gravely wounded. The wound is always emotional, and depending on the nature of the abuse, it may be physical as well. A sexually exploited and abused child suffers from feelings of shame, self-hate, fear, rage, and confusion. But the child's pain and suffering are not limited to these emotional states. Being sexually abused always has lifelong consequences for the survivor.

Sometimes children are sexually abused by people who unconsciously abuse their power or authority. Adults or bigger children may not realize that their behavior is abusive, even though their actions may seriously damage a child's future ability to trust, to love others, and to function as a whole person in the world. A parent may give daily enemas to a child, mistakenly believing that enemas are necessary to keep the child healthy. Although the parent is unaware of it, this practice is extremely sexually abusive to the child. Of course, enemas are also sometimes given to children in order to inflict harm, as punishment, to shame them during toilet training, or because it is sexually gratifying to the perpetrator. Such cases can hardly be called "unconscious" abuse. Still, other parents (especially those who were once abused themselves) can sexually abuse their children without realizing it. If you are a survivor who is also a parent, please refer to the guidelines given in Chapter 8 for further information on how to prevent unconscious abuse.

Obviously, not all, not even most survivors who are parents sexually abuse their children. Some do, however. If you know that you have sexually abused your children or any other children, immediately seek the help of a therapist and remove yourself from the presence of the children you have abused. You can stop the cycle of abuse now. You can start to heal now.

Of course, not all sexual interactions that children have are abusive in nature. Parents have an intimate physical/emotional bond with their children; they care for them when they are too young to care for themselves. Children are bathed, have their diapers changed, and their genitals washed. Parents and other adult caregivers have the responsibility of taking care of all of a very young child's needs. If very young children are not hugged and kissed, bathed, changed, clothed, and fed, they do not survive. Although some children are sexually abused during these activities, there is certainly nothing inherently unhealthy about parents hugging, kissing, washing, or dressing their children. If you think that, as a child, you may have been sexually abused at these times but you aren't sure, ask yourself why you feel uncomfortable about it. If you felt violated, you were violated. Whether or not your caregiver intended to harm you is unimportant. What is important are your feelings about what happened to you.

As children grow and mature, their needs change. Gradually they develop the ability to take care of themselves. Along with learning to take care of their own needs, children become curious about their bodies and their parents' bodies. They ask questions about their parents' sex organs and their own, and they want to know "where babies come from." This curiosity is part of normal, healthy development. Information about sex, and about our bodies, is essential to our health and safety.

Information, attitudes, and myths about sex are passed down from generation to generation. Adults—parents and other caregivers—teach by their own behavior and by directly giving information. Our primary caregiver (whether a parent, grandparent, nanny, or another relative) holds the responsibility for teaching us how our bodies work. This includes a responsibility to teach us about our sexual nature. Human beings are sexual beings. We are a lot of other wondrous things, too, but we are certainly sexual or we would all disappear! It is not only appropriate but healthy for parents to answer their children's questions about sex and reproduction. It is also helpful for parents to respond with calm understanding when children show curiosity by experimenting with each others' bodies.

In one form or another, children have "played doctor" with other children throughout history. Given the opportunity, healthy children will explore each other's bodies and talk to each other about the differences between girls and boys. Generally, if the interaction is between children within the same age range (one to two years apart) and there is no coercion or force involved, there is little likelihood that this sexual play is abusive or harmful.

Kathy had had a sexual experience when she was a child and had no abuse issues as a result of the experience. In a therapy group session Kathy related that at age eleven, she and a female friend (age ten) had masturbated each other. Whenever they stayed overnight together, they took turns rubbing each other's genitals. Kathy's sexual contact with her friend continued for about a year. When Kathy told this to the group, she also reported that she did not believe she was abused by her friend and that she and this friend were still very close. During the course of her therapy, Kathy spoke further about her feelings about her relationship with her friend and came to the conclusion that the sexual experiences they had had as children were not a problem for her.

Due to misunderstanding the naturalness of children's sexual curiosity (and often due to their own parents' similar misunderstanding), parents sometimes react abusively when children experiment with sexuality. Frank's experience with his father shows what can happen when innocent curiosity is met with abusive rage. Frank reported that when he and another boy had been found together without clothes on,

Frank's father had beaten his buttocks and genitals with a leather strap. The two five-year-olds, who had simply been curious about each other's bodies, had been looking at each other. Frank's father's brutal reaction was abusive and had far-reaching effects for Frank well into his adulthood. He reported that he still felt shame, anger, and embarrassment whenever he thought about the incident. Frank also experienced intense shame whenever he was seen naked. This consequence of Frank's childhood experience caused him extreme pain in his sexual relationships.

MYTHS AND REALITIES

The troublesome myth seems to prevail in our society that child sexual abuse is committed by an isolated group of "deviants" who hang around schoolyards, luring little girls and boys into their cars with offers of candy or toys. This myth easily accompanied the once widely held belief that child sexual abuse was a rare occurrence, committed mostly by kidnappers. The fact is that you were much more likely to have been sexually abused by a member of your family or by an acquaintance than by a stranger. The sexual abuse of children is not at all rare or unusual. Sexual abuse is happening to children today, and it has been happening to a lot of children for a long time.

Another persistent myth concerns incest. Many people still believe that incest occurs only in poor families or in "backwoods" communities where inbreeding is common. But incest happens in all kinds of families. Incest has been present for generations in families from every socioeconomic group. The neighborhood you lived in, the school you went to, your parents' occupations—none of these has any bearing on whether incest existed in your family.

Today, it is difficult to find an urban newspaper that does not contain a story about the sexual abuse of a child. But despite the increased attention it has received in the media, sexual abuse is still largely regarded as a rare occurrence. It may be that, because the media generally report only the most bizarre and horrible incidents of sexual abuse, many people assume that these are the only incidents of abuse. In reality, overworked child abuse caseworkers throughout the country are given many more reports of sexual abuse than they can possibly investigate. Still more cases of child sexual abuse are never reported at all. While it is true that sexual abuse and the sexual exploitation of children is receiving increased public exposure, it is good to keep in mind that the issue is not a new one. The sexual abuse of children has occurred throughout many generations. The brave people who are now coming forward to speak about their personal abuse were children decades ago.

Every time I do a public lecture or workshop on childhood sexual abuse, one or two people in their late fifties to early seventies come up to me afterward to share their experience. One woman in her sixties, a grandmother, told me she had never talked about what happened to her. She had been raped numerous times by her uncle when she was twelve. Although her uncle had been dead for many years and her abuse had happened over fifty years ago, she still had dreams about him and what he did to her. She told me, "I was so ashamed, I thought that I was the only one this had ever happened to. Now a lot of things I did, and choices I made in my life, make sense to me."

After another workshop, a man in his fifties told me that in child-hood he had been sodomized many times by his boy's club leader. At the same workshop, another man in his forties told the group that his abuse had started at age five, when a seventeen-year-old female neighbor forced him to perform oral sex on her numerous times over a two-year period. This abuse ended when the girl moved to a different neighborhood. Both men reported feeling continuing shame and anger about the abuse. Both men also reported believing that their experience was so unusual that no one would understand how they felt about it. These two men carried their shame and rage in secret for over forty years.

If you are a survivor in your forties or older, you are not alone. There are many survivors in your age group. Your abuse is as life-damaging and painful to you as it is to younger survivors. If you have not been able to share your experience or receive help for the effects of the sexual abuse, you still carry the wound of that experience, regardless of your age.

WHO COMMITS CHILD SEXUAL ABUSE?

No profession, race, nationality, religious affiliation, or any other group of people seems to be without members who sexually abuse children. Women as well as men commit sexual abuse, and children abuse other children. It is not my intention to make you see a sex offender hiding behind every tree. If you are reading this book, however, it is likely that you know or suspect that you were sexually abused as a child. It is also likely that you have a lot of unanswered questions, a lot of missing pieces in your memory puzzle. In your search for healing (and for memories), keep in mind that your abuse could have been perpetrated by people whom you may not have considered abusers. It is also not unusual for survivors to recall being abused by more than one person. Perpetrators could be family members (most commonly), acquaintances, or strangers who abused on a one-time basis. You may have survived incest, as well as abuse by an acquaintance or a stranger. Or you could have been molested by more than one member of any of these groups.

Family Members

You could have been abused by any member of your family.

Father

Mother

Brother

Sister

Uncle

Aunt

Cousin

Grandfather/great-grandfather

Grandmother/great-grandmother

Stepfather

Stepmother

Stepbrother

Stepsister

Other stepfamily member

If you were sexually abused by a member of your family, you are a survivor of incest. Incest is the ultimate betrayal. Ideally, the family is an atmosphere of love and protection where children can grow and develop in safety. In a big, confusing world, home is the child's safety net, a place to gain courage, love, and support. When someone is abused by a member of their family, "home" becomes a fearful place.

In the incestuous family the child is used as an object for sexual gratification. If your parent had sex with you, you were raped by someone who was supposed to love and protect you. Because your physical body was used and violated, your emotional life has been severely damaged. There is no excuse for your rape, and there is no justification for what happened to you. Your pain and confusion are real and justified. Even the term *rape* is too mild to adequately describe the betrayal you have suffered.

Kate's Story

Kate, a former client, intuitively knew that she had been sexually abused. She had no memories of any abuse, but when she listened to other survivors talk about their incest experiences, she felt extremely frightened and sad. She had "forgotten" much of her childhood. When Kate entered a sexual abuse survivors' group, she was, in her words, "looking for answers to questions I don't know how to ask." During the first session she told the group that she was not sure she belonged but that she was searching for the reasons for her nightmares and her inability to stay happy in a sexual relationship.

After her third group session, I received a telephone call from Kate. She had remembered being sexually abused. During the next session Kate told the group about her flashback:

> I was sitting in the bathtub relaxing before I went to bed when I suddenly had this flash of fear along with an image of being held under water. Then I remembered when I was about three years old, I was swimming with my father. He was floating on his back, and I was lying on my back on his stomach. I remember the sensation of floating and how good it felt to be with Daddy. Then he began to rub me against him. I felt his penis get hard. I started to get scared but didn't say anything. When he began to rub me faster and faster, my back started to hurt, and I started to cry and struggle. I don't remember how his bathing suit came off, but I do

remember feeling his penis against my back. He became more and more violent, and my head would go under the water. I began to choke and swallow water and thought I was going to die.

Kate began to cry. The group was respectfully silent. After a few minutes she continued her story:

All this time Daddy never made a sound. I was choking and crying and begging him to stop, but he never paid any attention to me. It was as if I were not even there. I don't really remember him stopping, I just remember being on the beach and him putting his bathing trunks back on. My suit was still on, but it was all twisted around. He never said a word. He stood up and walked back to the house. He never even looked at me. I might as well have been a doll.

During the next several weeks, Kate began to remember more and more of her childhood abuse. She remembered a night when her father raped her, holding his hand over her mouth and nose so she could not scream or make any noise. Again, she thought she would die because she was unable to breathe. She told the group, "I felt like an object, not a person. And that's how I feel when I have sex today. I feel like an object."

Kate's story is a violent example of father/daughter incest. Although physical incest is always a rape, a violation, incest does not always involve physical force. The absence of physical violence, however, does not diminish the serious effects the violation has on the child. And while father/daughter incest is probably the most widely recognized, incest is certainly not limited to fathers and daughters. I have had clients who were incested by one family member, and clients who were incested by several people in their family. I have had clients who were abused by their uncles, great-grandfathers, and mothers. Girls are not the only victims of incest; boys also fall victim to the abuser in the family.

John's Story

At the age of two, John was anally raped by his grandfather. Like most incest survivors, John lived in a family where the incest was kept secret. In his pain he could turn to no one for support. Even as a very small child, John was isolated and alone, suffering acute shame and fear. He repressed the memories of the abuse for many years. Although he had "forgotten" the abuse, John's experience affected his friendships and sexual relationships. He found it extremely difficult to trust people. When he found himself getting too close to someone, he would start a fight and end the friendship. John's sexual relationships were usually short-lived. He wanted intimacy, but he was afraid of it.

John became an alcoholic. During his recovery from alcoholism, he became aware of the rage he felt toward his grandfather and other members of his family. After two years of sobriety, John entered therapy for what he called "out-of-control bursts of rage" and his "fear of getting too close to people." During therapy he remembered how his grandfather had sexually abused him.

In the following excerpts from a long poem entitled "Dear Grandaddy," John vividly describes his feelings about being a survivor of incest:

Dear Grandaddy

You approached
me like jetliner, gave me an
asshole as big as a canyon,
and left a starfish, with
twitching little arms, bleeding.

Later in the poem, John powerfully confronts his abusive grandfather and describes the intense shame and anger he feels as an adult. Echoing many survivors of male/male child sexual abuse, John also writes about how the incest affects his view of himself as a man:

Now I'm incriminating you, grandaddy,
and saying that I hate you right
here in the open. And to this day
from the shame, my hips
are too wide, ugly, and I am
a man. And grandaddy, I fear men,
fear football, groundballs,
pulling hooks out of fishes' mouths,
afraid to clutch, to withstrain
their mucousy writhings, to rub
against the slant of their scales,
to expose my soul to lightning,
for fear of being struck.

Like most recovering survivors of violent incest, John's murderous rage toward the perpetrator seems enormous. His rage leads him to imagine shooting at strangers from a distance. But writing about this anger seems to bring John to the deeper truth about himself, that a part of him remains "inviolate," unharmed:

> *Today, I wanted to snipe people*
> *in the cable cars from the*
> *mountainside, knowing how good*
> *a shot I am, I could get them.*
> *The miracle of the hard apple, the*
> *inviolate plum, and the wriggling*
> *starfish are waiting inside my center.*
> *Today, your oceanic mass, your walrus*
> *presence above me is something*
> *I can shit out. You failed in*
> *all the levels of hell to love me,*
> *and you failed to scathe the best in me,*
> *but I have not known that*
> *for a very heavy*
> *long time.*

Although John's poem ends with expressions of rage and deep grief, it also affirms that he is on the path to rediscovering "the best in me." In this way, John's poem speaks to all incest survivors about the wound of childhood sexual abuse: no matter who abused you, and no matter how you were abused, there is a part of you that remains untouched by that abuse. That unhurt aspect of yourself is your greatest ally.

It is a myth that the perpetrators of childhood sexual abuse are always men. Like John, more and more men are becoming involved in self-discovery groups and are reclaiming their childhood experiences. Along with this greater awareness, an increasing number of men are remembering their childhood sexual abuse. As these men begin to talk about their abuse, we are learning of more and more incidents in which women (mothers, sisters, aunts, and other female caregivers) were the perpetrators of sexual abuse.

In some cases the child victim may even become a child perpetrator. Wounded children, in pain and afraid, with no place to turn or to express their feelings, sometimes commit sexual abuse on younger or less powerful children.

Gloria's Story

Gloria was incested by her father and her stepfather. The incest lasted from the time she was six years old until she was eleven. At age thirteen, Gloria seduced her eleven-year-old brother Tony, after which they continued to have sexual intercourse on a regular basis for four years. Gloria stated that in the beginning Tony did not want to have sex but that she forced him. After four years, when Gloria wanted to stop having sex with her brother, he raped her on two separate occasions. After that, Gloria and Tony had no further sexual contact.

As an adult, Tony had one marriage, which ended in divorce. He fathered two children. At the age of twenty-six, he committed suicide. Gloria does not know whether her brother was abused by anyone other than herself. She does not know whether Tony ever abused his children.

Both Gloria and Tony were victims of incest. Both of them became perpetrators as well. Who is to blame? Gloria, for abusing her younger brother? Tony, for raping his sister? The patterns of sexual abuse in families can be complex, and abuse committed child-to-child can be every bit as damaging as sexual abuse that is perpetrated by an adult on a child.

Once it begins, incest usually persists in a family. Some families have a history of incest that spans generations. As with a disease such as alcoholism, incest, as well as its consequences, can be passed from one generation to another. Survivors of child sexual abuse (both women and men) seem to have an increased potential to abuse children just as they were abused, or to unconsciously create situations in which their own children are sexually abused. Even if you go to great lengths to protect your children from sexual abuse, if you don't seek recovery for yourself, you are extremely likely to pass on the fear and dysfunction you learned as a child in your own family. You may not behave as a sexual offender, but you will still behave as a survivor of incest. You have to—that's the way you've learned how to live. Ann's case history and family tree (see Chapter 11) illustrate multigenerational incest.

The most important thing to know about the incest family is that you can break the cycle of sexual abuse. You can teach your children healthy and constructive ways of being in the world. You do not have to be chained to your past, and your own children do not have to suffer what you endured as a child. Chapter 8, which discusses healthy parenting, love relationships, and friendships, may be of particular interest to you. As a survivor of incest, you may want to make special use of the "Family Members" section of the Healing Journal (Chapter 12). If you have not yet taken the opportunity to begin work in the journal, you may want to turn to Part Three of this book and consider starting your Healing Journal now.

Acquaintances

Besides your own family, the next group most likely to have abused you is people with whom you came into contact on a fairly regular basis. Here is a partial list of possible acquaintance sexual abusers; you may add to it anyone else in your life who belongs there.

Friend of your family

Neighbor

Babysitter

Nanny

Friend of older brother or sister

Your own friend (from school, church, camp, etc.)

Teacher or coach

Clergy

Doctor or other medical professional

An acquaintance sexual abuser may have been a caregiver—a person who was charged with protecting you, teaching you, and otherwise caring for you. Your caregiver may have been someone you knew for a long time—a teacher or a friend of your parents—or someone you had just met, such as a new babysitter.

In the absence of your parents, your caregivers acted as substitutes; they had as much control over you as your parents did. If you were abused by a caregiver, you were betrayed by a person occupying a position of trust. Unfortunately, most children are taught to obey all adults without question. This teaching can be extremely harmful; it makes children easy targets for sexual abuse. As a child, you had no control over what happened to you at the hands of adults who were placed in positions of authority over you.

There is another reason why so many children are molested by acquaintances. Perpetrators of child sexual abuse frequently spend months or years "grooming"—creating a bond with—the children they intend to abuse. Once the child knows the perpetrator as a trusted friend, the child is extremely likely to comply with a proposal of sexual activity. An ongoing relationship of this type can be similar to long-term seductive incest, in which the child may be given gifts or special treatment in exchange for sexual favors.

Children who are sexually abused are never at fault for the abuse, regardless of the circumstances. Sometimes even a child's natural curiosity can result in an abusive situation if the adult or older child involved responds to it inappropriately.

When parents leave a child with a babysitter or take the child to school, then (consciously or unconsciously) they are granting those caregivers a position of power over their child. Your parents' implicit trust in your caregiver would have made the sexual abuse even more confusing for you: "My parents wouldn't have left me with someone 'bad,'" the child often reasons, "so I must be the 'bad' one." Caregivers who wanted to sexually abuse you could easily have done so without much risk to themselves. Like any adult placed in a position of authority over you, a caregiver could easily intimidate you into keeping silent—by threatening to kill you or someone you loved, or by telling you that you had done something "bad" and that you would be severely punished if anyone found out. Your caregiver may have insisted that no one would believe you if you told that you had been abused.

Carol's Story

Carol entered a survivors' group because she had been molested by her family doctor from age seven until she was nine years old. The molestations stopped when her family moved and changed physicians. During routine examinations her doctor, who insisted on seeing her alone, would insert his fingers into her vagina while he masturbated. He told her that all doctors did this with their patients, and that if she told anyone what went on in the exam room, she would get in "big trouble." Carol lived in fear of going to the doctor. Because she was a child and believed his threats, Carol was too afraid to tell anyone what he had done to her.

Carol's experience clearly illustrates how someone in a position of authority may use that power to molest and intimidate a little child. Carol was understandably afraid to challenge the doctor's authority or to expose him as a sexual offender. All she was able to do was try to avoid visits to the doctor and to survive the visits she had to make. Carol did not tell anyone about her molestations until she was in her early twenties.

In the course of my clinical practice, I have heard many variations on Carol's story. One man was molested by his priest, another by his female babysitter.

Other acquaintance sexual abusers are not caregivers. These could include your friends, friends of your family, neighborhood children, your newspaper or postal carrier, bus driver, and so on. Although these people did not have direct authority over you, their familiarity would have given them opportunities to abuse you.

Jean's Story

Starting when she was six years of age, Jean was repeatedly raped over a two-year period by a "gang" of four older boys. The boys ranged in age from ten to twelve years. Jean's parents knew the boys, all of whom lived down the street from their home. The four boys had built a clubhouse in some nearby woods. At first they lured Jean into their clubhouse by offering to show her their "special place." After showing her some pornographic magazines, the boys forced her to act out the pictures. These boys continued to molest Jean until she was eight years old. Jean did not remember this abuse until she was forty years old. Prior to this time, she had remembered the boys but not the molestation she had suffered. When she began to recall that the boys had raped her, she also remembered that all of them had been friends of her older sister and that they often visited her house. Jean had kept silent because the boys had threatened to kill her if she told anyone.

Jean came from an alcoholic family. Due to the active dysfunction in her family, she received very little parental supervision. Jean's sister, who was only two years older, was expected to take care of Jean when her parents were too busy or too drunk to watch her. Jean was an easy target for abuse by older, more powerful children. They frightened her into silence. Having experienced repeated abandonment and neglect by her alcoholic parents, Jean had no reason to believe that they could or would prevent the boys from abusing her. Jean did not have adequate protection—her eight-year-old sister was not a suitable caregiver. As in many cases of sexual abuse by a noncaregiving acquaintance, lack of adequate adult supervision directly contributed to Jean's abuse.

As she did further memory recovery work in therapy, Jean also remembered that the four boys who raped her had also abused other little girls in her neighborhood.

Strangers

Sexual abuse by a stranger is generally a one-time occurrence. If you were sexually abused by a stranger, you experienced serious trauma. Stranger abuse usually occurs without warning. In a public park, a naked stranger suddenly appears before a child who has wandered off from a group. In a public rest room, a man makes obscene gestures and attempts to kiss a small boy. If you suffered sexual abuse by a stranger, a tornado roared into your life. One moment you were playing and daydreaming, and the next moment someone frightened, terrorized, and hurt you. Just as suddenly, as in a bad dream, the whole incident was over. But it is not over for you. Unless you received help and support to heal your terror and fear, the effects of your sexual trauma are still with you.

Survivors of single-event sexual abuse by a stranger often try to minimize the effects of their experience by telling themselves (and others), "It only happened once. I lived through it. I'm okay now." Unfortunately, it does not help that the sexual abuse occurred only once, nor does having "lived through it" indicate that everything is all right. In fact, the effects of a single incident of sexual abuse can be as devastating as abuse that continues over an extended period of time.

Survivors who were sexually abused by a stranger often manage to repress, or "forget," the incident altogether. But such trauma is never completely forgotten. If this is your situation, you may intuitively feel that something sexually inappropriate happened to you, but you're not sure what it was. You relate easily to other survivors, but you're certain there was no incest or other sexual abuse in your history. This can be very confusing. Trust your intuition and the facts about your life. Do you relate easily to survivors of sexual abuse? Are you drawn to

survivors, and are you comfortable at sexual abuse survivors' meetings? If so, it is highly likely that you were sexually abused as a child,
and I would encourage you to begin your healing process as if you
were certain of it. One of the most difficult challenges for any survivor
is learning to believe yourself. In survivors of sexual trauma, years of
denial have dulled (or erased) this natural self-trust.

Don's Story

When he was eleven years old, Don and his friend were hitchhiking
when they were picked up by a police officer. Both boys sat in the front
seat of the police car. During the ride the officer reached across and put
his hand down Don's pants and fondled his genitals. Both Don and his
friend were terrified and could not believe what was happening. The
police officer told the boys he wanted them to perform oral sex on him.
He also told them that if they ever told anyone, they would be arrested
and locked up. The officer said that it would be his word against
theirs, and that no one would believe them. The car pulled off the road
behind a group of trees. When the three of them got out of the car, Don
was forced to have oral sex with the police officer. Then the officer
drove off and left the boys. Neither of them ever spoke to each other
about what had happened, and they never reported the incident.

The terror, shame, and guilt that Don experienced stayed with him
for more than thirty years. Most of the actual experience Don repressed. He did not know why he felt shame and fear without apparent
reason, and he did not know why he hated the police so much.
Sometimes Don would get drunk and look for a cop to fight with. Of
course, most of the time Don lost badly. But he continued to pick
fights with police officers. In therapy for sexual abuse, Don regained
complete memory of the abuse incident and was able to focus his rage
and hurt at the police officer who had molested him rather than at all
police officers.

In terms of your recovery, it does not matter so much whether you
were sexually abused by a family member, an acquaintance, a friend, a
caregiver, or a stranger. If you were abused in childhood, you were
traumatized. In one sense, it is impossible to measure your pain to find
out how severely the abuse has affected you. You may look at outside
indicators in your life—your fulfillment, or lack of it, in relationships,
for example—but this method is not always reliable. A one-time

violent abusive incident by a stranger may seem to severely affect one survivor, while another survivor's years of ongoing incest may not appear to have affected him as severely. Whatever the circumstances of your abuse, you will not be fully aware of how badly you have been injured until you actively begin the process of healing. Still, "measuring" your pain is not the point. What is most important is that, a long time ago, a precious child was sexually hurt and betrayed. That child deserves to be comforted, and to heal.

The Accomplice

All of the examples of sexual abuse I have given thus far have discussed only you and the offender. It is important to know that your feelings of anger, rage, hurt, and betrayal are valid, and it is healthy to direct these feelings toward the offender. Naturally, you will feel betrayed by the person who abused you, but you may also feel betrayed by the adults in your life who were supposed to protect you but either could not or would not do so. If your father sexually abused you, you will feel that your mother betrayed you by not protecting you. If your aunt sexually abused you, you may feel that your parents betrayed you by not stopping the abuse. If you were molested by an acquaintance or by a stranger, you might feel that your family betrayed you. It is important to know that feelings of anger toward the "protectors who did not protect you" are very common among survivors. Whether or not your feelings "make sense" to you, they deserve to be heard and expressed.

Don't worry about what is fair and what is not fair. Your feelings are real. Even if your parents could not have done anything to prevent your being molested by a stranger, you will probably still feel angry at them for not protecting you. A child's understanding is very simple: They know it is always the responsibility of adults to protect children. So when you feel angry at the adults who didn't protect you as a child, you are feeling the betrayal you felt as a child, feelings that arose from that innocent and natural expectation. Emotional responses to sexual abuse are not always rational, but these feelings are still valid, and part of your recovery is to experience them.

Unfortunately, it is a common experience to have been betrayed by family members who did, in fact, know or suspect that you were being sexually abused. Because most sexual abuse happens within the family system, it is a secret that no one talks about but everyone knows. It is healthy to feel rage at the members of your family who were silent accomplices to your abuse. When Alice began to process her rage at her father who raped her, she also began to feel intense anger and rage toward her mother. Despite Alice's clear memory of her abuse, her mother angrily denied that the sexual abuse had ever happened. Alice told her therapy group, "It's impossible that she didn't know what was happening to me. I remember. She let him have me so he would stay away from her." Alice continued, "I always felt sorry for my mother because of the way my father treated her, but now I don't care. She should have stopped him."

Alice's response echoes the feelings of many survivors of sexual abuse, whether or not the abuse was incestuous. In the next chapter we will look at specific categories of child sexual abuse and the impact they may have had on your life.

CHAPTER 2

Categories of
Child Sexual Abuse

Brenda's Story

"When I was six, my mother found me and my uncle in bed together. He was fondling me, and I was rubbing his penis. Mom yelled at me, called me a 'little whore.' It was a terrible scene. I got punished, and then nobody ever talked about it again. My family was pretty crazy. We never talked about anything important. My uncle was twenty-two years old when we 'got caught.' He was my favorite uncle; he bought me ice cream and toys. He always had time for me. For years I wondered what I had done wrong. Even now, I still feel guilty about it. I didn't know I was sexually abused. No one ever told me that. Sometimes I feel so stupid. How could a thirty-five-year-old woman not know that that was sexual abuse?"

On entering therapy, Brenda, like many survivors, had almost no information about sexual abuse. In Brenda's family, incest had been present in at least two generations, but it was never acknowledged. The barrier of secrecy was total. And since her mother had blamed Brenda (a six-year-old!) for the encounter with her adult uncle, Brenda had accepted that she was at fault. When Brenda entered therapy, she did not really believe she had ever been sexually abused.

The process of recovery from childhood sexual trauma involves a rediscovery and a retelling of your personal story as you experienced it. Often mysterious in its unfolding, this process will take you deep inside yourself to find your reality. Rediscovering your personal story means rejecting the artificial history created by your denial (or your family's denial). Learning about different kinds of sexual abuse is a crucial first step toward finding out your truth. Her mother's response led Brenda to believe that she was responsible for the abuse; Brenda was unable to recognize that she herself was the one who had been injured. In the absence of specific information you, like Brenda, may dismiss sexual abuses you have experienced, or you may minimize the impact that the abuse has had on you.

We will look at two categories of sexual abuse: physical sexual abuse and emotional sexual abuse (see figure 1). As we will see, both physical

FIGURE 1: Categories of Child Sexual Abuse

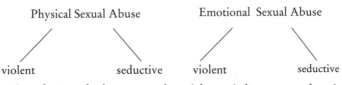

and emotional sexual abuse can be either violent or seductive. It is important to remember that even though "seductive" types of sexual abuse are not categorized as "violent," all kinds of sexual abuse are harmful to the child, both at the time of the abuse and in later adult life.

Some children survive emotional sexual abuse without experiencing physical sexual abuse. All survivors of physical sexual abuse, however, suffer emotionally. If you were physically abused, you suffered emotional abuse as well. You may have felt horror, shame, rage, and agonizing grief. These powerful emotional states have affected your life profoundly. The child who is unable to heal stores up these natural emotional responses to the abuse, and the "unfelt feelings" produce damaging results later in life. Even if you experienced nonphysical sexual abuse, in your adulthood the consequences of that abuse may manifest in the extreme. (To find out more about the consequences of sexual abuse, see Chapter 3, "Living with Secrets".)

This chapter will discuss in detail many types of sexual abuse. I will describe emotional as well as physical forms of sexual abuse, seductive as well as violent abuse. As you read this section, keep in mind that it is important not to "gloss over" the details of sexual trauma. Child sexual abuse can be brutal, or it can be subtle. In either case, the details must not be understated or avoided. If you begin to feel emotionally overwhelmed as you read, please put down the book and take a break, or call someone who can support you. You don't have to read the information all at once. You can skip parts of the book and come back to them later on. This is an opportunity to practice taking care of yourself.

PHYSICAL SEXUAL ABUSE

You were physically sexually abused if there was physical sexual contact between you and the perpetrator. Physical sexual abuse can include being forced to watch, or participate in, sexually explicit behavior. Sexual abuse often includes more than one type of physical activity; your abuse may have included different combinations of sexual activities between you and the abuser(s). If you experienced frequent abuse of long duration, it is particularly likely that you were abused in a variety of ways.

As you read the descriptions below, remember that you were a child when the abuse took place. If an adult, or a more powerful child, acted sexually toward you, you were sexually abused. Any penetration of your body was rape. You were not mature enough to make an adult decision about sexual behavior. You were not in any way at fault for the abuse you experienced. Throughout this book, I will continue to repeat this statement—not only because it is true but because many survivors deeply believe that they were somehow to blame for being sexually abused.

Common Physical Sexual Abuses

Some of the most common physical sexual abuses are listed here.

Oral abuse

Anal abuse

Vaginal/Penis Abuse

Inappropriate touching or rubbing

Privacy violations

Sexual behavior with an animal

Being dressed in adult sexual clothing

Being made to participate in pornography

Watching or hearing someone else being sexually abused

Unnecessary medical procedures

Inappropriate health procedures

Oral Abuse

Oral rape occurs if the perpetrator made mouth-to-genital contact with you, or if you made mouth-to-genital contact with the perpetrator. This kind of contact can take the form of kissing, licking, or sucking on or around your vagina, breasts, or anus. If you are a man, oral abuse would include any kissing, licking, or sucking of your penis and testicles. If you had any oral contact with the abuser's genitals, you experienced oral sexual abuse. When an adult engages in mouth-to-mouth sexual kissing (French kissing) with a child, that is also physical sexual abuse. A finger, or any object or sexual apparatus introduced into your mouth in order to mimic the adult act of sexual intercourse, is also oral rape.

Anal Abuse

If you were anally penetrated with a penis, finger, or other object, you were anally raped. An adult sexual "toy" such as a vibrator, or another object such as a broom handle or hairbrush, could have been inserted into the anus. Penetration of the anus by any object, for purposes of sexual stimulation, is anal rape. Anal abuse includes any oral-anal contact with the perpetrator.

Vaginal/Penis Abuse

Any penetration of your vagina was vaginal abuse. Any fondling of your pelvic area was also abusive. Sexual intercourse with the abuser, forced or not, is vaginal abuse. If the perpetrator inserted hands, fingers, penis, a vibrator, or any object into your vagina, you were vaginally raped. Any oral-vaginal contact with the perpetrator is also vaginal abuse. If as a boy you were seduced or forced to penetrate another person's anus, vagina, or mouth with your penis, you were physically sexually abused.

Inappropriate Touching or Rubbing

If your genitals were touched, rubbed, or stroked, or you were asked or forced to touch, rub, or stroke the person who abused you, you experienced physical sexual abuse. If you and the abuser rubbed and stroked each other's genitals at the same time, then sexual abuse still occurred. If the abuser rubbed his or her genitals against your body, you were sexually abused.

Inappropriate sexual touching is one of the most common forms of sexual abuse, and it occurs in many more and subtler forms than can be listed here. If you felt ashamed or uncomfortable, or if you felt that "something was wrong" while the touching occurred, then you were probably being sexually abused (whether or not the perpetrator was aware of abusing you).

Privacy Violations

If you were continually and intrusively interrupted while going to the toilet, bathing, or dressing, you were sexually abused. If you were manipulated or forced to watch an adult bathing, going to the toilet, or dressing, you were sexually abused. Being continually stared at in a sexual way (someone looking at your groin or "mentally undressing" you) is abusive and can be very frightening.

Parents' attitudes and behaviors about privacy establish the family's "code of conduct" regarding nudity. Routine family nudity is nonabusive so long as each member of the family is comfortable with the nudity. As you got older, you gradually formed your own set of boundaries. If these boundaries were ignored by your parents, then your privacy was violated. It isn't really possible to set specific rules about family nudity—there is great variety in it among healthy families. But if in your home you felt shamed, abused, or manipulated concerning your own or your parents' nudity, you may assume that you were sexually abused.

Sexual Behavior with an Animal

You may have been forced or manipulated into touching or licking an animal's genitals, or forced or manipulated into letting an animal lick your genitals. Any other type of sexual activity with an animal, including being asked to put your fingers into an animal's anus or vagina, is physical sexual abuse.

Being Dressed in Adult Sexual Clothing

If you were dressed in sexually titillating or revealing clothing, or if you were made to "cross-dress" (wear clothing you considered inappropriate to your gender), you were physically sexually abused. If the offender looked at you and masturbated, you were physically sexually abused. Whenever you were made an object for sexual gratification and were aware of the offender using you, you were being abused.

Being Made to Participate in Pornography

It is not my intention to attempt to define pornography. It is important, however, for recovering survivors to be aware of how sexually explicit pictures and other sexual information was introduced to them. Fine art or educational materials showing nudity can be introduced to a child in a nonabusive way; on the other hand, such materials can also be used abusively. If, for purposes of sexual stimulation, someone took sexually explicit photographs of you, or if you were shown sexually explicit photographs intended to sexually arouse you, you were physically sexually abused. If someone took pictures of you engaging in sexual activity with another child, you were sexually abused. (Naturally, this does not include parents taking the usual pictures of their babies bathing or running naked through the house.)

Watching or Hearing Someone Else Being Sexually Abused

Witnessing another person (either a child or an adult) who is being sexually abused is a terrifying experience. Even though the offender may not actually have touched your body, you experienced the implied threat of abuse by that person. Overhearing or seeing an act of sexual abuse can be as damaging to a child as if that child had been the physical focus of the abuse.

Unnecessary Medical Procedures

This kind of abuse includes unnecessary probing and examining of the vagina, anus, breasts, penis, or testicles. Sexual offenses of this type are generally committed by a doctor or other medical professional. Such abuse may take a variety of forms, with the perpetrator justifying their actions to the child under the guise of carrying out a "medical procedure."

Inappropriate Health Procedures

Unnecessary and/or frequent enemas, suppositories, vaginal douches, or rectal temperature-taking by parents or others is physically sexually abusive. This kind of abuse also includes compulsive or unnecessarily rough washing of your genitals by a parent or other caregiver.

The list of ways in which children are physically sexually abused is both long and complex. It would be a hopeless task to attempt to describe every possible kind of abuse. Whenever I think I have finally heard everything, one of my clients relates to me something I have never heard before. I have attempted to cover a broad spectrum of abuse in the hope that you may find some validation and recognition of your experience. If you are still unsure whether you were sexually abused in a physical way, I can tell you this: You were physically sexually abused if there was *any* physical contact, or physical intrusion, between you and the sexual offender (including sexually threatening behavior occurring in close proximity to you). If your body was made an object for the sexual gratification of another, you were physically abused. Being forced to submit to sexual explorations by more powerful children is also physical sexual abuse.

Violent Physical Sexual Abuse

By its very nature, any sexual act with a child is an act of rape, an act of extreme aggression. Compounded by the use of physical force, violence, and coercion, the abuse becomes even more brutal and terrifying. The higher the degree of violence you experienced with the sexual abuse, the more severe an impact your abuse is likely to have had on your life and relationships. Violent behaviors that you could have experienced during sexual abuse include:

Physical force

Holding/restraining

Tying or handcuffing

Choking

Hitting

Punching

Slapping

Kicking

Biting

Sexual beating

Torture

Ritual sexual abuse

The abuse you experienced may have included other forms that are not listed here. Being held or restrained can mean someone holding you down with their body weight, tying, or otherwise restraining you. Because they are outside the range of ordinary knowledge, I will explain the terms *sexual beating, torture,* and *ritual sexual abuse.*

Sexual Beating

Sexual beating includes being whipped or hit on or around your genitals. Sexual beating is sometimes accepted by society when it occurs in the context of "discipline" or punishment. Such beatings are a violent form of sexual abuse. If your pants or skirt were removed and you were beaten or spanked on your bare buttocks, your natural response of shame and embarrassment places this kind of hitting in the category of sexual abuse. This type of punishment is even more severely abusive when it takes place in front of another person(s).

Torture

Sexual torture is one of the most severe types of sexual abuse. During sexual torture your genitals may have been burned with matches or cigarettes. If you were penetrated with an object that was specifically intended to be painful to you, you experienced sexual torture. Not only were you sexually abused, but the person who abused you also intentionally inflicted pain on you. If you were forced to watch another person or child being tortured, you psychologically experienced the effects of their torture. The terror inflicted upon survivors of sexual torture is extremely damaging; such experiences are often so bizarre that the survivor represses the memory completely for many years. If you experienced sexual torture as a child, it is important that you take the recovery process slowly and gently, with the help of a therapist who has experience working specifically with victims of sexual torture. By a miracle, you survived your abuse; you deserve an expert to help you in your recovery. You *can* recover from this kind of abuse. It will take time and courage and a qualified guide to help you, but you *can* heal.

Ritual Sexual Abuse

Ritual sexual abuse of a child occurs when a child is used by one or more people as an object/sacrifice during a sadistic or satanic ceremony. Here the child is forced to participate in bizarre and cruel activities. During these ceremonies forced group sex, sex with animals, and ritual killing of animals (and sometimes human beings) is practiced. Torture and sexual beatings are often part of ritual abuse. This type of sexual abuse does occur. If you have survived this kind of abuse, you can heal. I strongly suggest that you work with a qualified therapist during your recovery.

Violent sexual abuse is not limited to physical acts. It also includes shouting and physical intimidation. A more powerful person (an adult or a bigger child) may use the threat of violence to force a child to participate in sexual activity. Children who are too small to adequately defend themselves experience threats of violence as direct violence. These are some common threats made by perpetrators of violent sexual abuse:

Coercion/Intimidation
"I'll hurt you if you tell."

"I'll kill your family."

"You will be punished if you tell anyone."

"I will go to jail, and you will be punished if you tell."

"If you talk, everyone one will know what you did."

The fear and terror instilled in you by the threat of violence to you or to your family was enough to have forced you, or any child, into participating in abusive sexual activities. Your terror was as real and as intense as if you had been physically beaten. On the other hand, your abuser may not have made direct threats but yelled and shouted at you in order to terrify you into compliance. Verbally or physically threatening actions compound the severity of the abuse.

Brad's Story

Like that of many survivors of violent physical sexual abuse, Brad's experience contained more than one element of violence. Brad did not remember any part of his abuse until he was twenty-seven years old. When he finally began to remember what had happened to him, the memories came in bits and pieces, over a period of one year.

When he was nine years old, Brad was raped several times by his best friend's father. Brad believes his friend had also been sexually abused by this man. The first rape occurred on a Saturday afternoon. Brad was at his friend's house, and he believes that his friend was hiding in his bedroom. Brad's friend's father was the only adult in the house. He asked Brad to help him in the attic. Once they were alone, he slapped Brad and told him to undress. Brad remembers that when he tried to resist, the man knocked him down and told him that no one would hear him if he screamed. The man hit Brad again and made him undress, ordering him to fold his clothes so they would not be wrinkled. Then he raped him anally.

When Brad was raped, he felt intense pain, shame, and fear. He remembered being choked until he almost blacked out. The choking happened several times during the rape. Brad believed he was going to die. He felt terrified and confused; he could not understand why the man would choke him when no one could hear anyway. After the rape, Brad felt "dirty and scared." The abuser/rapist made him continue to lie on the dusty floor while he rubbed Brad's body and talked obscenely to him. Brad remembers trying to hold his breath while spiders crawled onto his legs and across his stomach. His friend's father laughed at the spiders and told Brad not to move, or he would die. Brad did not remember how long he was forced to lie naked on the floor, "but," he said, "it seemed like forever."

Brad was then ordered to go to the bathroom, wash off, and put his clothes back on. He remembers bleeding and feeling intense pain in his anus and rectum. The offender then drove him home. He told Brad that if he told anyone what had happened, he would kill him and his family. Brad believed him and told no one. He remembers at least two other rape incidents in which this man slapped him, choked him, and forced him to perform oral sex. Of these repeat offenses, Brad says, "I was afraid not to go [to my friend's house]. He scared me so much, I thought he would come and get me if I didn't go back. He had told me that if I didn't come back, he would kill me." The abuse stopped when Brad refused to visit his best friend anymore. In a therapy session, he told the group, "I remember being so frightened that he would come for me, that for months I kept looking over my shoulder. I would get up at night to make sure the doors were still locked."

In therapy, when Brad was processing his terror and rage at his attacker, he said, "That bastard not only stole my childhood, he stole my family." After Brad was raped, he never again felt close to his father, mother, or sister. From that time on, he always felt "different" and "distant." Although Brad still has some memory loss surrounding the year of his abuse, he remembers consciously trying to act as if nothing had happened to him. His family seemed to know that something was wrong, but they never found out that he had been raped. His father was an alcoholic, and his family did not communicate much anyway, so he survived the experience without talking to anyone about what had happened to him.

Although Brad was violently raped at the age of nine, eighteen years later the terror, shame, and confusion were still present in his life. Before he remembered this violent abuse, he could not understand why he was so terrified of spiders and attics. He had attacks of severe anxiety whenever he saw spiders, and he would never willingly go into an attic, either alone or with others.

Many other survivors were abused by an acquaintance as Brad was, but it is important to note here that violent sexual abuse often occurs in a child's own home, in the very place where the child should be safest.

Seductive Physical Abuse

If you were abused physically in a way that involved little or no violence, you may be left with a sense of confusion and a strong feeling that somehow you caused the abuse. Along with your feelings of shame, rage, and fear, you may have the recurring thought, "I enjoyed it, so it was my fault. I must have wanted it to happen." You may believe, "I am as responsible for the abuse as the abuser was." But remember this: You were a *child*. In your innocence and immaturity, it was easy for the abuser to manipulate and control you.

In seductive abuse, the perpetrator lures the child into taking an "active" part in the abuse. A seductive abuser often spends months or even years gaining a child's confidence, setting up an abuse situation long before actually physically abusing the child. Because children are naturally trusting, they are extremely vulnerable. As a natural part of their development, children want to please and to be important to adults. A seductive sexual offender betrays this simple and natural trust.

The emotional, and sometimes physical, damage caused by seductive abuse can be as painful and far-reaching as the effects of violent rape. If you were seductively sexually abused, try not to minimize the effects of this violation of your body. Of my clients who experienced seductive physical abuse, many have spent years carrying feelings of guilt and shame for "their part" in the abuse. Do not fall into the trap of taking on *any* of the responsibility for the abuse you experienced. You were a child, and you were not to blame. An adult who manipulates a child into sexual behavior is committing a serious crime. No matter what took place physically and no matter what the abuser told you, if you were a child who was seductively abused, you were a victim, not a perpetrator.

Paula's Story

Paula's abuse started when she was ten years old. She remembers lying on the couch with her stepfather, watching TV. Their closeness seemed very innocent to Paula. He would rub her back and sometimes her legs. Every once in a while, Paula's stepfather came into her room at night and gave her a massage. Paula enjoyed the "special attention," even though sometimes she felt uneasy when he touched her.

The occasional massages gradually became sexual. Paula's stepfather would tell her how pretty and "sexy" she was. When he massaged her, he began to rub her genitals, too, and sometimes he would kiss her. Paula felt too afraid to stop her stepfather, and at the same time she wasn't sure she really wanted him to stop touching her. "I was real confused so I didn't do anything," Paula later told her survivors' group. This fondling continued for months. One night her stepfather came into her room and massaged her, telling her how beautiful she was and how he needed her. Then he had intercourse with her. Of this abuse, Paula stated, "It didn't hurt and it did feel good, but I felt dirty inside."

After that night, Paula's stepfather began to come into her room several nights a week to have sex with her. By the time Paula was twelve, she was participating in a wide range of sexual activities with him. He gave her special presents. Sometimes, when she wanted new clothes or spending money, she would sexually tease him. "I knew that what I was doing was wrong, but I liked the attention and the presents. I thought I was ugly and dirty anyway, so I continued to participate in the incest."

Paula's stepfather continued to abuse her until she was sixteen years old. At that time, she ran away from home and got married. Paula told her therapy group that she had always blamed herself for the abuse. She believed her stepfather was "weak-willed" and could not control himself. Besides, she said, sometimes *she* had seduced *him*, which seemed to prove to her that she was at least partly to blame for the incest.

Paula's story is not unusual. Seductive sexual abuse can happen to children as young as three or four years old, or in their middle teenage years. Boys as well as girls are seductively sexually abused. The perpetrator is generally a family member or a trusted caregiver. Due to the seductive nature of Paula's abuse, it was easy for her to forget that she was raped. She may not have been beaten or directly threatened, and she may not have felt *physical* pain as is usually the case with rape; nevertheless, Paula was raped. She was a child. A person she trusted, who had power over her, raped her. When Paula began to think of her experience as a rape, she could begin to feel her repressed rage toward her stepfather.

These are some phrases I have heard frequently from survivors of seductive sexual abuse.

"It felt good."

"I felt needed and special."

"I liked having a secret."

"I knew it wasn't right, but I did it anyway."

"Sometimes I looked forward to having sex."

"I would act seductive on purpose."

These statements are part of the denial necessary to survive the trauma of being seductively abused. It is important to examine these statements more closely to understand the reasoning behind them, and to challenge the denial they represent.

"It felt good."

Our bodies are wired to enjoy the physical act of sex. It feels good to be rubbed, kissed, and otherwise sexually stimulated. Although children do not have fully developed sexual organs or the hormones that accompany sexual maturity, their genitals still respond to stimulation. As a child you would not have responded to sexual stimulation the same way an adult would, but if you were sexually stimulated, it probably felt *physically* pleasurable.

Even if your thoughts were, "Please don't do this," your body may still have responded to the sexual touching and rubbing. I have worked with clients who reported having orgasmlike experiences as early as infancy. Your body did not betray you if your abuse felt "good." Your body was just doing something it was designed to do—feel sexual pleasure. The betrayer was the abuser, not you or your body.

"I felt needed and special."

The person who abused you played upon your desire to be loved and to feel important. All children have these wishes. If you were a child who was often discounted or did not get the attention or nurturing you deserved, then you were easy prey for a seductive sexual abuser. Such a perpetrator used your natural need for love and attention in order to seduce and abuse you. Even though you were being betrayed and used, you may have felt "needed" by the abuser. Many survivors report that they enjoyed this "special status." Often, seductive sexual abusers will say "I need you" to their victims, but what they need most is help for the problem that causes them to seek sexual interaction with a child. When you think of your abuse, remember that you were a child then; you were unable to fully understand what was happening to you. As a child, your enjoyment of being "special" only indicates that you had a natural need for love and affection, and that you trusted your perpetrator to fulfill that need.

"I liked having a secret."

Having a secret also may have made you feel "special." Knowing your secret gave you a sense of power in a situation where you were, in fact, powerless. Even though you may have chosen never to tell your secret to anyone, just having that choice can give survivors a sense of control. Desperately trying to get control over some part of your life is a natural response to being sexually violated.

"I knew it wasn't right, but I did it anyway."

Because your abuse had to be kept secret, you probably sensed that what was happening to you was not good for you, and that it was wrong. But even when a child has the knowledge that something is wrong, that child cannot be expected to make an adult decision about it. Children learn *from adults* what is appropriate and inappropriate. It is unrealistic to expect that a child could correct an adult abuser's inappropriate behavior.

Because you were physically sexually abused, you were "sexualized" at an early age. Being "sexualized" means that, because of your experience of sexual abuse, you acted out sexually in ways that were inappropriate for your age. You may have engaged in compulsive masturbation or constantly touched your genitals. You may have sexually abused younger children or acted sexually seductive. A child who is aggressively sexual with adults or other children is showing evidence of having been sexually abused.

"Sometimes I looked forward to having sex."

Even a young child's body will respond to sexual stimulation—it feels good. If this was true for you, it is natural that you would look forward to having sex. It may be that sex was the only contact you had with another person. Out of loneliness, a need for attention, emotional or physical neglect, or any number of reasons, sex may have been a way for you to make that contact.

Remember that *you* were the one who was abused. You learned or were taught to use sex as a way to get your needs met, or even to survive. You were blameless, though you may have looked forward to having sex. You were a child. You were not responsible for being sexually abused.

"I would act seductive on purpose."

Because you were sexually abused, you were "sexualized" at an early age. Being "sexualized" means that, because of your experience of sexual abuse, you acted out sexually in ways that were inappropriate for your age. Acting sexually seductive, or sexually teasing, are behaviors that you learned would gain you some attention, or a gift, or perhaps something else you wanted. Remember that you are a survivor, and would have used anything you could to make your life more livable. When your behavior was sexually seductive, you were a *child acting out adult behavior.* The adults in your life held the responsibility to guide you into age-appropriate behavior. When you were sexually abused, you received the false message (spoken or unspoken) that being seductive was appropriate for someone your age. Again, you were innocent.

EMOTIONAL SEXUAL ABUSE

Emotional sexual abuse can be as painful and as damaging as physical sexual abuse. Although you may have been emotionally abused by someone outside of your family, most emotional abuse will have been perpetrated by members of your own family. If you were abused by a family member, you were emotionally incested. The more you trusted the abuser, the more painful and damaging the abuse was to you.

Emotional sexual abuse (sexual abuse without physical contact) is not as easy to identify or to define as physical sexual abuse. If you were sexually shamed, ridiculed, harassed, or intimidated, then you were emotionally sexually abused. If you were forced, coerced, or expected to assume a level of sexual maturity that was beyond your years, you

experienced emotional sexual abuse. Any physical contact at all between yourself and the abuser redefines emotional sexual abuse as
physical sexual abuse.

If you were emotionally sexually abused in childhood, you may tend
to minimize and discount the effects of your abuse now. When you
hear survivors of physical sexual abuse sharing their experiences, you
probably say to yourself, "That never happened to me," or, "My
experience wasn't that bad." Measuring your experience against someone else's will always lead you to incorrect assumptions about the
effects of your own abuse experiences. The most meaningful way to
find out how the abuse has affected you is by experiencing your own
feelings, and by discovering the dysfunction that exists in your life as a
result of being abused. Then you can begin to heal.

Violent Emotional Sexual Abuse

When you were a child, intimidating tones of voice, harsh ridicule, and
sexual shaming by a parent or other important caregiver would have
been enough to cause you to feel extreme guilt and shame. A parent's
sarcastic comment is as painful and humiliating to a child as a slap
across the face. Being laughed at, hearing degrading remarks or sexual
jokes about your body, being called a "slut," "whore," "tramp,"
"queer," "fag," or other sexually derogatory names seriously erodes a
child's self-respect, especially regarding body image and sexuality.

This type of abuse is categorized as "violent" because, as a child, you
would have responded to this kind of abuse just as if you had been
physically assaulted. The resulting fear, terror, hurt, shame, and guilt
you would have experienced—and internalized—could have severe
consequences for you (in both your childhood and adulthood). Carla,
a former client of mine, was a survivor of violent emotional sexual
abuse.

Carla's Story

An only child, Carla reported having had a close relationship with her
father. "He always treated me special," Carla said. When she reached
puberty, however, her relationship with her father changed dramatically. He began to make crude jokes about the size of her breasts, and
he teased Carla about getting her period. He told her that all boys

wanted to do was "fuck her." Carla's father made a rule that he had to meet every boy she went out with. When her father met her dates, he made jokes about her body in front of them.

Carla felt such shame and embarrassment when her father ridiculed her that she quit bringing boys home. Her father effectively stopped her from dating. He still watched her closely and accused her of dating behind his back, calling her a "slut" and a "tramp." By age fifteen, Carla was sneaking out of her house at night and had become sexually promiscuous. At seventeen, she was pregnant: "I got pregnant and got married just to get out of the house and away from my father. He was smothering me."

Carla experienced violent emotional sexual abuse. Although her father never touched her, his verbal assaults were devastating to Carla's self-esteem. She survived this harassment, but she internalized her father's cruelty: "Even after fifteen years, whenever I have sex I still hear his voice in my head telling me I'm a tramp," Carla told her therapy group. "He really has made it almost impossible for me to have a good relationship with a man."

Carla's abuse started at the onset of puberty. For some, the sexual shaming and ridicule may have begun at a much earlier age, continuing throughout childhood. As in Carla's case, constant verbal assaults on the sexual self-image of any growing child interrupts the growth of a healthy sexuality, leaving an invisible wound that becomes more painful the longer it is ignored.

Seductive Emotional Sexual Abuse

Seductive emotional sexual abuse occurs as a result of inappropriate sexually charged interactions between you and the abuser. The most common example of this kind of abuse is parent/child sexual equalization: when a parent treats a child as if that child were a sexual equal. In such a case, the child is being used to meet the parent's emotional need for an adult partner. If, as a boy, your mother elevated you to the position of "man of the house" or talked with you at length about her problems (sexual or otherwise) with her husband or her lover, then she sexually abused you emotionally. By drawing you into confidence about her sexual relationship(s), your mother placed you in the damaging position of expecting you to provide her with emotional support and sexual understanding beyond your years. You were made to assume the inappropriate role of caretaker to your mother. Such behavior on the part of parents is extremely confusing to children, often causing them deep feelings of sexual inadequacy and insecurity that they carry into adulthood.

If you are a woman who, as a child, became your father's "little girlfriend," you were emotionally sexually abused. Even if your father did not speak to you about his sex life but treated you as a "surrogate spouse" by using you in place of an adult female companion, you were still emotionally sexually abused. This kind of emotional sexual abuse can also occur between mother and daughter, or between father and son. It is not confined to the "surrogate spouse" scenario.

Whenever a child is used by a parent to fill the parent's emotional sexual needs, emotional sexual abuse is occurring. A healthy adult will seek out other adults to confide in and to be with rather than abuse their child in this way. It is natural for a parent to spend time alone with a child—to go out to dinner, to movies, or on camping trips. But when a child is being used to fill a parent's need for the kind of companionship typical of adult sexual relationships, emotional sexual abuse is taking place.

As a child it was natural for you to try to meet your parents' needs. All children love their parents and want them to be happy. Children have a basic need for their parents to be whole and capable. Their survival depends on it. Often, if a child detects illness or suffering in a parent, the child will try (without being told or asked) to "put the parent back together again," so that the parent will again be able to take care of the child. Even though you may not have understood what your parent confided to you, and even though you may not have understood fully what you were doing, you still would have tried to meet your parent's need. But simply because you were a child, you naturally "failed" to be an adequate "partner." Such emotional sexual abuse creates feelings of frustration and inadequacy. If this happened to you, that childhood feeling of inadequacy is the cause of your feeling emotionally and sexually unequal to your sexual partner in adulthood. In this way, emotional sexual abuse has *physical* consequences.

In one therapy group, a survivor named Will described his feelings about parent/child sexual equalization: "I hated it when my mother told me about her sexual frustrations with her boyfriends. I just wanted to be her son; I didn't want to know all that stuff. It made me feel like I should do something for her, but I didn't know what. I felt inadequate and confused then, and now I feel the same way with my lover. But at least now I know where these feelings came from, and I can work on letting them go."

COMBINED PHYSICAL
AND EMOTIONAL SEXUAL ABUSE

In typing and categorizing childhood sexual abuse, I have tried to simplify a complex phenomenon in order to help you to identify the type of sexual abuse you may have suffered. It is not unusual for survivors to report that they experienced more than one type of abuse in childhood. Your abuse may have been a combination of physical and emotional abuse, or it may have involved a blend of violence and seduction. You may have experienced violent emotional abuse by one family member and seductive physical abuse by someone else. Some survivors are physically sexually abused by their mothers and emotionally sexually abused by their fathers. Still, no matter how or by whom you were sexually abused, you are a survivor whose wounds can heal.

By now, it should be evident that it is impossible to draw the line between physical and emotional abuse, though I've tried to do so here for the sake of clarity. Your emotions and your body are not separate; your emotional pain is felt physically, and vice versa. Even if your defenses currently prevent you from feeling the emotional pain of the abuse you suffered, that pain is still within you. Whether the abuse was primarily emotional or primarily physical, you probably had some kind of physical response to the abuse. Such physical responses can manifest as sexual dysfunction, panic attacks, backaches, headaches, or a number of other physical ailments. In the same way, however you were sexually abused, you have probably experienced emotional responses of fear, terror, rage, and shame. In Chapter 4, the relationship between the body and its emotional states will be discussed in more detail.

Regardless of the type of sexual abuse you experienced, you have survived and you can recover. Simply by reading this book, you have made a conscious decision to begin, or to deepen, your own healing.

CHAPTER 3

Living with Secrets:
The Effects of Childhood Sexual Trauma

Alan's Story

I never knew what was wrong with me. I just thought I was messed up. I knew there was something different or strange about me. I looked successful from the outside—I was married, I had a kid, I had a good job. But I had a secret life. I'd sneak around and have affairs, go to porno shops, sometimes masturbate three or four times a day. No one ever knew about this "other life" I had. I felt ashamed and afraid about my compulsive sexual behavior, but I just couldn't stop it.

I was kind of a lonely kid. My dad drank a lot, and my mom had three nervous breakdowns, so she kept going to the hospital. When I was eight or nine, I started singing in the church choir, and I got to know the minister real well. I liked him. It felt good to have a friend. One day I was the last one to leave the building, and he asked me to come into his office. He told me he wanted to show me a secret, but I would have to take off my pants. As soon as my pants were off, he took my penis in his mouth and started sucking on it. It felt good. I liked it—a lot. But I felt sneaky; I guess I knew it was wrong. He told me never to tell anyone and I didn't.

After that, the minister would make excuses to be alone with me, and we would take turns sucking on each other. Even though it felt good, I always worried that someone would find out. When I would suck on him, I pretended like I enjoyed it, but most of the time I was disgusted. I would try to think of something else, or just shut off my feelings until it was over—I got to be good at that. I was so ashamed, but the minister seemed to be the only one who cared about me. I hated him, but I needed him. I was confused, I felt guilty, and I was constantly fearful. I was utterly miserable, but my parents never even noticed.

This minister and I were sexually involved for three years, until I was about twelve. Then he got another little boy. It was the only homosexual relationship I had ever had. I didn't have sex with anyone else until I was about seventeen, but I masturbated three or four times a day. Sometimes I'd do it so much that I got sores on my penis where I rubbed the skin off.

I never talked to anyone about this. For a long time I thought, "Well, it just happened. It wasn't such a big deal." But it was. When I think about it, I still feel guilty and dirty. And I'm ashamed of my secret sex life—I used to tell myself that it didn't really affect anyone but me, but it did. I've been married for ten years. When my wife found out about my last affair, she left me and took my little boy. I miss both of them. Those secrets cost me everything that was important to me. At least now I can talk about what happened to me and what I did. It's a relief to have my story out in the open.

Before Alan entered therapy, his childhood abuse experience had consumed his life and had cost him his marriage. Even though the minister/perpetrator had offered Alan the companionship he craved, the fear, shame, and compulsive behavior resulting from the sexual abuse crippled Alan in his adulthood. The sexual secrecy established by his childhood abuse experience became an uncontrollable pattern that ultimately shattered his family life. Like Alan, survivors who still carry the secret pain of childhood sexual abuse live in perpetual reaction to their past trauma.

If you, like Alan, were sexually abused as a child, the pain and fear you experienced are still with you. Left untreated behind a veil of repression and secrecy, this pain will not go away. The trauma will stay with you until you release it.

THE TRAUMATIZATION PROCESS

To survive the trauma of sexual abuse, you developed defenses that helped you survive emotionally (and sometimes physically). In adulthood, these defenses continue to operate in your life, keeping you in a "survival mode." Figure 2 illustrates the effects of your childhood sexual trauma. Starting with the sexual trauma itself, it charts the

FIGURE 2: Sexual Traumatization

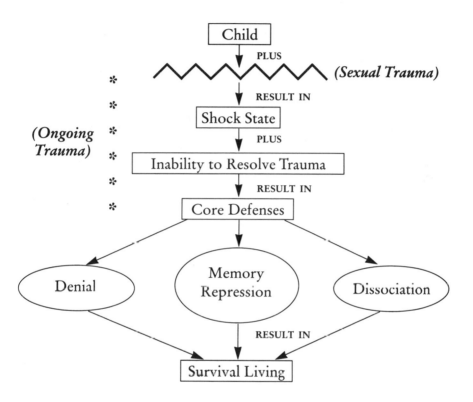

development of the survival defenses that have helped you to continue to function in the world, despite the pain you carry.

The Child

In figure 2, "the child" represents your basic state of innocence and trust before the sexual abuse occurred. Generally speaking, no matter what kind of family environment you grew up in, you learned to adapt to that environment. Your family may have been mildly (or even severely) dysfunctional. In any case, you adjusted to it and learned to live in it.

Sexual Trauma

"Sexual trauma" in figure 2 represents the point in your life when you were first sexually abused. If you were subjected to one single sexually abusive incident, here lies the source of your pain and fear. If you were subjected to ongoing or periodic sexual abuse, it represents the first time that you were sexually abused.

The asterisks on the left side of figure 2 represent ongoing sexual abuse or periodic sexual abuse. Each time you were abused, you suffered additional trauma. Your body may have learned to go numb, you may have learned to "switch off" your emotions, you may even have believed you had gotten used to being abused, but you were still experiencing a trauma. The feelings and experiences you repressed during each abuse incident are still with you.

Remember, sexual abuse can be physical or emotional, violent or seductive. Regardless of how you were sexually abused, you were traumatized by the experience. A trauma is defined as "a catastrophic emotional/physical event that is outside the normal range of experience." Sexual abuse of any kind falls far outside the range of normal childhood experiences. It was a catastrophic jolt to your system. Like all wounded human beings, you responded to this trauma by going into shock.

Shock State

The shock state is a natural response to being sexually abused. During the abuse your physical, emotional, and mental faculties became overloaded by what was happening to you. Each of these systems responded in a way that would ensure your survival. *Physically*, you may have experienced feeling separate from (or hovering over) your body, or your body may have felt wooden or numb. Such defenses arose to protect you from the physical pain of the sexual abuse. *Emotionally*, you may have shut down in order to protect yourself from the overwhelming terror and shame you were feeling. *Mentally*, you may have "gone blank" or directed your thoughts to other things, to distract you from the painful realization of what was happening to you. Most survivors of sexual abuse employed all of these defenses, to some degree, as they entered the shock state. If you experienced physical sexual abuse that was not painful but pleasurable, the emotional overload you experienced as a result of being sexually used was enough to cause you to go into the state of shock.

Inability to Resolve the Trauma

All human beings must deal with trauma or crisis as part of life. The death of a friend, the divorce of one's parents, and life-threatening illnesses are all examples of trauma. We human beings are remarkable creatures. We have a natural tendency to return to health, to recover from—and even to be strengthened by—our personal traumas. The trauma of sexual abuse, however, is not resolvable by a child. You needed (at least) the help of supportive adults and family to heal from what happened to you. If you are reading this book, it is unlikely that you received the support you needed to resolve your trauma at the time it occurred.

There are two common reasons why children do not receive the support and help they need to recover from sexual abuse. If you were abused by a family member, it is highly likely that the incest was kept secret. The people to whom you would have gone for comfort and healing were themselves part of the problem. In an incest situation, children have no choice but to deal with the sexual trauma as best they can.

If you were not an incest survivor, there may have been other reasons why your family was unable to give you the support you needed: Alcoholism or another compulsive-addictive disorder may have been active in your family system. Your parents may have been cold and distant, uninterested in you. If you grew up in a dysfunctional family system, you probably didn't tell your family you had been abused; if you did, they may have handled it in a way that didn't help you heal. In either case, you would not have been able to resolve the sexual trauma.

To determine whether or not you grew up in a *dysfunctional family*, ask yourself the following questions:

1. Did you try to hide your true feelings and thoughts from your parents?

2. Did you believe your parents could not handle the truth?

3. Did you experience your family as an unsafe place where you could not find protection and support?

4. As a child, did you try to take care of your parents, or protect them?

Answering yes to any of the above questions indicates that your family was dysfunctional. Remember, for you, a dysfunctional family is a family who could not protect you and assist you in healing from your experience of sexual abuse. There are many definitions of *family dysfunction*, but for the survivor of childhood sexual abuse, the definition is very simple and subjective. If you were sexually abused as a child, and if you are still in pain from that experience, it is highly likely that you came from a dysfunctional family.

The Core Defenses

To live with the pain of ongoing abuse or a single incident of abuse, you had to develop defenses. It is of great importance to understand—and even to appreciate—your defenses: They protected you from the pain and horror of the abuse you experienced as a child, and they continue to protect you from feeling that intense pain. Because your defenses operate mostly on an unconscious level, you will probably remain unaware of them until they are pointed out to you. The unfortunate paradox about these defenses is that, while they protect you from the pain of your past, they greatly diminish your ability to have a full and happy life as an adult. For this reason, healing from your childhood sexual trauma must include discovering and discarding defenses that are no longer necessary. There is no doubt that this is a scary proposition. Even with lots of loving support, the process hurts a lot. But it is by walking through the old pain that you will reach your natural state of joy. Once you put down some of that armor, that feeling of heaviness will leave you.

Three major defenses commonly used by survivors of childhood sexual abuse are:

Memory repression

Dissociation

Denial

These core defenses helped you survive your childhood sexual abuse. Even as an adult in recovery, your core defenses will help you maintain a balance between feeling and expressing your stored pain, and continuing to function in your daily life. Remember that your defenses are powerful allies, not enemies. As you move through the process of learning about and discarding them, sometimes these defenses may actually seem to be stumbling blocks to recovery. They aren't. Accepting your defenses by acknowledging the part they played in your survival will help you release them more easily.

Now we'll look at each of these core defenses individually.

Memory Repression

The feelings of shame, horror, and other overwhelming emotional states you experienced during the sexual abuse were so strong that you repressed the memory of them. This "forgetting" has kept you from living in constant painful awareness of the abuse. Remember that you were a child when the abuse occurred. You were not emotionally or physically capable of dealing with the abuse as an adult would. There are two major factors that contribute to memory repression as a survival defense: your age at the time of the abuse, and the level of violence you were subjected to at that time.

The younger you were when you were sexually abused, the more likely it is that you experienced memory loss around the abuse incident(s). If you were abused between birth and seven years of age, your memory loss around the abuse may be total. You simply will not remember what happened to you. In very early childhood, your ability to protect yourself was almost completely limited to memory repression. If the abuse occurred sometime between age seven and puberty, you are more likely to have partial, rather than total, memory loss around the incident(s). Children age seven or older are much more sophisticated emotionally and mentally—they tend to use a combination of core defenses. If you were sexually abused at puberty or after, you probably used defenses other than memory repression. The chart on the next page illustrates the relationship of age range to the degree of memory repression (MR) you may have.

Age 0 to 7	7 to 11	11 or older
Most Memory *Repression*	*Partial Memory* *Repression*	*Least Memory* *Repression*

The presence of violence (whether implied or carried out) along with the abuse also relates to the repression of memories. The more violent the abuse, the greater the likelihood that the survivor of that abuse used memory repression as a primary defense. Being beaten, tortured, and/ or violently sexually penetrated is severely traumatic. Where extreme violence was present, repressing the memory of the experience may have been the only way to survive the experience and still be able to function. Violent sexual abuse includes intimidation, seeing others violently abused, and hearing sexual threats or other verbal assaults. Severe "emotional" violence often triggers memory repression as a survival defense. Although seductive abuse can also lead to memory repression, it is the type of abuse least likely to trigger this defense. The chart below shows how memory repression is related to the kind of violence experienced with sexual abuse.

Physical Violence	Coercion	Seduction
Most Memory *Repression*	*Partial Memory* *Repression*	*Least Memory* *Repression*
Beating	Threats	Manipulation
Torture	Seeing others beaten	Not overtly violent
Violent penetration	Verbal assault	

In addition to memory loss around the abuse itself, long periods of time surrounding the abusive episode may be missing from the survivor's memory. If the abuse was violent, began at an early age, or continued over a long period of time, you may not remember most or all of your childhood.

Dana, a man who was sexually abused by his grandmother and his father, remarked during group, "I never thought it was odd that I didn't remember my childhood. I didn't think anyone remembered their childhood. Sometimes when I heard people talk about having birthday parties and going on vacations as children, I would feel uncomfortable, but I would shrug it off and forget about it. Now I can see how strange that was. It was as if I'd been born at the age of eleven or twelve. I didn't remember anything before that."

You may have partial memory of the abuse, or only a feeling that "something happened" to you. In either case, it is not necessary to have total memory recall in order to heal from childhood sexual abuse.

Dissociation

Dissociation means that, although you remember being sexually abused, you feel emotionally disconnected from the experience. When you recall the abuse, your emotions "go numb." It is as if your connection to yourself has been severed. You may experience the numbness as a feeling of being distant or far away, or as feeling physically numb or cold. Or you may speak of the abuse as though it happened to someone else.

Dissociation is a very powerful defense. It helped you survive by "switching off" your feelings and body sensations during the sexual abuse. The dissociation response protected you from a frightening and confusing experience at a time when you were too young to defend yourself otherwise. It is a simple but effective defense: If you do not feel the pain, then you feel "safe," no matter what is happening to your body. And children need very much to feel safe.

Another form of dissociation is often referred to as "splitting off." Some survivors report the feeling of leaving their body while they were being sexually abused. They have the physical sensation of disconnecting and moving away from their body entirely, so as not to feel their overwhelming terror. Especially common among survivors of violent sexual abuse, such out-of-body experiences sometimes include the ability to watch the abuse from a safe distance, often from the ceiling of the room where the abuse took place. Dissociation includes the memory of the trauma, but not the pain of the experience.

As with memory repression, survivors can experience dissociation regardless of their age at the time of the abuse. But it is my observation that survivors who were sexually abused as older children (and who therefore remember more of their abuse experience) are more likely to use dissociation as a defense. If you were sexually abused frequently over a long period of time, there is a high probability that you used dissociation to help you survive that ongoing trauma. Survivors of seductive sexual abuse (who are often older children) effectively use dissociation to endure their feelings of betrayal and shame.

One survivor described her dissociative experience this way: "It was actually a relief when he finally came into my room. Then I stopped being afraid. During the abuse I would leave my body; it was like I wasn't even there. I would just drift away. Sometimes I could even see what was happening to me. But it was as if it were happening to somebody else, or as if I were watching it on TV. It all seemed unreal. When he was finished, I would go back to my body. That's when I would feel dirty and sometimes even throw up. But during the abuse I didn't feel a thing."

Denial

The third core defense, denial, defends a survivor mentally against the pain of the abuse. It is the little voice inside your head that tells you "it wasn't that bad" or that "it was no big deal." Denial tells you that what happened to you really did not happen to you at all. It is your mind's way of hiding the truth about the sexual abuse. The logic of denial runs this way: If you say to yourself that "it wasn't that bad" or "I must have made it up," then maybe you will never have to experience the pain of what happened to you. Denial is a state of mind that you talk yourself into. If you tell yourself over and over that nothing happened, eventually you will believe that you dreamed or imagined the whole thing.

The survivor using denial is not entirely conscious of this process, which clouds the memory of the abuse and the feelings associated with it. But as recovery begins, the survivor learns to recognize the mind's denial statements when they arise and to heal what is false by continually applying reality to it.

Denial is a formidable defense. In spite of the survivor's actual memories of sexual abuse and validation from other survivors about the impact of abuse, denial minimizes and discounts the survivor's real experience. Denial is a way to avoid experiencing pain. If you were sexually abused by a parent or other trusted person, the pain of your betrayal is so intense that denying the experience sometimes seems the only way to live with it. If you were abused by a stranger, denial has protected you from intense terror. Denial is your attempt to return to feeling that the world is a safe place, in spite of the trauma you experienced.

In general, denial takes two forms: total denial and denial by minimization. *Total denial* exists when, in the face of overwhelming evidence, in the face of logic, and in spite of actual memories of the sexual abuse, you continue to deny that it happened. The truth is so painful and frightening that you simply refuse to believe it. With *denial by minimization* (which is more common), you downplay the extent of the abuse or the impact it has on your present life. Although the denial defense can be present in a sexual abuse survivor at any age, minimization is most often used by survivors who were older children at the time of the abuse.

Corinne was seductively abused by her uncle when she was eleven years old. Although she had clear memories of the abuse and could relate in detail what had happened to her, she denied for fifteen years that the abuse had any impact on her.

> It only happened four times, so I thought that it was no big deal. Besides it didn't hurt and felt good, even though I was ashamed about it. I remember when my friends talked about sex and boys, I felt dirty. They giggled and whispered about things I had already done. I felt ashamed, but I just told myself, "It was no big deal." Now I feel enraged when I think about my uncle. How could he do that to me? I was just a little girl! I wanted to giggle and whisper with my friends instead of feeling dirty and used.

The three core defenses often work in concert with one another. It is quite common to have memory loss, dissociation, and denial all operating at the same time to ensure your pyschic, and even physical, survival of the sexual trauma. Your powerful feelings during the abuse were contained by these defenses. Eventually, however, containing so much pain and terror becomes extremely uncomfortable, even impossible. In adulthood, the situation is reversed: In order to survive, to be healthy and free, you must acknowledge your past pain and feel it so that it can be released from your mind, your body, and your life.

Even if you are a survivor who does not consciously remember being sexually abused, all the fear, shame, terror, grief, horror, loss, and rage that you experienced when you were abused are still stored in your body. Whether you were abused once or many times, you still hold the pain you experienced as a child. Carrying these raw emotions within you is like having an open but invisible wound. Though it is hidden deep inside, it still desperately needs to be healed. The energy it takes for you to contain so much intense emotion causes you to experience another kind of physical overload, which results in survival living.

SURVIVAL LIVING

The term *survivor* accurately describes the state of a sexually abused child who has grown to adulthood. Simply by living through your experience, you moved from being a child victim to an adult survivor. The core survival defenses of repression, dissociation, and denial kept you mentally and emotionally intact during and in the years following the sexual abuse. Now that you are an adult, you continue to use the defenses you employed as a child to protect yourself from the pain of that sexual trauma. Survival living means that you are simply continuing to *survive*, without being able to fully *live*. Survivors' unhappiness springs from the fact that they intuitively know they are only surviving rather than unfolding their potential for a contented and rewarding existence. Being happy and fulfilled is impossible when the body and mind are trained to remain on "survival alert" twenty-four hours a day. More will be said later about the physical aspects of survival living.

The Tensions of Survival Living

Survival living greatly diminishes your emotional and physical resources. Being sexually abused threw you into a confusing constellation of emotional and physical experiences. Even an adult would have been overwhelmed by such abuse, but for a child the effects are devastating. Because the pain you felt was intolerable, your defenses walled off your awareness of the trauma. To the extent that you were unable to process your experience of the sexual abuse, that pain remains with you. As an adult still carrying this wound, your situation has changed. The crisis has passed, but your body and psyche still don't "know" that yet. In order to get you to recognize your need for healing, a great pressure builds up inside you between the reality of your experience and the defenses that hide that reality.

Figure 3: Held Pain

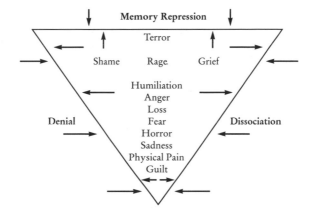

The diagram in figure 3 shows the "war" between the emotional pain of sexual abuse and the defenses that arose to protect you, the child, from being overwhelmed by that pain.

The walls of the triangle represent the three defenses enclosing the original pain of the sexual trauma. Outside the triangle, the arrows pointing inward show the force the core defenses exert to hold this pain. In turn, all the emotional responses associated with the sexual abuse exert force on the defenses (arrows pointing outward). So the unhealed survivor of sexual trauma faces an ever-present dilemma: Your defenses helped you to survive, but to heal—to feel fully alive— you must consciously experience the anger, fear, shame, grief, and other emotions associated with the sexual abuse. No matter how many of the three core defenses you used or how strongly they are constructed, this inner struggle will persist until you recover.

This is a natural process. Though it can be very uncomfortable at times, we human beings have an inner force always urging us to be as pain-free and as healthy as we can be. But we can never be pain-free as long as our defenses hold back our emotional experience. In addition to this natural *internal* pressure to release and experience the pain, survivors experience *external* pressure on the core defenses. This external pressure can come in the form of crippling feelings or a persistent frustration in sexual relationships. In this way, the pressure of our real experiences (both within and without us) works to erode and overcome our defenses so that we can begin to heal. At first, the defenses will respond by increasing their efforts to "protect" you from feeling the pain of the sexual abuse. Why can't survivors just continue to strengthen their core defenses and avoid the pain altogether? The answer is that, as the conflict between reality and the defenses becomes more and more intense, eventually survivors are using nearly all of their available energy just to keep containing the pain. Living in a survival mode is not like living on a battlefield; it's more like *being* a battlefield:

"One day I was driving home from work and I felt a sharp knot right at the top of my stomach," recalled Martha, a survivor. "I was having trouble breathing, it was such a thick knot of pain. I had the sense that something was about to explode, not just in my body but in my life. I knew that this knot was going to burst open, and that when it did, something big was going to happen. It was a strange feeling. I felt 'caught,' as if 'the jig was up.' Within a month, I started therapy because I was having 'flashbacks' of the sexual abuse from morning till night."

Secondary Consequences

When the pressure to release the pain becomes stronger than the defenses, a survivor like Martha begins to experience *secondary consequences* of the sexual abuse. These "symptoms" actually signal the beginning of healing, as the survivor begins to experience (if indirectly) some of the pain of the abuse. Here are some common secondary consequences of childhood sexual abuse:

Narrow range of emotional experiences

Emotional flooding

Emotional numbing

Shortened attention span

Confused thinking

Feeling hopeless and helpless

Nightmares

Flashbacks

Body memories

Panic attacks

Body objectification

Chronic fatigue

Compulsive-addictive diseases

Multiple personality disorder

Chronic minor illnesses

Sexual dysfunction

Intimacy dysfunction

Offender behavior

Remember that, for a survivor, all these secondary consequences are the direct result of having been sexually abused. The sexual abuse is the origin of the pain. As long as survivors remain unaware of (or disregard) their sexual abuse experience, they remain confused about their own behavior, beliefs, and feelings. For this reason, many survivors believe they are "going crazy."

If you are a survivor experiencing some or all of the symptoms on this list, you are not crazy or insane. You behave and feel as you do because of what happened to you as a child. Your held pain is so intense that it makes you volatile. It is as though your powerful emotional and physical reactions to your abuse simply cannot stand to be ignored any longer, so they begin to manifest in the form of these secondary consequences.

It is no wonder that you are often tired, confused, and frustrated. The original pain has now multiplied into so many different forms! When survivors experience secondary consequences of sexual abuse, they usually seek help for these "symptoms," since they appear to be the primary problem. But treating the secondary consequences of the abuse—rather than healing the original trauma—will not solve the problem permanently. It would be like taking cough syrup to cure a case of pneumonia: Your cough may quiet down for a while, but your body will continue to be weakened by the illness.

Now we'll take a closer look at some of the secondary consequences. It is impossible to include all the secondary effects of childhood sexual abuse, and you may have experienced some that are not listed or discussed here. On the other hand, you probably will not have every single one of these symptoms. The important thing to remember is that these feelings and behaviors are the result of the sexual abuse; they do not appear without reason.

Narrow Range of Emotional Experience

Some survivors swing between anger, rage, deep grief, and sorrow, but they are unable to experience the broader range of human emotional experience. Emotions like happiness, bliss, annoyance, sadness, hurt, and fondness are unavailable to them. Although survivors may experience some emotions in the extreme (especially rage, grief, and terror), the subtle nuances of these emotions are missing from their experience. Instead of feeling annoyance at misplacing his car keys, for example, one man I worked with would fly into a rage and punch walls or hit himself. The feeling of mild annoyance was simply not available to him. Another client reported that she sometimes became depressed and cried for long periods of time if she thought that a friend disapproved of the way she was dressed.

If you have a narrow range of emotions, you probably do not experience extremes of "good" emotions such as happiness and joy. A narrow emotional range is usually confined to more painful or "negative" emotions. Many survivors live in a state of relative absence of feeling, but they occasionally launch into extreme emotional states with little or no provocation.

Emotional Flooding

Emotional flooding is another way in which survivors may begin to experience held emotions associated with sexual abuse (or the time period surrounding the abuse). At times, for no apparent reason, a survivor may sink into a deep grief and sorrow or fly into fits of rage. The sudden onset of these powerful emotional states is baffling to survivors and to those around them, because often it cannot be connected to a particular event (or it may occur in response to an event that is seemingly insignificant). Emotional flooding happens when survivors' defenses temporarily collapse, causing them to feel overwhelming emotional pain, even though they may still be unaware of the source of that pain. Unlike the narrowing of emotional range, such flooding can include any emotion: joy, sadness, fear, anger, or a complex combination of emotion and compulsion.

Hilary was a working mother whose daughter stayed at day care during the week. Hilary had bouts of overwhelming fear and dread that came on quite suddenly. Her fear was always accompanied by a powerful compulsion to "do something" to ensure the safety of her five-year-old daughter, so Hilary made frequent calls to the day-care center. Sometimes her fear and compulsion were so intense that she would immediately leave work and drive directly to the day-care center to check on her daughter. Not only were these episodes stressful for Hilary, but it was extremely frightening for the little girl to see her mother in such an anxious state. During therapy, Hilary discovered that she herself had been molested at the age of five. Once she was able to understand the source of her feeling of dread, Hilary could begin to work directly on her recovery. Her intense fear and the compulsion to check on her daughter gradually disappeared.

Emotional Numbing

When faced with the possibility of remembering their abuse, survivors often become emotionally numb. At these times, all emotional feeling and even some physical feeling will be suppressed. Because some survivors used emotional numbing to survive the original sexual trauma, they become emotionally numb when faced with remembering their past. Emotional numbness is the inability to experience one's emotions as they occur—it does not mean the absence of emotion.

When he was a boy, Mark's mother stripped him and beat him with a belt. He was sexually abused this way many times over a period of years. Sometimes the abuse occurred in the presence of his older sister and her friends. Mark's shame and embarrassment were so painful that he eventually shut off his feelings entirely. In therapy he reported that during the beatings he would "stand there like a piece of wood," feeling nothing. As an adult, he would automatically go numb whenever he felt threatened. He would even go numb when he was excited or very happy. Mark told his therapy group that he went numb even when he didn't want to—he couldn't help it.

Some survivors become emotionally numb only when they begin to feel uncomfortable, but others stay emotionally shut down nearly all the time. These survivors "think" their feelings rather than physically experiencing them. When asked how they feel, these survivors mentally *decide* what they should be feeling, then report having that emotion.

Pat had survived frequent violent incest by her father over a period of eight years. As a child, she had learned to "stop feeling" and go numb while she was being abused. As an adult in therapy, Pat reported, "I know I have feelings sometimes, but most of the time I just feel numb." Being numb was not unpleasant for her, but she had a vague sense that she was "missing something." As Pat began to identify her buried feelings, little by little she rediscovered her emotional experience. She learned to differentiate between what she *thought* she felt and the emotions she was *actually feeling.* Pat soon began to focus on her rage at the father who had raped her. After doing her first anger work in therapy, Pat commented, "It's like someone pulled the rug out from under me. I feel kind of shaky, but I don't have to think about it. I can feel it!"

Shortened Attention Span

Some survivors have difficulty concentrating, and their attention moves rapidly from one subject to another. Such mental "jumps" prevent their mind from focusing on any single topic, including the sexual abuse. In some cases, this lack of focus seriously interferes with their ability simply to communicate. Others may complain, "Didn't you hear what I just said?" and tire of repeating themselves.

In early stages of treatment and recovery, the survivor's inability to concentrate or focus will often worsen as the defenses make a last-ditch effort to guard against the terror and rage that must surface so that healing can take place. The intense energy of the pain of the abuse forces the survivor's mind to wander, to avoid the reality of the past suffering.

"I couldn't seem to concentrate on anything for more than a few seconds," Juan, a survivor, reported. "I'd get in the car and forget where I was going. I had several minor auto accidents. Sometimes I would be driving on the freeway and start thinking of a million things, and before I knew it, I'd be nearly out of town! My poor car looked like it had been in a crash derby. I had lots of fender-benders because I just couldn't hold my attention on what I was doing."

If you are having difficulty concentrating, or if your ability to mentally focus seems to be getting worse, this is highly likely to diminish as you continue in recovery.

Confused Thinking

Survivors who are holding intense pain often become confused because their pain is so large that it cannot be safely examined by the mind. Their thoughts may become disjointed and disorganized, as though internal defenses rise to prevent further awareness of the abuse. Such confusion is usually intermittent, but it may become particularly intense when the survivor attempts to think directly about the sexual abuse.

"Every time I tried to talk about my childhood or think about him touching me that way," said Chris, "I would get totally confused, as if somebody just stirred up my thoughts with a big stick. Everything would run together. It was weird." During a therapy session, Chris described this secondary consequence of his abuse experience. "I'm pretty organized most of the time," he continued, "but if I try to remember or talk about being molested, I get confused. It seems like the closer I get to the details of what happened to me, the more confused I get. It's started to affect my job and everything else in my life. It scares me."

Chris's description of his confusion may echo your experience. It is useful to remember that the confusion will lessen as you continue to recover. As the past surfaces, so does the held pain. When you begin to feel your held pain, all the secondary consequences (including confusion) will have outlived their usefulness. Once you begin to heal your wound directly, the symptoms will leave.

Feeling Hopeless and Helpless

Because survivors had no power to control what happened to them as sexually abused children, they often have a persistent feeling of hopelessness about life in general. At the time of their abuse, children are in a hopeless situation: They are severely wounded without any power to stop what is happening to them. A child cannot be expected to get away from an abuser. Children must rely solely on internal defenses to help them survive sexual trauma. Survival is not experienced by children as a triumph; their state of helplessness is real. In adult life, long after the abuse, the survivor's helpless or hopeless feeling continues until the original childhood pain has begun to heal.

This feeling of hopelessness and helplessness can invade all areas of life, robbing survivors of their motivation and their sense of usefulness in the world. As one survivor reported, "Everything seemed out of my control. Whatever I did or however successful I was at anything, sports, my job, anything, it was never enough to completely wipe away that helpless feeling. Sometimes I would fantasize being rescued by someone who would take care of me, but then I would feel even more helpless. There was no way I could win."

Feeling helpless and hopeless arises from the belief that nothing one does will change things for the better. A sense of stagnation sets in, and it may prevent survivors from taking ordinary risks such as asking for a raise at work or simply picking up the phone to call a friend. Another survivor said that, to her, life had been "like trying to walk through molasses. Everything I did seemed so hard." Still another survivor described her hopelessness as "a heavy dark weight in my chest."

The survivor who feels hopeless and helpless develops the attitude, "Well, things aren't working out, they're never going to work out, and there's nothing I can do about it." This attitude can lock survivors into a habitual course of action long after it has proven unworkable, often causing them to remain in unfulfilling, sometimes abusive relationships.

For some survivors, feelings of hopelessness and helplessness come and go, while for others these feelings develop into deep depression. Like the other secondary consequences, the hopeless-helpless feeling can intensify during early recovery, as it did for Eve: "I always had a nagging feeling that everything I did was futile—you know, 'What's the use?' But it never got so bad that I couldn't get over it. After I found out that my father sexually abused me, it got a lot worse. Sometimes I stayed on the couch all day. I wouldn't even move. Everything in my life just seemed too difficult. It lasted several months, but I kept coming to group and the depression gradually lifted."

Nightmares

Many survivors have extremely frightening nightmares. They may wake up screaming, sweating, and with a deep feeling of terror and fear. Nightmares may involve genitalia (a penis or vagina) or being raped or chased. Sometimes a survivor's nightmares consist of apparently harmless images (such as small details of clothing or a tuft of hair), but to the survivor the dream is still terrifying. It is still a nightmare, whether or not anyone else might be scared by it. During sleep the core defenses sometimes weaken and the original memories of sexual abuse, along with severe emotional pain, come into the survivor's dreams.

"I keep having the same dream over and over," said Karsten. "I'm in a house and there is someone outside trying to get in. I'm so afraid. I run from room to room, quickly closing and locking all the windows and doors. I'm terrified. I know he's going to get in no matter what I do. I just can't get to that last door. I see it open. Then I wake up screaming." Karsten had been having this recurring nightmare for several years when she told it to the people in her survivors' therapy group. At that time, two other group members shared that they had had the same nightmare.

If you are having similar nightmares, your unconscious mind is trying to give you information about the abuse you experienced. This happens to many survivors. As recovery deepens, your nightmares will become much less intense and less frequent. (To use your dreams and nightmares as opportunities for healing work, see Chapter 17, Dreams.)

Flashbacks

Flashbacks are spontaneous memories of sexual abuse that surface without warning. They can be extremely vivid and terrifying. Bits and pieces of memories of the abuse suddenly flash forth into the survivor's consciousness. The survivor does not understand the source of the spontaneous memories; therefore when a flashback occurs, the survivor often feels "crazy" or "out of control." Once flashbacks begin, they may become more frequent and more intense. Then, as though the dam had burst, memories of the abuse flood the survivor's consciousness. At this point the core defense denial often appears, and survivors say to themselves, "This couldn't have happened to me. I must be going crazy."

Flashbacks can come in many different forms. One survivor began to "see" telephone poles turning into penises as she was driving down the highway. This flashback was accompanied by extreme fear and horror. Another described a flashback this way: "I just suddenly saw a snapshot of me being forced to have sex. The flashback just happened," he said. "There was no warning. I was just talking to this woman, and suddenly there it was—a picture of me being forced to have sex with my uncle. It was so strange. I just stopped talking, and I guess I must have looked scared. The woman asked me if I was all right. I said yes, but really I thought I was losing my mind."

Body Memories

Body memories are closely related to flashbacks and are mostly experienced by survivors of physical sexual abuse. During body memories the physical body will, without apparent reason, reexperience the abuse. Body memories generally parallel the type of physical abuse the survivor experienced in childhood. A survivor who was anally raped may have extreme anal soreness or swelling, a sudden onset of severe constipation, or unexplained rectal bleeding. A survivor who was choked or orally raped may experience a choking sensation without warning, especially when trying to talk about the sexual abuse. Like flashbacks, body memories can be terrifying. Survivors who have body memories often report feeling that their body is "out of control."

Many adult survivors experience body memories during sexual activity with their partners. This usually occurs without warning. You may have been enjoying sex for years and suddenly have a body memory of the abuse, which seriously affects sex with your partner.

This happened to Melanie. "Everything was normal," she said. "We were making love just as we always did. It felt good—but then suddenly I felt smothered. My husband's weight on top of me felt like a ton. I couldn't breathe. I panicked and began to hit him and told him to get off of me. My body felt like wood. It felt as if I were being crushed. I had intense pain in my vagina. It was horrible. When my husband rolled off of me, I curled into a ball and sobbed. I couldn't believe what was happening. Neither could he. We had made love hundreds of times before, and nothing like this had ever happened."

As she told her therapy group this story, Melanie explained that she had never known she had been sexually abused. Suddenly, during sex, her body had "remembered," and she had reexperienced the abusive incident from her childhood. If you have had a physical memory such as this one, it is your body's way of letting you know what happened to you. Whether your experience seems to you to be more or less intense than Melanie's, your feelings about it are real and valid. You are not crazy.

Panic Attacks

Panic attacks begin with intense feelings of dread and panic. The survivor may experience shortness of breath, rapid heartbeat, tightness in the chest, and a belief that death or insanity is imminent. Feeling loss of control over the ability to stay alive is common during these attacks. When memories of childhood abuse surface without warning, the survivor may become overwhelmed by feelings of helplessness that result in a panic attack. Panic attacks can also accompany flashbacks or body memories.

"My heart would race and I couldn't catch my breath," said Craig. "I was so frightened. It was this sense of impending doom. . . . I thought I was going to die. One time I went to the emergency room because I thought I was having a heart attack. They hooked me up to an EKG machine and did all these tests. The doctor told me my heart was fine and suggested I see a therapist. It seemed so unreal. I never knew what might trigger one of these episodes. Now I know they happened because my grandmother sexually abused me. When I used to have panic attacks, though, I wasn't at all aware. Now when I feel one coming on, I know where it's coming from, and it either goes away or else it just isn't that bad."

The kind of panic attack that Craig described is fairly common among survivors. Craig had never experienced a panic attack until he had been in recovery from alcoholism for two years. Like many survivors who are addicted to alcohol, drugs, food, or other destructive compulsions, Craig had used his addiction to shield himself from the pain of the sexual abuse. When he stopped the addictive behavior, he was confronted with the past. His panic attacks were a signal of the unresolved pain of his childhood sexual trauma. Not long after he entered therapy specifically to deal with the panic attacks, Craig began to work on sexual abuse issues, and his panic attacks stopped.

Body Objectification

Many survivors have the belief that their physical body is an object. You, too, have a deep feeling that your body is not your own. Some survivors who experience body objectification report that they did not care what happened to their body and would even mutilate or scar it. Psychically disconnecting from the body in this way is a direct result of having been used sexually in childhood. When a child's body is used as an object, the child continues to experience the body as an object. Rather than feeling that your body is to be loved as an expression of yourself, you may treat your own body as a thing that exists for the use of others.

"One day I stepped out of the shower and looked in the mirror, and there was this real person standing there," says Mona. "It was *me*! I was *there*! I just stood there and looked and looked into my own eyes. I was so amazed that I was there in that body. I realized then that all my life I had only looked at pieces of my body, checking to see which parts needed improvement, which parts I'd like to get rid of, and so on. I just saw my body as this machine with all these separate parts—no feelings, no *being*, really. Suddenly I saw that my body was my *home*. I felt what it meant to really love myself."

A twenty-two-year-old survivor of violent incest, Mona had been actively working in a therapy group for two years when she shared this story. Seeing one's body as an expression of oneself, rather than as a meaningless object, signals the beginning of deep and lasting recovery from childhood sexual trauma.

Chronic Fatigue

It takes a great deal of energy to hold inside the pain associated with childhood sexual abuse. The struggle to contain such suffering is exhausting, both emotionally and physically. Many survivors are constantly fatigued, no matter how much they sleep. They simply do not have the energy to participate fully in life. For such survivors, daily existence is gray and tiring. All they want is to be left alone.

This is how Pam, a survivor of long-term emotional incest, described her chronic fatigue: "I wasn't depressed, I just didn't have the energy to do the things I wanted to do. I was tired all the time. Everything seemed so hard. My friends would call me to do things, and I just didn't have the energy to go out. I didn't even feel like talking to anyone. It wasn't just emotional—I was physically tired. I wasn't able to do much of anything. I was completely exhausted."

If you experience chronic fatigue, and you know or suspect that you were sexually abused as a child, the fatigue may be directly related to the repression of your pain. When you begin to release your repressed emotions, the chronic fatigue will lessen and, in time, will go away completely.

Compulsive-Addictive Diseases

Survivors are highly susceptible to compulsive-addictive diseases. Eating disorders, drug addiction, alcoholism, compulsive sexual behavior, workaholism, and compulsive gambling are some of the compulsive-addictive behaviors often used by survivors to blot out the pain of the sexual abuse. Although it has the opposite effect, the survivor's compulsivity is an attempt to repress the pain and gain control. Often survivors stop practicing one addiction only to go on to another. An alcoholic survivor may stop drinking, then develop an eating disorder. An anorectic survivor may return to more regular eating, but then engage in compulsive sexual behavior. Without addressing the unresolved childhood sexual abuse, the survivor will continue to develop new compulsions.

A survivor named Eric told me how he went from addiction to addiction until he discovered that the source of his pain was sexual abuse: "When I stopped drinking and taking drugs, I thought I would 'live happily ever after.'" My life did improve for a time, but then I began compulsively buying things and acquired a lot of debt. When I got that under control, I started trying to get my body into perfect shape. I went at it with a vengeance. I'd work out every day for three or four hours. I felt sort of frantic and agitated a lot of the time. One day my sponsor in AA suggested I try going to therapy. After five sessions, my memories of sexual abuse came up. Then a lot of things started making sense to me."

Childhood sexual abuse is not the source of every addiction or compulsion. But if you have developed a pattern of moving from one addiction to another, I strongly suggest seeking out a therapist who can help you find out whether you may have been sexually abused.

Multiple Personality Disorder

This complex disorder was once considered extremely rare. As more and more survivors come forward to tell about their past and the effects it has had on them, more cases of multiple personality disorder (MPD) are beginning to appear. MPD is the result of the most severe kinds of sexual abuse, such as torture and ritual abuse. If you were abused this way, you may have MPD. If this is the case, you can be healed, but you will require the assistance of a qualified therapist.

MPD means that you have developed two or more personalities that at times alternate interacting with the world. You may be aware of some or all of these personalities, or you may not be aware of any of them. Generally, each personality displays unique characteristics: One personality may have a different eyeglass prescription than another, personalities may represent different ages, or have different sexual preferences. One personality may be competent and functional, whereas another is incompetent and dysfunctional. Shifts between personalities can come about as a result of stress (when memories of abuse are regained, or in new situations). The possible combinations of various personalities are limitless and cannot be adequately described here. If you suspect that you have multiple personality disorder, seek professional help. You can heal from this disorder. Don't give up hope.

Chronic Minor Illnesses

Some sexual abuse survivors have various kinds of chronic illness. Migraine headaches, lower back pain, recurrent health problems involving the reproductive organs, gastrointestinal disorders, and frequent colds and flu are a few of the kinds of chronic illness that survivors endure. You may also suffer from a general low grade of health without being able to pinpoint any particular illness as chronic. You may tend to have more than your share of accidents (falls, minor cuts, and bruises). These problems can be caused by the repression of sexual trauma. Once the pain is released, a survivor's general state of health usually improves dramatically. Kyle's history was filled with sickness and accidents. He had no idea that they were in any way related to the abuse he experienced until he began to work on these issues in therapy. Here is an excerpt from his journal:

Up until the age of eight or nine, I remember being very healthy. I got all the childhood illnesses, but nothing out of the ordinary. Then all of a sudden I started to get sick a lot. Every Christmas I had a flu or a cold, and several times a year I would get a very high fever and be sick for several days. I was really accident-prone, too. I was always falling out of trees, stepping on nails, things like that. It was always something, I was always at the doctor's office. My mother really complained about it. This kept up until my late twenties. Somewhere I read or heard that accident-prone people sometimes cause their own accidents. I was sexually abused by my stepdad—I remember the first time. I was around eight or nine—just about the time I started to get sick and have accidents. I know there had to be a connection between the abuse and all the physical problems I had. Since I've been talking about the abuse in group, it's a lot better. I know I'm having fewer accidents.

Sexual Dysfunction

Not surprisingly, adult survivors of childhood sexual abuse often suffer from sexual problems, ranging from compulsive sexual activity to feeling no sexual desire at all. You may "act out" your past abuse by engaging in undesired sexual behavior, or by getting involved in sexually abusive relationships.

"My ex-husband was a pig," says Lisa. "God, I really hate him. He would read these 'swinger' magazines and then set us up with other couples so we could have group sex. I would get so loaded, I didn't feel anything. In those days I really didn't know how to say, 'No, I won't do that.' I remember doing oral sex on some guy while another guy was having anal sex with me. My husband watched and masturbated. There were all these disgusting combinations. Finally it got to where I was drunk or loaded all the time, and he left me. What a relief! I never knew it had anything to do with being sexually abused as a child."

Having been sexually abused has a direct and immediate impact on your sexual identity. Your sexual boundaries have been violated, and your sexual identity distorted. The natural beauty and pleasure of sex may be unavailable to you. One survivor described his sexual self in this way: "Either I'm a sex machine, and all I want to do is have sex, or I'm a piece of wood, and I don't feel anything." Some survivors report not really liking sex but "doing it anyway" because they love their partner and are afraid not to have sex: "After several weeks of no sex, my husband begins to drop hints about it. Then I force myself to have sex with him. Sometimes it's good, but most of the time I feel dirty."

If you are a survivor experiencing sexual dysfunction, no amount of sex therapy will end your problem. Healing your childhood sexual wounds will heal your current sexual life.

Intimacy Dysfunction

Becoming emotionally vulnerable—being willing to feel hurt and needy sometimes—is the foundation of intimacy with friends, with a sexual partner, with your parents, with your children, and in any relationship. When you were abused, you spent a lot of energy becoming "invulnerable" to try to insure that you wouldn't be hurt any worse than you had been hurt already. To be invulnerable means to "wall off" your feelings and consequently to become less conscious of who you are. Constantly protecting your emotional self seriously limits your ability to experience intimacy. Intimacy dysfunction among survivors of childhood sexual trauma often takes these two forms: terror of intimacy, and emotional unavailability.

For Jane, it took the form of terror of intimacy: "There comes a point in every relationship where I become afraid. Things will be just fine. I'll really feel in love with the man I'm with, I'll begin to think, 'This is it,' then the fear will start up. I don't know why, but the fear just takes over. It doesn't make any sense. I start noticing all the things I can't stand about him. I start fights. The more afraid I feel, the more we fight. I want to be in the relationship, but I sabotage it. I don't know why this keeps happening. I keep losing people I love because of this fear."

Jane was talking about her most recent relationship, which had ended in an explosive physical fight. Her fear of becoming intimate ruled her behavior and her relationships. She yearned for intimacy, but the betrayal and pain she had experienced as a result of incestuous abuse by her father caused her so much distrust and fear that she had not been able to become emotionally close to anyone.

Another incest survivor, Collin, experienced a lack of intimacy most profoundly with his family: "It feels like I have a wall around my heart. I want to be close to my family, but I just can't be. Even when my daughter was killed I didn't cry. I wanted to and I could almost feel the tears, but I couldn't really cry. I know this can't be right. Sometimes I'll feel like there's a pack of emotions deep down inside me, just out of my reach. I think I'm a pretty good father, a good husband. I try not to ever hurt anyone. Recently my wife told me that she loved me but she felt she couldn't get close to me because I'm so distant. I do feel distant, but I don't want to be."

Like so many other survivors, Collin suffered from an inability to experience his emotions. He had been married for more than fifteen years and had three children, but had never really experienced intimacy with his family. He loved them, but he could not "feel" the love because of "the wall around my heart." Collin's abuse had begun when he was around seven years old. He was constantly sexually shamed and sexually beaten by an aunt who stayed with him while his parents worked. Collin suffered in silence so that he wouldn't "add to his parents' problems." In his pain he shut down his emotions, vowing never to allow anyone else ever to hurt him. Although this worked well enough to get Collin through his childhood, later on his emotional unavailability robbed him of the intimacy he could have formed with his family.

Offender Behavior

Becoming a sexual abuser of children is another secondary consequence of having been sexually abused in childhood. Strictly from my own clinical experience, it appears that most survivors do not engage in active offender behavior, either to sexually abuse their children or other children.

Committing sexual abuse involves making a choice. At some point the abuser has chosen to sexually harm children. No matter how horrible their own past has been, the choice to abuse is their own. Survivors who commit sexual abuse are accountable to their victims and to society for their behavior. The statement, "I was abused, therefore I abuse," is no defense at all. It is as invalid as a drunk driver saying, "I was drunk and passed out at the wheel, so I wasn't responsible for killing those people who were hit by my car."

If you are a survivor who is engaging in sexually abusive behavior, *stop*. Remove yourself from the children you are abusing and get help for yourself and for them. You can heal your current sexual behavior by healing your past. But you must *stop abusing first*. Remember, you cannot stop this behavior by willpower alone. You must have professional help. If you are a survivor who has thought about or fantasized about sexually using children, get professional help now, before you act out the abuse. You don't have to wound another child the way you yourself were wounded. But you will need support.

Looking over these secondary consequences of sexual abuse, you may have discovered clues to the root cause of your own pain. Your own memories, flashbacks, or other symptoms of the sexual abuse may become more pronounced as you read this book. These are strong messages from your inner self, shouting at you to take notice of your "unfelt" feelings. As you seek help and begin to progress in recovery, the secondary consequences of the sexual abuse will gradually disappear.

The shock and trauma of your past have caused you a great deal of pain. Over the years you may have behaved in self-destructive and self-defeating ways. Remember that you were not at fault for having been sexually abused. You were not responsible. You could not have prevented the sexual abuse. You were innocent. Survival living has kept you going—you've made it this far, thanks to your ability to adapt and survive. But, as you recover, as you become increasingly aware of yourself as an adult, you will become less and less satisfied with "just surviving." You will naturally begin to want more out of your life. When you begin to feel this dissatisfaction, take it as a good sign! It means that you have taken back your life, that you are healing.

Part One of this book has given you information about what may have happened to you. For most of you, reading this book has probably been a painful experience, so far. But in order to proceed with recovery, you need as much information as possible about sexual abuse. The rest of the book is about healing from the wound of childhood sexual abuse. Remember as you continue in recovery that tens of thousands of other survivors are also healing from their past. You are not alone.

PART TWO

HEALING
AND
RECOVERY

Go with *the pain, let it take you.* . . . *Open your palms and your body to the pain. It comes in waves like a tide, and you must be open as a vessel lying on the beach, letting it fill you up and then, retreating, leaving you empty and clear.* . . . *With a deep breath—it has to be as deep as the pain—one reaches a kind of inner freedom from the pain, as though the pain were not yours but your body's. The spirit lays the body on the altar.*

—ANNE MORROW LINDBERGH
War Within and Without

If Winter comes, can Spring be far behind?
—PERCY BYSSHE SHELLEY
"Ode to the West Wind"

CHAPTER 4

Recovery:
An Unfolding Process

THE THREE STAGES OF RECOVERY

Recovery from childhood sexual abuse is not easy—the wounds are deep and extremely painful. To stop carrying this deep pain that has invaded every avenue of your life, to be free of this pain, you must first feel it. The terror and rage that you can expect to encounter are intense, to be sure, but time makes a difference: You are now an adult, no longer a small and helpless victim. The pain you will feel in recovery is the cleansing pain of healing. No matter how intense your emotions may become, a feeling of hope and empowerment will accompany their release. As you continue working through the old feelings, the pain will become less intense, while the feeling of hope will steadily increase. You will begin to realize that your past is losing its power to direct your life.

Of course, no amount of therapy or work can erase the facts of your past. You will always be a survivor of sexual trauma. As you heal, however, this trauma will become integrated into your life. You will come to accept it as part of the intricate fabric of your life, as part of what makes you who you are. I would never presume to tell you, or any survivor, that *all* your pain will go away. Through your recovery work you will, however, find freedom from your past trauma: It will lose its grip on you, and the pain will diminish. This is the very essence of recovery—to reduce your inner pain to such an extent that it has no control over your adult life.

For most, beginning recovery is a highly mysterious process. But it doesn't have to be this way. Having a general idea of what is in store for you in recovery is vital. Understanding the stages of healing and knowing how to facilitate your own recovery help to ease the fear of the unknown. You are not entering completely foreign territory (although it may feel this way at times). Other survivors have cleared the path for you, and their recovery experiences can offer you invaluable guidance. Although, in one sense, recovery is a highly individual process, it also contains predictable elements. Learning about these similarities or "stages" can help you form a general picture of what your healing will involve.

Before we move deeper into a discussion of healing, I must point out that this book has certain limitations. What I have to say about recovery from childhood sexual abuse is written from my point of view as a therapist. The people I describe in these pages have been or are currently my clients. Although I believe that not all survivors must have professional therapy to recover, my own experience has been with those who have come to me for professional help.

Most of what I know about healing from childhood trauma is gathered from a combination of clinical training, direct work with clients, and my own personal recovery. I have studied a wide range of therapeutic techniques over the years, and consequently, my clinical style is eclectic. Although the methods described in this book center mainly on the body, breath, and energy for healing, many of the concepts presented here are also based on my studies of the structure and dynamics of family systems. Of course, there are other viewpoints, other avenues of healing. Most effective therapists, however, will have had a wide range of experience and training. Chapter 8, A Safe Place, gives some guidelines for selecting a therapist.

The healing techniques described in the following chapters were originally designed for use in a therapeutic setting. I include them here so that you may adapt them for your own use, either privately or with others. You may want to teach them to your own therapist, if he or she is unfamiliar with this kind of personal work. Often these exercises and meditations produce a strong emotional response, so I strongly suggest having a support group with whom you can talk about your experience. The experiences of hundreds of sexual abuse survivors around the country, and of many other counselors and therapists strongly affirm the effectiveness of the healing techniques shared in this book.

I have observed three major stages in the process of healing from childhood sexual trauma: I call these stages discovery, active healing, and integration. The discovery stage was the focus of Part One of this book. As you read Part One, you probably learned more about your past and the abuse you experienced. The rest of this book will focus on active healing and integration. Of course, recovery is not neatly divisible, and some of the stages will overlap at times. That is, you may experience being in discovery and active healing at the same time; this can be true for any combination of the three stages. But generally speaking, the stages of healing follow the progression given below. Recovery is not really linear, however, and it cannot be predicted how long each person will work in any given stage. Each survivor works through sexual abuse on a time schedule perfectly suited to that individual's healing process.

Figure 4 shows the overlapping progression of the three recovery stages. An overview of each stage follows, as well as a more detailed account of how the healing stages flow together.

Figure 4: Stages of Recovery

Stage One: Discovery

"I want to remember what happened to me. I want to know how it affects my life now."

Through flashbacks or dreams, memories that were repressed or temporarily forgotten begin to surface to the conscious mind. These memories, in turn, trigger other memories. At this time, you will begin to experience extreme feeling states: fear, rage, deep grief, shame, hurt, and disbelief.

You will begin to discover how your abuse has affected your adult life. Up to this point, you may have remembered the abuse, but without realizing its persisting effect on you. As you learn how much the abuse has affected your relationships, your goals, and your physical health, your feelings of rage and hurt may be so powerful that you think of little else. In "meeting" your wounds, you are meeting long-lost parts of yourself. You slowly come to understand yourself and your actions more fully. Survivors often report that the discovery stage is like "putting together a puzzle." You have always had all the pieces of your experience, but some of them were hidden from your conscious mind. When you begin to piece together your past experiences with your natural responses to those experiences, then your feelings, choices, and behaviors begin to make more sense. It is a great paradox: You may feel excited to finally understand all these things, yet at the same time feel frightened because the process of recovery involves many tears, so much rage, and such intense feelings of fear and shame.

Despite these strong emotions, from time to time you may still have difficulty believing that you were abused. One day you may feel absolutely certain, then only a day or two (or an hour) later, you may change your mind and think you are "making the whole thing up." During this stage you may sometimes lose control of your feelings and cry without apparent reason, or you may fly into a rage at little or no provocation. Such emotional "roller-coaster rides" are quite common.

The discovery stage gradually leads you toward acceptance of your abuse. You understand that it really happened and that it has affected your life. This is a scary time for many survivors. At the beginning of this stage you may start and stop therapy, join and drop out of support groups for survivors, both believing and disbelieving that you are a survivor. As discovery progresses, you can expect to move in and out of denial this way, and to want to run away from your feelings. It's all right when this happens. Resistance is part of the healing process.

Unfortunately, it is impossible to predict how long each stage of recovery will last. One thing is certain, however: The roller coaster doesn't last forever. There is an end, and as you begin the active healing stage, as you are able to translate your emotions into action, you will start to get a glimpse of "the other side."

Stage Two: Active Healing

"I am a survivor of childhood sexual abuse. What can I do to heal?"

During the active healing stage you will begin to focus less and less on whether you were abused and more on what you can do to heal. Your healing will become a primary focus in your life. At this stage, it is not uncommon to experiment with different approaches to healing. You may try various therapies, twelve-step groups, and spiritual approaches. Some of these methods may not appear to work, and you may go on to something different. Anything that you experiment with will contribute to your healing—even if you simply find out that a particular method or group is not for you. This is a process of getting to know yourself in a new way. Everything you do toward this understanding is helpful and applicable, especially if you understand that your healing is a process that happens *inside you*, and not elsewhere.

One of the most important goals of the active healing stage is to establish an ongoing support group. A good support group consists of people whom you trust and who unconditionally encourage your recovery. It will be a group of your own choosing, and it may or may not include members of the family you were born into or the family you have created as an adult. (More will be said about this in Chapter 8, "A Safe Place.") At this point, it is vital that you make contact with other survivors of sexual abuse. Sharing your experience with other survivors adds an invaluable dimension to your healing: validation. No matter how clear it becomes to you that you were abused, sharing with other survivors and receiving their supportive feedback is essential to help you hold on to the reality of your past. Denial is tricky—it can crop up when you least expect it. When you're tempted to disbelieve your experience, it's good to have friends around to remind you.

Further on in the active healing stage, you will settle into consistent work with a specific therapist, group, or combination of support groups. The work of active healing involves releasing those pent-up emotions associated with the abuse, finding personal boundaries, and learning self-nurturance. Each survivor has a personal blend of issues to work through; these issues often include sexual intimacy, risk-taking, and simple physical health. At this stage the previously frantic search for healing becomes calmer and more stable. Although your emotions will still be intense, the emotional "roller-coaster ride" will begin to level off.

In this stage you will come to know your individual blend of issues and be able to consciously work on them. As you continue your healing, wonderful things will begin to happen. Your feelings of helplessness and hopelessness will begin to diminish. By practicing new, healthier behaviors, you will begin to break old patterns of self-abuse and self-sabotage. Although your healing will continue to be a major focus in your life, you will also engage in other interests and activities. Your relationships, both at home and work, will improve significantly. The main work of active healing generally lasts several years. At the "end" of this stage, you will have learned living and self-healing skills that you can use for the rest of your life.

Stage Three: Integration

"I am a recovering survivor, continuing to heal. My life is no longer just survival—it is a steadily unfolding creation."

As you move into the integration stage, you will experience a profound sense of freedom. Rather than feeling victimized and driven by your past, you will begin to view your history of sexual abuse as one of the many events and changes that have shaped your life. Although you will always be a survivor of past abuse, that abuse will cease to control your feelings and actions. At this point, the pain that you experience as a direct result of being sexually abused will diminish *dramatically.*

Integration is a most gratifying stage of recovery. It is the point at which survivors can actively recognize (and marvel at) the healing that has taken place. Your personal recovery work will begin to change during this time: You will do less of the deep emotional expression work that was so important in the active healing stage. You will have done a great deal of healing already, and your work in therapy will reflect this change. You may occasionally discover additional memories of being sexually abused, but you will have acquired the experience and insight (as well as a good support group) to be able to integrate this new information into your life without a great struggle. If you find that a new memory is "too much," you will be able to care for yourself and work through the memory by returning to therapy or otherwise seeking support.

As part of integration, you will establish quality relationships with the kinds of people you enjoy having in your life. Your life will be filled with many other activities besides recovery work. It is not uncommon for some survivors to direct their energies toward spiritual activities during this time.

Integration means that you reclaim your feelings and your history, and the personal power that comes with fully meeting the reality of your past. If you choose, you can be of help to others who are coming to terms with their sexual abuse history. The integration stage is the part of your healing that lasts for the rest of your life.

Laura's Story

Although your recovery is likely to follow the general pattern just described, your individual story of recovery will be unique to you. You may feel that you spend a lot of time in one particular stage, or that you appear to move from one stage to another, then back to a previous stage. There is nothing wrong with this. You will heal on your own schedule. Steady work on these issues eventually leads to integration, at which stage your life will become much more fulfilling and joyful.

About seven years ago, Laura (then thirty-three years old) entered one of my therapy groups for adult children of alcoholics. During the first six months, Laura worked on a variety of issues, including her feeling of lack of intimacy in her sexual relationship and a growing anger at her mother, an alcoholic. Then Laura began to have flashbacks of being sexually abused by her stepfather. Over the next few months, Laura focused on uncovering what had happened to her. She found that from the age of nine to twelve, her stepfather had repeatedly fondled her genitals. The sexual abuse had stopped when Laura's mother divorced her stepfather. Like so many survivors, until she entered therapy Laura had completely repressed the memory of sexual trauma.

For Laura, the *discovery stage* lasted about six months. As she gradually rediscovered her memories, she experienced a "denial/belief cycle," in which some of the time she was able to believe her memories, and some of the time she was in denial. During this time, Laura reported to the group, "It feels like my emotions are taking over my life. I can hardly believe this happened to me, even though I know it's true."

In the *active healing stage*, Laura sought validation from other sexual abuse survivors by attending meetings of incest survivors' support groups and ACOA twelve-step groups, and by continuing with therapy that focused on healing sexual trauma. At different times over the next two years, Laura took part in art therapy workshops, had some rebirthing and breathwork sessions, did journal writing, had a series of deep tissue bodywork sessions, and continued in her primary therapy group. As Laura worked on the issues surrounding her sexual trauma, she began to experience a sense of accomplishment and a growing feeling that she was "getting better." After four years of hard work on these abuse issues, Laura decided she wanted to end professional therapy. Laura continued with her incest survivors' support group and her ACOA twelve-step group. She also became active in helping recovering newcomers in both groups.

During the active healing stage, Laura's life changed dramatically. She ended the unrewarding relationship with her husband and, two years later, met another man whom she eventually married. "I have never been happier," she told me then. After three years Laura returned to therapy for a short time because she wanted to confront her stepfather about his abuse of her. She moved through the confrontation process in less than ten weeks and again stopped therapy. Laura told the group that she might be back again in the future but that she felt "really complete" with her work. Laura had moved completely into the third stage of healing: *integration*.

Laura's recovery story is much like those of many other women and men who have survived childhood sexual abuse. Though each person's story is different, each has essentially the same difficulties, the same dance between belief and denial, the same hard work and rich rewards. The last time I saw Laura, I asked her what she would most like to say to other survivors. Her message was this: "Whatever happened to you, and wherever you are in your recovery, please don't give up. There is hope and healing. Your life will not only get better—it will get better than you can imagine."

Figure 5 traces the key elements of Laura's recovery process. The specifics of your own recovery may differ from Laura's but, overall, your own healing process will be similar to the progression depicted there.

FIGURE 5: Laura's Recovery Process

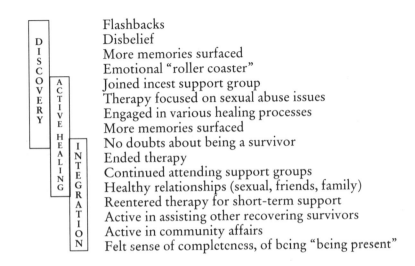

Flashbacks
Disbelief
More memories surfaced
Emotional "roller coaster"
Joined incest support group
Therapy focused on sexual abuse issues
Engaged in various healing processes
More memories surfaced
No doubts about being a survivor
Ended therapy
Continued attending support groups
Healthy relationships (sexual, friends, family)
Reentered therapy for short-term support
Active in assisting other recovering survivors
Active in community affairs
Felt sense of completeness, of being "being present"

Having learned self-nurturance, Laura reserved the right to reenter therapy whenever she felt the need. She knew that over the years more memories of abuse might be revealed to her. Having already felt the satisfaction and empowerment that comes with healing, the prospect of additional work did not frighten her. Laura felt she could handle just about anything.

Keep in mind that Laura's story is only one illustration of the healing journey. It is not advisable (in fact, it is impossible) to measure your recovery against Laura's or anyone else's. Your process is unique to you and to your set of circumstances—even though your story may be similar to others' stories, and you may feel a lot of the same feelings reported by other survivors. You will change and recover in your own style, according to your own internal time table, in the way that is best suited to you.

THE WHOLE PERSON

We human beings are complex, and understanding the human system is a multifaceted process. At this point, it is enough to consider four basic facets of human experience: Each of us has a physical body, a wide range of emotions, and a mind whose job it is to think. We also have a "spirit," or a spiritual aspect, which is difficult to define but which is central to our recovery. Of course, these simple terms—*spirit, body, mind,* and *emotions*—actually represent intricately interrelated processes that occur continuously in and around our physical selves. We cannot fully explain these different aspects of ourselves, but we can observe a fascinating truth about them: They are always working together to lead us toward health. The diagram in figure 6 is a simple picture of our human experience. Like anyone suffering a severe trauma, survivors of childhood sexual abuse sustain damage that touches the physical, emotional, and mental dimensions of their human existence. In recovery, each of these three aspects of oneself must be healed.

The fourth dimension, the spirit, remains untouched by the experience of sexual trauma.

FIGURE 6: The Whole Person

WINDOWS TO THE PAST

In survivors of childhood sexual abuse, the extent of memory loss can range from limited recall of specific details of the sexual abuse to the complete repression of one's childhood experiences. But the physical body, the emotions, and the cognitive mind all "remember" past events. Because the release of repressed memories is crucial to healing, it is important to know how these different aspects of ourselves recall past traumatic experiences.

Your memory is much more than a "bank" in which bits of information are stored. Memory is a fascinating process that is interwoven throughout the entire human system. Even if you do not have visual (mind) memories of your sexual abuse, you will still "remember" through your body and emotions. Traumatic memories can surface cognitively, emotionally, or physically, or in any combination of these three processes. The body, the emotions, and the mind each have a unique way of "remembering."

The Body

Your body accompanies you from the moment of birth until the moment of your death. Everything that has happened to you in your life has also happened to your body.

If you were *physically* sexually abused, you experienced the abuse through your body. You "felt" the abuse as a physical experience. You saw what was happening to you. You heard what was happening to you. You tasted and smelled your experience, and you felt the violation of your physical body. How much *physical* trauma you carry depends upon the level of violence you were subjected to when you were abused. But no matter how "nonviolent" the physical abuse may have appeared, you were being sexually used, and this causes physical trauma for any child.

Even if you experienced emotional (nonphysical) abuse, your body was still there and was affected by your experience. The lash of a cruel tongue, of ridicule and sexual shaming, leaves not only emotional scars. Every time you cringed, thought you would "die of shame," or tried to "become invisible," your body experienced this state. The memory of this abuse is etched into your body just as it is for a survivor who experienced direct physical abuse.

Body Memories

Recovering survivors sometimes report having physical reactions or symptoms directly related to the way they were sexually abused as children. These are "body memories." Survivors just beginning the healing process are often surprised to find that, even though they may have repressed their conscious memory of the abuse, their bodies have not "forgotten." Your body is capable of remembering everything that has happened to it. The memory of the sexual abuse is stored in your physical body, and these body memories may surface unexpectedly. Headaches, nausea and other digestive problems, sexual dysfunction, pain in the genital region and sudden fatigue are a few ways in which body memories sometimes manifest.

For most of his life, Jim had chronic constipation and occasional rectal bleeding. Repeated visits to the doctor did little to relieve these symptoms. After he began therapy, Jim remembered that when he was a child, his grandmother had given him enemas in a brutally abusive way, sometimes two or three times a day, for a period of three years. Jim's symptoms were a physical expression of his abuse: His physical body "remembered" what had happened, even though Jim had repressed the memory. It is encouraging to note that, once survivors consciously, actively seek to heal the source of these physical symptoms, they usually vanish. A few months after Jim began to work through the issues surrounding his sexual abuse in childhood, his constipation and rectal bleeding stopped.

The Emotions

Our emotions bring depth and color to our experiences, enriching our lives. By feeling our experiences, we connect with the world and with our fellow beings. We are fulfilled in love, laugh with joy, grieve at our losses, feel bliss in moments of peace, and are content when we feel fully understood. These, along with a host of other emotional states, give us the *felt* experience of being alive. Our emotions are a natural expression of who we are. Sharing these emotions with others is one of the ways in which intimacy occurs in our relationships. If we are unable, or only partially able, to make emotional contact with others, we suffer from loneliness. Conversely, when we are most freely able to spontaneously feel our experiences and to share them, we are at our happiest and strongest.

The wound of sexual abuse is an emotional wound. Being physically violated, sexually ridiculed and shamed, or placed in a sexual role that was beyond a child's maturity causes the child feelings of shame, guilt, rage, fear, and many other strong emotions. The repression of these feelings causes what I have called the secondary consequences, or "symptoms," of sexual abuse. If you experienced sexual abuse as a child and were not helped to work through your trauma, then your ability to express your emotions freely and openly has been dramatically limited.

Emotional Memories

Emotional memories are the experiential recall of your emotional states during the abuse. These felt memories can include fear, terror, shame, hurt, grief, bewilderment, surprise, rage, anger, resignation, and relief. During the abuse, and immediately after it, you probably experienced a wide range of intense feelings. As emotional memories surface, many survivors report that their feelings are confused or "jumbled up."

The intensity and complexity of your emotional response to sexual trauma can seem overwhelming at first, as they were for George: "I remember waiting for him to come into my room. I was always afraid. Afraid and resigned. I knew he would come, I just didn't know exactly when. My fear was so intense it was hard for me to breathe. I would jump at every little noise. I knew I couldn't hide. I was almost relieved when he came. Then the waiting, at least, was over."

George was talking to his therapy group about the continuing abuse he had endured from his older stepbrother. He could recall very vividly what he felt before, during, and after he was sexually abused.

Often survivors experience emotional memories without cognitive information about their source. This phenomenon is baffling to many survivors. If this happens to you, you will experience the emotional impact of the abuse without remembering the actual event. You may experience waves of terror and outrage without remembering the event that prompted these feelings. A survivor well into the active healing stage of recovery described an emotional memory this way:

> I was brushing my hair in front of the mirror. I was naked, having just stepped out of the shower. Suddenly my lover, who was already dressed for work, walked briskly past the open bathroom door. I felt instantly nauseous and burst into tears. I went to my bed and cried for ten or fifteen minutes, feeling deeply hurt, abandoned, frustrated, hopeless.

Then, as quickly as it had started, all these feelings just went away. I felt okay again, but all day I kept wondering, "What was that all about?"

It may seem that you are having overwhelming emotions without reason, but this is not the case. Your childhood sexual trauma is quite probably the source of these strong feelings, and these emotions can surface in many ways. At such times, you are simply experiencing emotional memory without the actual recall of a specific event of abuse. Emotional memory is every bit as valid as cognitive memory. As you move through the healing process, you will intuitively begin to recognize these emotional memories as stemming from the sexual abuse you experienced in childhood.

The Mind

We are thinkers, dreamers, and planners. Using the power of the mind, human beings build communities, make life-saving medical discoveries, and shape visions for the future of our world. Our mind is a great vehicle for our creativity. It is largely through our ability to think and reason that we determine the nature of our reality and our place in it. We use our minds to perceive what is in this world and to interpret what happens within us and around us. The power of the mind is awe-inspiring. What we believe, how we look, and what we feel—all of these originate in the mind. It is important not to underestimate the power of your mind to heal and to create.

Being sexually abused as a child has altered the way you perceive yourself and the world around you. As a child you were helpless to protect yourself. Due to that trauma, at times you may still think of yourself as a helpless person. If the sexual abuse occurred in your home, you may find it impossible to feel safe in your own home, even now that you are an adult. You may believe that the world in general is not safe. Our feelings of self-worth also begin in the mind. Survivors who have been used and "discarded" as sexual objects often continue to think of themselves as worthless, as objects. Sexual abuse, in any of its forms, profoundly affects how you see yourself and how you relate to others.

Cognitive Memories

Cognitive memories include mental pictures, thoughts, and visual impressions of past events. You are remembering cognitively when you "see" a specific mental picture of the sexual abuse that you experienced as a child. Cognitive recall of the abuse may be vividly detailed: You may remember the time of day, the clothes you were wearing, and your surroundings. You may recall what you were thinking while the abuse occurred.

Survivors often experience purely cognitive recall of the abuse without the associated emotional or physical feelings. One survivor described a vivid memory of sexual abuse this way:

> I remember everything about it. I can remember hearing the TV in the living room—I even remember what program was on. I remember seeing my uncle's face, the lines around his eyes, and hearing him breathing hard in my ear. I remember everything. Even his smell. The strange thing is, I don't feel anything when I talk about it.

It is possible to have only partial cognitive recall of abuse. If you were abused continuously over a period of time, you may have only fragmentary memories of it. Or you may remember certain episodes, but repress other incidents of your abuse. Your cognitive memory can help you piece together the truth about what happened to you. But you do not have to have cognitive memories in order to heal. Your physical and emotional memory systems are sufficient for your healing to take place.

Most recovering survivors of childhood sexual abuse recall past trauma in all three ways: as cognitive, emotional, and physical memories. In early recovery, from stage one (discovery) through early stage two (active healing), you may experience intense emotional and body memories before you regain direct cognitive recall of the abuse (which sometimes does not surface until late in the active healing stage).

As you move into stage two, your memories will become more and more directly associated with the abuse incident(s). Later in your healing, you will experience the emotional pain, body memories, and mental awareness of the sexual abuse in a more integrated way. Late in stage two, most survivors who have not had a clear cognitive memory of the abuse begin to regain partial—and sometimes complete—cognitive recall of the sexual abuse they experienced. Some survivors, however, never regain cognitive memories of the sexual abuse. This is not a barrier to healing—with the help of a good therapist and the continuing support and validation of other survivors, those without cognitive recall are still able to heal their invisible wounds.

During the third stage (integration), the emotional intensity of the pain will diminish considerably, and the body memories (for the most part) will end. When you remember what happened to you, you may still have an emotional response, but the destructive power of the abuse will have left. The three memory systems—cognitive, physical, and emotional—are central to healing in the life of the recovering survivor. Coming back to wholeness is a multifaceted process, simultaneously puzzling, painful, and deeply beautiful. It is nothing less than the miraculous unfolding of all that you can become.

The Spirit

The spirit is the center, the essence of who we are. It is so close to us, in fact, that it is extremely difficult to define. Nevertheless, it is always present. We are much more than just our physical body, our emotional experiences, and our mental abilities.

For three years I worked as a counselor in the emergency room of a large urban hospital. During that time I witnessed the deaths of many people. The causes of death were numerous, but one common element existed in all those cases: When a person's body ceased to function, there was a sense that their vital energy was "leaving." It was not something that could be seen or measured with any conventional instrument, but I felt its presence and felt it as it "left." The movement of this "spirit," or essential energy, was accompanied by a feeling of quiet respect and awe. There would be a short pause, and then the usual pandemonium of the emergency room would start up again. Thereafter, I no longer saw the body on the table as a person, but as a hollow shell. I felt that the "spirit" was elsewhere, untouched by the wounding of the body.

Your body may have been violated; your emotions may have been repressed and turned inward; your mental view of yourself may be filled with fear, shame, grief, and rage. Still, your spirit remains untouched. No matter what your experience has been, your spirit remains beautifully free of it all. And ultimately it is your own powerful spirit that will heal you.

Though we speak of them as distinct entities, body, mind, and emotions are inseparable—what affects one, affects the others. The spirit, however, stands free and possesses a powerful force for healing. It is important to remember that despite the often chaotic process of working through sexual abuse issues, everything you need for your recovery is contained at the center of your very own self. Your spirit has brought you this far, and as long as you live, it will continue to work for your healing. One survivor described this aspect of the "spirit" this way:

> When I began my recovery, I was overwhelmed. I thought every part of me was wounded and hurt. I felt that everything about me had been molested by a monster. It was comforting to find a part of myself that remained impervious to the shame and fear I felt. Even though I was unsure about "God," I could sense, inside me, an essence of self that transcended my emotions, mind, and body. The core of me was pure and uninjured. I liked that. It gave me hope.

CHAPTER 5

The Experience of Healing

THE HEALING CYCLE

During the active healing stage of recovery, a lot will be happening in your life. It is important to understand the details of healing, so that you can be prepared for this experience. There is no single event or milestone that heralds healing; it is a process that takes place over time, in cycles. The active healing stage consists of many of these cycles. With the completion of each healing cycle, a part of your past abuse is healed and resolved.

Each healing cycle consists of four phases: (1) exposing the wound, (2) reexperiencing the trauma, (3) externalizing the pain, and (4) healing the wound. If your recovery follows this framework, you will be able to heal at a deep level. But if your recovery work does not include complete healing cycles, you will tend to stay in your pain longer and may experience only limited recovery. It may be that you are already experiencing complete cycles of healing. This is good. The cycles are a natural healing process. I have not invented the healing cycle; I have observed it in survivors who were recovering from their childhood trauma. Even though the healing cycle is a natural event, your internal defenses can still inhibit you from allowing the cycle to complete itself. Therefore, it is critical that you understand how the healing cycle works, so that you can consciously cooperate with the process, especially during the active healing stage of your recovery. Now we'll look at each part of the healing cycle.

1. Exposing the Wound

Throughout your life you have been experiencing the pain of child-hood sexual abuse, in the form of secondary consequences described in Chapter 3. During the discovery stage, and in the early phases of the active healing stage, you began to consciously expose your wound. You were searching for the source of your pain and for an explanation of your actions and feelings. This global search for the hurt you carry now becomes very specific. At this point, you consciously seek to see the wound you bear. You actively search out the incidents of sexual trauma in your past. When you expose this wound, you open yourself to the pain that goes with it. In the process you will breach the strong core defenses (memory repression, dissociation, and denial) that you built to protect yourself from the feelings that overwhelmed you when you were sexually abused. You will then be able to make a conscious decision to stay with your feelings and to reexperience the trauma.

When you reach this point in a healing cycle, an experienced thera-pist (who is knowledgeable about the interrelatedness of the body, mind, and emotions) can be of great assistance. If your emotional memories are repressed, or if you have no cognitive recall of the abuse, such a therapist can help you reclaim your past by focusing on your present physical experience, especially if there is tension anywhere in your body. Often these tense areas are physical patterns which devel-oped to hold the pain of sexual abuse, and focusing your attention on them can release your emotional and cognitive memories. Then it is possible for you to continue the cycle of healing until it is completed. Here is a common example of using body awareness in therapy.

THERAPIST: What are you feeling now?
SURVIVOR: Nothing. I feel numb.
THERAPIST: Scan your body to see if you can find a place of tension.
SURVIVOR: My chest feels tight. My heart hurts.
THERAPIST: Focus on your heart.
SURVIVOR (*tears in eyes*): It hurts.
THERAPIST: What emotions are you having?
SURVIVOR: I feel sad.

This survivor was not aware of having any emotions at first. But when encouraged to focus on the body, the survivor became aware of a feeling of sadness.

Another common example tells a somewhat different story.

THERAPIST: What are you feeling right now?
SURVIVOR: I'm feeling angry.
THERAPIST: Why are you angry?
SURVIVOR: I don't know.
THERAPIST: Where in your body do you feel anger?
SURVIVOR (*hands clenched in fists*): I don't know.
THERAPIST: Focus on your hands.
SURVIVOR: I wanted to hit him but I couldn't. He held my arms so
          I couldn't. I never remembered that before.

In this example, the survivor was aware of an emotion (anger) but
was confused about why the anger was there. After consciously focusing on the bodily location of the anger (the hands), the survivor
remembered that her arms had been held back during a particular
incident of sexual abuse.

Another survivor was asked to focus in a different way.

SURVIVOR: I remember watching myself being abused, as though I
          were across the room. But I don't feel anything.
THERAPIST: Scan your body. What does it experience?
SURVIVOR (*body appears rigid and tight*): I don't know.
THERAPIST: Focus on how rigid your body is.
SURVIVOR: I was afraid to move. I pretended to be asleep. My
          heart's beating faster.
THERAPIST: Keep focusing on your body and your heart.
SURVIVOR: Why did you do that to me? It hurts! (Begins to cry).
THERAPIST: What are you feeling?
SURVIVOR (*through tears*): Hurt and afraid.

Here, the survivor had remembered the abuse incident but felt no
emotional connection to the memory. By focusing on the rigidity in
the body, then on the rapid heartbeat, the survivor was able to reconnect with the emotions that accompanied the original experience.

When I work with clients in therapy, I continually remind them to
be aware of what they experience in the body. Body awareness plays a
central role in reclaiming repressed and denied memories. Once the

wound has been exposed through attention to the body, the next step is to reexperience the trauma.

2. Reexperiencing the Trauma

This is the place of pain; it will hurt for you to stay here. When you are reexperiencing the sexual trauma, you are allowing yourself, as an adult, to feel the pain you felt as a child. This is often a terrifying prospect. The reason you repressed the pain in the first place was that it was unbearable. But as long as the pain is repressed, you will keep that pain. To be free, you must experience it. You will probably feel rage, deep grief, shame, and (most intensely) fear. Fear is the core emotional experience of sexual abuse. It is terrifying to a child to be sexually violated, whether or not the violation was physical. As you are reexperiencing your past pain, a qualified therapist can help you remember that you are experiencing a *memory* of the abuse, and not the actual abuse—an important distinction. Experiencing the pain, however, is not the end of healing. You must take the next step: externalize the pain.

3. Externalizing the Pain

For you to heal, your internal pain must be brought out of hiding. You have held the pain of a sexually abused child inside you for years. This is original pain. If you are to have relief from it, this hidden pain must be expressed. Of course, it is possible to reexperience your pain, remain stoic, and not express it. If you do this, you will keep the pain inside. You must externalize it to be free of it. As you express more and more of this emotional pain, your defenses will begin to weaken, making it increasingly easier to release these strong feelings. Remember that these emotions were once so overwhelming that you needed to contain them just to function. When you express them now, your experience will be very intense. This catharsis, or release of pain, will involve bursts of extreme emotional experience: sobbing, raging, crying, screaming, or hitting pillows with your hands or a tennis racquet. Sometimes, however, catharsis takes place in gentler ways, such as by quiet crying, writing about what happened to you, or doing artwork about the abuse you experienced. (The use of writing and artwork is explained more fully later, in Part Three.)

There are many ways to externalize your pain. Most important of all, remember that the emotions you experience are healthy; there is nothing wrong with having feelings. Problems arise when emotions are repressed or are expressed indirectly. The terror and/or shame you experienced at the time of the sexual abuse were normal, healthy feelings, but because you didn't have a safe place to feel them, you held the pain inside. Holding in the feelings creates the difficulty—not the feelings themselves.

During deep cathartic experiences, it is important to be with people who can assist you through your experience. Your emotions will be powerful. It is essential to have someone with you so that you do not accidentally hurt yourself or get stuck in a place of fear. Your best guide is usually a professional therapist who is very familiar with helping survivors to release their repressed emotions.

When I speak to groups about externalizing repressed emotions, someone always asks me, "Isn't it easier for men to express anger and for women to express grief?" My answer to them is no. Making generalizations about gender-specific behavior in recovery only creates another barrier to the healing process. Each individual expresses held emotions somewhat differently.

Remember, the *child you once were* experienced sexual abuse. A little boy is no less tender, vulnerable, or hurt by the experience of abuse than a little girl is. Little girls, on the other hand, are just as capable of feeling—and repressing—rage as little boys are. An adult male survivor experiences intense fear, anger, and grief, just as an adult female survivor does. I have worked with men who were unable to express their anger, and with women who were unable to cry out their grief. Both men and women must externalize these feelings in order to recover. Neither sex has an easier path to healing than the other.

The focusing and healing techniques described in this book work equally well for men and woman. Remember that it is the pain of a wounded little child that you are experiencing. Later, in Chapter 6, I will more fully describe the role of this wounded child in healing.

4. Healing the Wound

After you have externalized the pain of the abuse, the next step is to actively heal the wound. This is where a transformation begins to be felt, where the sense of personal empowerment returns. This crucial part of the healing cycle is also the most often neglected. Without consciously healing your wound, there is little likelihood that complete healing will take place. When you consciously seek to heal the wound you have just reexperienced, you draw the energy of healing into your body and direct it to the place in your body where you held or experienced the original wound.

Now, as you read Jenny's story, you'll be able to see how one survivor moved through the four phases of one complete healing cycle: exposing the wound, reexperiencing the trauma, externalizing the pain, and healing the wound.

Jenny's Story

From age four to age seven, Jenny had been molested by her maternal uncle. The molestations began when her uncle, age twenty-five, moved in with her family. Jenny's uncle was planning to move into the area where she and her family lived, and he was to stay at Jenny's house until he got a job. He slept in Jenny's room. At first she was excited to have her uncle stay with her. Jenny liked him, and he was always willing to spend time with her.

After about a month, Jenny awoke in the middle of the night to find her uncle kneeling next to her bed with his hand between her legs. Shocked and frightened, Jenny pretended to be asleep. She heard him breathing heavily, and she felt his hand rubbing her thighs. After what seemed a long time, her uncle stopped touching her and returned to his bed. Eventually, Jenny fell asleep again.

The abuse continued for about a month. Jenny was afraid to tell anyone what was happening. One afternoon while Jenny was home alone with her uncle, he told her to "stay put," took off her pants, and began to fondle her. As he did this, he exposed his penis and masturbated. After he ejaculated, he told Jenny she could move. He also threatened her, saying she had better not tell anyone what "they" had done. He told Jenny that no one would believe her if she did and that if her parents found out it would "kill them."

Terrified, Jenny avoided being alone with her uncle whenever possible. Then, after nearly six months of continued molestations, her uncle moved out. He had gotten a job in a different city. Jenny was happy and relieved, believing the abuse would stop. The abuse did not stop, however. Whenever her uncle visited during holidays and in the summer, he molested her. His pattern of abuse seldom varied. He would arrange to be alone with her, then he would tell her to "stay put" or "be still," and he would remove her pants and rub his hand between her legs while he masturbated. Each time, he would instruct her "not to say anything to anyone." He would molest her two or three times during a visit, and sometimes more frequently. During these visits, Jenny's uncle would wink at her and make remarks that only she understood were related to the sexual abuse.

These molestations continued for over three years. Before she was sexually abused, Jenny remembers herself as a happy child who "laughed a lot." During the time that she was molested, Jenny became quiet and withdrawn. She sometimes had nightmares about her parents finding out what her uncle had done to her.

When Jenny was seven, she remembers one day "blurting out to my mother what was happening, and why I didn't like my uncle." Jenny's mother seemed shocked, but she did not disbelieve her. After that, the sexual abuse stopped. Jenny's uncle still visited for the holidays, and she saw him even more frequently because he joined the family business. But no one in Jenny's family ever said anything further about the fact that her uncle had sexually abused her.

Jenny entered therapy for this abuse at the age of twenty-nine. In our initial interview, Jenny stated that she did not think her abuse was "bad enough" for her to be in therapy, but that she was trying therapy at the advice of friends. Jenny related that it had become more and more difficult for her to go home for the holidays, when she would see her uncle. She also said she had difficulty trusting men in her sexual relationships. She had sex with various boyfriends but did not enjoy it, and she felt ashamed after having sex: "I can't ever really relax during sex. I'm always tense."

Although Jenny remembered being abused, she did not consciously realize how deeply she had suffered since that time. In her search for healing, Jenny was willing to consider that the sexual abuse had deeper consequences than she had imagined. She became willing to expose her wound. By entering therapy, Jenny opened a window in her past and exposed the physical and emotional trauma she had experienced. To do this was a great act of courage and faith. The following history, which took place during a group therapy session, illustrates one cycle of healing in Jenny's story of recovery.

The five other women were quiet. Jenny, who had joined the group two months earlier, was having difficulty breathing. Her breath came in shallow, ragged spurts. Even in the soft lighting of the group room, Jenny looked pale. When she tried to talk, her voice broke into uncontrollable sobs. Seated on a floor pillow, Jenny wrapped her arms around herself in an attempt to protect and to comfort herself. Between sobs, Jenny said, "I feel so dirty," and, "I feel so ashamed."

We had begun the group session with Jenny telling the group, "I don't know why I'm here; I feel like I'm wasting my time." When I asked Jenny what she was feeling, she replied, "I guess I feel ashamed for taking up time when others could be working on their issues." We were quiet for a moment. I asked her if she would be willing to explore the feeling of shame she was experiencing. "Yes," she said.

At this point Jenny made a decision to *expose the wound* she had had since childhood. In working with Jenny, I continuously reminded her to focus on how her body felt and what she was experiencing emotionally. (When you focus on your body or your emotions, you will eventually be led back to your original wound even though you may have repressed the cognitive memory.)

"Jenny," I asked, "please focus on the shame you feel. Allow yourself to fully experience the shame."

"Okay," she said. "It feels big."

"Where in your body do you feel the shame?"

"In my heart—it feels like it's going to break."

"Is it okay for you to stay with this feeling?"

"Yes."

"Okay. Try to focus on your heart area."

"Oh God, I'm feeling so scared and cold. I want to throw up. It really hurts. Now I'm starting to go numb."

"Keep breathing, Jenny. Focus on your body. Where in your body do you feel tension?"

"My chest and gut feel very tight, but I don't have any feelings."

"Focus on your heart and belly area now."

"I feel scared again. It's like a black hole of fear."

"Can you stay with the fear?"

"Yes. I feel so terrified, he touched me between the legs, and all I could do was stand there and hold my breath."

Jenny was exposing the wound of her abuse. She stayed with her experience and felt the feelings she had had when she was a child being abused. As Jenny began to *reexperience the trauma*, her voice trembled.

"I keep wanting to get away, but I'm scared. I just lay there frozen. I'm looking up at the ceiling and pretending to fly around the room to escape. He stuck his finger in me. It hurt, but when he rubbed me it felt good. I'm so confused. I loved him. We played games, and he bought me things. I want to get away and hide so no one will see me. I can smell him and hear him breathing hard. It hurts and I'm scared. I'm going numb, my body is going numb! I'm scared, he told me not to tell anyone. It's hard to breathe and my heart is pounding. I feel cold. I'm scared."

"Jenny, you're experiencing a memory. You're safe here with the group. Do you want to continue?"

"Yes, I want to go on."

"It's okay if you want to stop."

"No, I want to finish this."

"Okay, is there anything you'd like to say to your uncle?"

As Jenny reexperienced this trauma, she remembered more of the details of the abuse. Up until this time, Jenny had not remembered that her uncle had inserted his finger into her vagina. As is often the case, Jenny's defenses were so strong that she didn't remember the full extent of the abuse until she began the experimental work of recovery. (A few weeks later, Jenny also remembered being forced to perform oral sex.)

At this point in the session, Jenny decided to *externalize the pain.*

"Why did you do that to me?" Jenny cried. "I feel dirty and ashamed. You stole my childhood. I always feel different and soiled." Sobbing, Jenny pulled her hands into fists and screamed, "I hate you, I hate you, you motherfucker!" A pillow and a plastic bat were placed in front of her, and she began to beat the pillow with the bat. Screaming and cursing her uncle, Jenny raged for over twenty minutes. When she was finished her eyes were red and swollen from crying. She was soaked with sweat, and her hands were cramped from holding the bat. Jenny's rage then subsided into deep grief. She curled into a ball on the floor and sobbed, "Why? Why? Why?"

When Jenny externalized her held feelings by physically hitting the pillow, sobbing, and raging, she released the energy of her fear, rage, and grief. She showed the group what she really felt about the abuse. In doing this, Jenny was able to receive their empathy and support. Having poured out some of her pain, Jenny had created an "empty space" in herself where the wound had been.

Her next step was to *heal the wound.*

After several minutes, I asked Jenny if there was anything she would like from any member of the group, and she asked if someone would hold her. Kara, sitting next to her, gently took Jenny in her arms, cradling her like a little child. Still crying, Jenny held onto Kara, and after a short time she stopped crying.

"I feel safer right now than I can ever remember. I never want to leave here." Jenny laughed. "I feel so light, like I just dropped a fifty-pound rock. I'm still pissed off at that son of a bitch. But I feel good, too. I can't believe it. I've never felt so relaxed." Jenny sat up and thanked Kara. "This is the first time I've ever done anything like that," she said.

After she had expressed her feelings by crying, beating the pillow, screaming, and raging, Jenny felt a sense of release. What she had needed at that point was to be comforted by another human being. There is a healing power in human touch, and when Jenny asked Kara to hold her, she received that energy of healing from Kara. This also gave Jenny the experience of feeling loved and cared for. She could actively ask for help, something she could not do as a little girl. Jenny not only released her feelings, she healed a part of her wound. (Much more will be said about healing energy and touch in Chapter 7.)

For years Jenny had repressed her fear, anger, shame, and grief. Because she had repressed them for so long, she was unaware of the strength of these feelings. She was also surprised at how quickly her rage was replaced by grief. Throughout Jenny's therapy, the intensity of her experiences continually amazed her. Her outward expression of rage and hurt was an act of trust in the group, and an act of faith in the healing process. As Jenny continued to express her held emotions, she became more trusting and more vulnerable. As she experienced her vulnerability, she was able to feel more compassion for herself and for the abused child she once was.

Jenny had believed that her abuse "wasn't that bad" because she had not been raped or forced to do anything but "stay put" and submit to being fondled. Jenny's initial view of her abuse as "minor" was a way to minimize how angry and betrayed she felt about being sexually abused. In the months following, Jenny uncovered and expressed those deep pockets of shame, hurt, betrayal, rage, and fear. She continued to be surprised at the degree of the pain she had repressed and at how profoundly her "mild" sexual abuse had affected her life.

WORKING WITH HEALING CYCLES

When you are working at such a deep level, you cannot control the specifics of your healing. You may decide you want to work on the rage you have at your father for not protecting you from your abusive mother, but you may wind up experiencing your grief and loss over not having had a nurturing mother. It is also quite common to move from one traumatic experience to another during one healing cycle. This "bouncing around in your past" does not in any way diminish the power of the work you are doing. When you open yourself to a healing cycle, your natural inner process takes over, and you will work with whatever is most important for you to work on. When you consciously expose your wound and start a healing cycle, you never really know where you will end up. For this reason, healing requires a lot of faith and courage, as well as a certain amount of skill and flexibility on the part of the guide or therapist you choose to help you through this process.

Although each healing cycle is, in itself, a complete event, this does not mean that you must experience an entire healing cycle for each episode of abuse and trauma. If this were the case, survivors who were abused continuously over a period of years would be in therapy for decades! When you heal, you not only heal the traumatic event you are focusing on during that particular healing cycle, you also heal "globally." Upon the completion of each healing cycle, *all* your inner pain diminishes. Each of your traumatic experiences then has a little less emotional intensity than it had before. It is as if all of your trauma were contained inside you in a pressure cooker, with the pressure exerted by the three core defenses. When you release the pain of a single trauma, the overall pressure inside you is reduced. Six years after ending his group therapy, one survivor shared this with me about the overall nature of his healing:

I know I have received so much grace in my life. Just from the reading I've done since therapy, and from the little I know of my childhood, I'm sure I was abused many more times than I'll ever remember. I'm so grateful that I don't have to go back and experience everything! The little I did remember was frightening enough. And I know there was more. I used to wonder if I had "cheated" somehow, because I always felt intuitively that there was more to work on. I don't worry about that anymore. Out of great compassion, my Higher Power brought back just enough of my memories so that I could heal, so that I could be free.

If you want to heal your past but don't believe it is possible, try doing the work of recovery anyway. What have you got to lose? If you continue to "show up," to simply do what is suggested, you will discover that you were healing even before you became consciously aware of it. Although your mind may be clouded with doubts, the inner desire to heal is always stronger than any reservations you may have. I have seen this happen again and again in my work with survivors of sexual trauma. One man in a therapy group shared some advice he had heard in a twelve-step meeting: "They told me to 'bring the body and the mind will follow.'" If you simply engage in the process of recovery work, then (whether or not you believe it) you will get better. You will heal. Faith helps, but it's not essential.

CHAPTER 6

Healing Your Inner Child

Healing cycles will form the framework of your recovery. As you enter and reenter these cycles, it will become clear that you have an "inner child." The inner child is the essence of who you were when you were abused. When you expose the wound, you are exposing the pain of your inner child. When you reexperience the trauma, your inner child is experiencing that deep, original pain. When you externalize this pain, it is your inner child who reveals your pain to the world. When you heal, it is your inner child who heals. Your inner child is a very intimate aspect of who you once were and of who you are today. Coming to know and love your inner child will greatly facilitate your healing. This precious inner child appears in two ways: as the wounded child and as the magical child.

THE WOUNDED CHILD

Your wounded inner child has been hidden away since the time of the sexual abuse. Surrounded by defenses, this wounded child has been unable to heal, to grow, or to develop naturally. The wounded child remains stuck in the unresolved pain of that early betrayal. No matter how old you are—twenty, forty, sixty, or older—you still have a little wounded child within you. Through your courageous work in recovery, this child will be healed.

Figure 7 shows a picture of the wounded inner child that sexual abuse survivors carry inside them. Inside their defenses lies the pain of

FIGURE 7:
The Wounded Inner Child

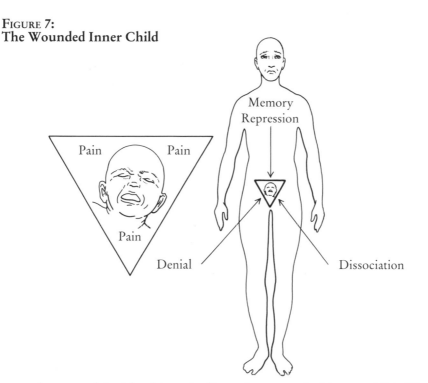

past abuse, and inside this pain lives the wounded inner child. The picture locates the inner child in the lower belly area, where the body stores most of the pain of sexual abuse. When the wounded inner child is trapped this way, little room is left for emotional experiences other than this held pain.

In the process of recovery, you will contact this wounded child to begin a healing relationship. Then gradually this child's pain will leave you. People experience their inner children in different ways, but most survivors are able to perceive their wounded child, either through imagery or by other ways of turning inward. The age of your wounded inner child is determined by the age you were at the onset of the sexual abuse. If the abuse you experienced began when you were three years old, then your wounded inner child is three years old. If you were ten when you were sexually abused, your wounded inner child is ten years old. Most survivors experience sexual abuse over a period of time, rather than only once. If you were emotionally sexually abused beginning at age seven, and later you were physically sexually abused at age ten, your wounded inner child is seven.

Even though you may have been abused over a period of years in childhood, your wounded child remains fixed at the age you were when the abuse began. If you experienced continuing sexual abuse or multiple incidents of abuse, your wounded inner child was rewounded each time you were abused. In this way, more and more pain is sealed behind the protective defenses.

The sexually abused child responds to additional sexual abuses by regressing to the age of the wounded child. This is one reason that abusers are able to wield power over a child survivor. Each time you were sexually abused, you responded as the wounded child, who remains emotionally frozen at the age you were when you first experienced sexual abuse.

Clara was an incest survivor whose father sexually abused her from the age of eight until she was sixteen. At sixteen, Clara ran away from home. She swore she would never let her father touch her again. When she was twenty-nine, she heard that her father was sick and wanted to see her. She had not seen him for over ten years. "I thought I might never see him again, and I wanted to. I hated him for what he did to me, but I still loved him because he was my father," Clara said. "I hadn't been with him more than an hour when he told me to 'do him,' which meant to perform oral sex on him. I suddenly felt as if I were eight years old and, without questioning him or saying no, I got down on my knees and 'did him.' I hated him, and myself, but I could not stop myself. Even though he was sick and I was physically much stronger than he was, I still couldn't stop. I felt like a little girl again."

Survivors will also regress to the age of their wounded child if they are abused by someone other than the original abuser. Clara said during a therapy session,

> I can't say no to sex. I don't feel I have a right to say no. I always feel like I'm about eight years old. All my sexual relationships have been abusive. My last boyfriend would come home drunk and demand to have sex. One night I was sick with the flu and felt terrible. I told him I was sick, but he just ignored me and we had sex anyway. I was too afraid to say no. Like so many other times, I just lay there and felt like a helpless little girl. Even when I enjoy sex, I still feel like a little girl. I realized, when I had sex with my father again after ten years, that every time I have sex, I'm

that same scared little girl. Enjoying it doesn't make any difference. I enjoyed it sometimes when I was a little girl, too, and I was scared at the same time. In a way I'm glad for what happened when I saw my father, because after that experience I realized I felt the same way every time I have sex. I'm tired of it. Looking back at my sex life, I can say that most of the time I've had sex I've been unwilling. It's like being raped again and again and again.

Clara's case may sound extreme or unusual, but it isn't. Until the wounded child is healed, the survivor can still be intimidated and controlled by the original abuser or by other abusers. Even survivors who are able to get help to stop the offender from abusing them often continue to feel like little children around the abuser. People who do not understand this aspect of sexual abuse often ask a survivor, "Why didn't you do something—run away, or tell your mother or father?" Survivors ask themselves the same questions. The answer lies with the wounded child. No matter how old you are, if you have not healed from the past, you will continue to respond to abuse as the wounded child would respond. This is why many survivors continue to fear their abusers, even long after that person is no longer in their life and no longer has any actual power over them.

Survivors of emotional, rather than physical, sexual abuse are often amazed by the intensity of their pain. Since emotional sexual abuse generally continues over a long period of time, the wounded child absorbs pain continually, year after year. Survivors of emotional sexual abuse often mistakenly believe that, because they were not physically molested, their wound is not serious. This personal myth is quickly shattered as they begin to acknowledge and experience the deep pain of their wounded inner child.

THE MAGICAL CHILD

In Chapter 4, I called the "spirit" of a human being that part of us that cannot be touched or hurt by the external events of life. The magical child is that part of you that remains untouched by the sexual abuse. This unwounded "spirit" is the essence of the magical child. It is our birthright as human beings to experience happiness, joy, love, play, laughter, spontaneous creativity, and bliss. These are a just a few of the "feel good" emotional experiences that humans contain within. All people, including you, are able to have these "feel good" experiences in abundance.

The tragedy of sexual abuse is that it not only causes us deep intense pain, it walls us off from our natural "feel good" emotional states. When painful experiences are repressed by the core defenses, our ability to experience the joys of life is also repressed. Because you spent so much of your energy and time trying to survive, you were not freely able to feel the joy of childhood. But the childlike ability to be amazed and joy-filled still lies within you in the form of the magical child. As you heal from your childhood abuse, a transformation will gradually take place. The wounded child, who seems at first so helpless and frightened, will be transformed into the powerful and wise magical child. Then you will reclaim the joys and wonders in your life.

Figure 8 shows this transformation: the inner child is freed from the core defenses and radiates the natural energy and power of joy that is every person's birthright.

FIGURE 8:
The Magical Inner Child

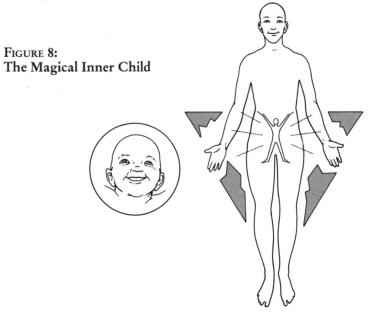

As you heal from the sexual abuse, it is the wounded child you are healing. This is where your pain is, and this is where the healing takes place. In the process of exposing this wounded child's pain, you will peel off some of your protective core defenses. Then you will relive, in part, the painful emotional—and sometimes physical—experiences you had when you were abused. You will feel as if you have become the age you were when you were wounded, while you reexperience the wounding. Although it is frightening and painful, this process is vital to healing. As your wounded child experiences the pain of the sexual abuse, you (as your "adult self") have the opportunity to allow your inner child to express those intense feelings. As you grow in compassion for yourself as a child, you create a pathway through the defenses so that your wounded child can heal this long-held pain.

When the wounded child is allowed to scream out the fear and rage at the injustice and betrayal and to sob out the deep loss and grief, the internal pain diminishes in intensity. As a result of this release, your ability to experience your natural joy and wonder will manifest through the magical child. When your inner magical child is realized, you will gain the ability to see the world through the eyes of wonder, and the spontaneous play and innocent awe of this inner child will be available to you. This transformation process is the essence of recovery from childhood sexual trauma.

Max was a survivor who had been raised by his mother and grandmother. Throughout his childhood, he was emotionally sexually abused. He was told he was a "dirty little boy" and that his penis was "evil" and "ugly." Max was frequently compared with his father, "the man who got his mother pregnant and left." Max was subjected to constant ridicule and shame about being a boy. He ran away at fourteen and became a prostitute, working the streets of a large city. Max also developed alcoholism. At the age of twenty-eight, Max joined one of my therapy groups. There he gradually felt safe enough to reexperience the shame, fear, and anger of his wounded inner child. Each time he worked through more of these feelings, Max was surprised at the intensity and depth of his pain. But one evening Max came to group smiling. Max shared that he had dreamed he was a bird, that he was flying high in the air. Then he had "turned into a little child who was able to fly and soar and laugh." As this little child, Max felt he could do anything, but mostly he just laughed and felt happy.

Max had recognized his magical child. He said that he felt so light and free that his feet "almost don't touch the ground." Although Max's wounded inner child still needed more healing, Max had discovered a source of contentment, wonder, and strength inside of him, in the form of his magical child. Max's experience makes it clear that you don't have to wait until you are "through" with your work to experience joy in recovery. Like Max, that natural joy will come to you as you heal the wounded child within.

FINDING YOUR INNER CHILD

Here is a guided experience designed to assist you in meeting your inner child. If you have done inner child work before, use this experience to deepen your relationship with your inner child. When using images to heal, it is important to understand that it is not your ability to see pictures in your mind's eye that causes healing. What is important is your willingness to concentrate on your healing process. Many people do not see "pictures" when they close their eyes. Each of us experiences our inner vision in a different way. For some people, inner vision is a "knowing" unaccompanied by images. Some, however, "see" extremely vivid pictures in their mind's eye. Once again, it is your *intent to heal*, rather than your ability to see mental pictures, that is important.

This guided inner vision is one I have used many times with survivors of childhood sexual abuse. You may want to use this exercise in a group setting by having one person read the written imagery to the rest of the group. Or you can use it alone by recording the words on an audiocassette tape and then playing it back. I would also suggest using soft background music to help you relax and become more receptive to the healing in the imagery. In order to get the most from this inner vision experience, repeat the process several times. An ellipsis (. . .) suggests a pause of approximately three seconds.

Begin this experience by finding a comfortable position, either sitting upright in a chair or lying down on the floor or other firm surface. Make sure that you will not be disturbed for about an hour. Lower the lighting in the room. Play soft instrumental music while you do the exercise.

"The Gift of the Star"

Become aware of your breath . . . Relax . . . Let your breath move freely in and out of your body . . . Use your breath as a way to focus your attention on your body . . . With each inhalation become aware of your lungs filling with life-giving air . . . With each exhalation let your lungs empty . . . Let go and relax . . . Now focus on your breath for the next minute or so.

Imagine yourself in the middle of a forest . . . You are surrounded by towering trees . . . Feel the wisdom of these large old trees . . . Become aware that you are standing on a pathway . . . You are wearing the same clothes you're wearing right now . . . Begin to walk along this pathway . . . As you walk, become aware that you are moving deeper and deeper into the forest . . . As you continue walking you realize that, off to each side of the pathway, there are scenes from your past . . . The farther down the path you go, the earlier the scenes from your life become . . . If you wish, you may leave the path and enter any period of your life.

Move deeper and deeper into the forest . . . Go farther down the pathway until you are at a time of your life when you were a young child . . . Look into your past and see yourself as a young child . . . Notice what you, as a young child, are wearing . . . Notice what your younger self is doing . . . Become aware of what this child, your inner child, is feeling . . . Step off of the path and go to the child.

Introduce yourself to the child . . . Begin to walk with your child, explaining who you are and that you won't hurt the child . . . Hold the child's hand . . . Feel the warmth and experience the trust of this little child . . . Pick the child up and hold the child to your chest . . . Tell your inner child they never have to be alone again . . . Tell them that you will be there whenever they need you . . . Tell your inner child that you will not abandon them. Ever.

Walk with your inner child . . . Feel the clear and simple love of this wonderful little being . . . Using the power of your imagination, look up and see a sky full of bright stars . . . Show the stars to the child . . . Now reach up and gently touch one of these shimmering stars . . . Hold the star in your hand . . . Bring down the star and give it to your inner child . . . Feel the healing warmth of the star . . . Experience the healing glow of this magical star . . . Tell the child that this magical star will never burn out . . . Tell the child this is their star . . . The child will always have its light of healing and hope to carry with them . . . No one can ever take this gift from them . . . Tell your child that, no matter what happens to them, the light from the magical star will always be there for them . . . Tell your child that the star's light will light the darkness and the shadows . . . and that you and the magical star will always be there for them.

You are holding your inner child and the child is holding the healing star . . . See the glow and feel the warmth from the star . . . As the child holds the star to their chest, the star begins to melt into the child's heart . . . healing and warming your inner child . . . Carrying your child, you walk back toward the path . . . You step onto the path and begin walking back in the direction that you came from . . . Holding your inner child, you once again reaffirm that you will never abandon them.

Returning up the pathway, holding your child, you feel the little child melting into your heart . . . You continue along the path, passing the early scenes of your life . . . You are aware of the truth that you and your inner child are one and the same . . . that you truly will not abandon your child . . . that together you will both heal and give each other love and understanding . . . The healing light of the magical star is for you, and for your inner child . . . You will always have it to light the way through your recovery.

Walking farther up the path, you become more and more aware of your breath . . . You begin to focus on your breath . . . You are aware of the flow of your breath . . . You are aware of the movement of your breath as it flows in and out of your body . . . You become aware of your body and of your surroundings . . . You are aware of being at the same place where you began this journey . . . When you are ready, slowly and gently allow your eyes to open.

If you have done this exercise in a group or with another person, take some time to talk about your experience. If you were doing the exercise alone, go to the Healing Journal (Part Three of this book) and write about your experience, using the section in your journal titled "The Inner Child."

If this is your first introduction to your inner child, you may have the experience that the child does not like you, or does not trust you. Do not become overly concerned if this happens. Some people need to take time to build trust with their inner child. Their inner child has been so wounded that the relationship takes time to grow and develop.

Some survivors find that they do not like their inner child. They feel betrayed or even repulsed by their inner child. Simply keep in mind that if you work on establishing this relationship, healing will occur. The love is there, regardless of how things may appear at first. All you need to do is to give that love time to unfold and express itself.

PARENTING YOUR INNER CHILD

Now that you have met your inner child, you can take further action that will contribute a great deal to your recovery. Your wounded child acts out of pain and fear, and some of this behavior is self-destructive. Now that you, the adult, have met your wounded child, you can "parent" that child. You can begin to treat your inner wounded child like a gentle and loving parent treats a child: with patience, humor, and compassion. This is important, because the wounded child in you will continue to act out its pain, and without the gentle discipline of a good parent, it will continue to behave self-destructively. Only a loving intervention on your part, as the adult, will change your wounded child's tendency to self-destruct.

The more you heal, the more clearly you will see your life choices and behaviors. You will begin to realize that you need to change the behaviors that cause you pain or endanger you. You will be healing from the inside out. Even though releasing your childhood pain is fundamental to your healing, the destructive habits developed in the past must be broken to complete your recovery. Loving your inner child does not mean giving it permission to act in any way it pleases. Just as responsible parents do not allow their little children to play on a busy street, you will learn not to let your "inner kid" walk into danger.

This means applying gentle discipline. In recovery you will see your destructive behaviors. These can range from putting yourself at risk by associating with people who abuse you, to committing systematic suicide by living a lifestyle that insures poor health and an early death. Now that you have met your inner child, it is your job to parent and protect this child.

Clara, the survivor who could not say no to sex, had developed a pattern of putting herself at risk by going out to bars and going home with men who were drunk and who abused her. "It was crazy," she said. "I didn't drink or do drugs, but in between boyfriends I would go to these sleazy bars and hang out. Sooner or later, some drunk would make a pass at me and we would leave together. I don't know how many cheap motels I wound up in, but it was a lot. Half the time I would get slapped around, and a couple of times I was beaten badly enough to need medical help."

Clara's high-risk behavior changed dramatically after she was introduced to her inner child. "I began to ask myself questions like, 'Would I take a little girl into this bar?' and 'Would I let this guy take care of a little girl?' I don't know much about parenting, but I do have common sense! If I answered no to any question about the safety of my inner child, I just wouldn't do it. I stopped going to bars completely, and I stopped being with men who abused me. Inside I still felt unworthy, but I changed anyway. After a while I felt a lot better about myself."

Even though her wounded child did not want to change, Clara began to protect her inner child by acting in a way that reduced her self-destructive behavior: "Those times that I returned to my old patterns and went to bars, I felt rotten that I would do this to myself. In fact I felt so lousy about putting my inner child in dangerous situations that it really became pretty easy to stop. Even now I test my decisions by questioning the safety of my inner child: I ask her, 'Do you feel safe with this person?' and if she says no, then I don't see them anymore. This goes for women as well as men."

Some survivors do not make changes to protect their wounded child. One man, Ike, acted out his childhood sexual abuse in a lifestyle that was systematically killing him. When I met Ike, he had a heart condition, was sixty pounds overweight, and smoked two packs of cigarettes a day. A recovering alcoholic, Ike had fifteen years of alcohol- and drug-free living and was in his early fifties. For almost a year in therapy, Ike and I talked about the inner child and about how important parenting his inner child could be for his recovery.

Ike wrote letters and did visualizations about his inner child. He tried to love his inner kid and take care of him, but he refused to make any lifestyle changes. During one session, Ike even told me that his inner child was angry at him for smoking and for being overweight. I told him I, too, was deeply concerned about his self-destructive habits. Ike soon decided to quit therapy, saying, "I'm content just to stay sober." Within a year, Ike had a massive heart attack. His doctor told him he wouldn't live unless he lost weight and stopped smoking. I saw Ike several times after that heart attack. Each time he said he was soon going to cut down on the fats in his diet and stop smoking. But he didn't do either, and in three months he was dead.

Ike had been a counselor who worked with people who had been sexually abused as children. He taught his clients some of the techniques I had taught him, so they could begin to parent their inner children. I spoke to several of Ike's former clients after his death, and they told me how much he had helped them to reclaim and parent their inner child. Unfortunately, he had not been able to put into practice what he had passed on to others. His death was a great loss to the community where he lived and worked.

I tell Ike's story because what happened to him happens all too often. There will be times in your recovery when you will have to act in spite of your fear, in spite of your habits, and in spite of the pressure you feel from those around you. You will have to take a stand for your own health and for the health of your inner child, who was wounded and who needs direction and guidance. When you change those self-destructive behaviors, then together you and your inner child will heal. Then the miracle of the magical child will fill your life and speed your recovery.

If you have been working in the Healing Journal, now is a good time to turn to the "Inner Child" section (Chapter 16) to write a letter to the little child who lives within you.

CHAPTER 7

Healing Energy

A crucial but often neglected part of healing from childhood sexual abuse is directing healing energy to the wound after externalizing painful repressed emotions. This is the "forgotten step" in the healing cycle that I mentioned in the previous chapter. By directing this energy to your invisible wound, you fill the void left by the pain, replacing it with warmth, light, and health. Doing this dramatically reduces the time you spend doing intense emotional release work. It is possible to release your pain and then draw it back to yourself over and over again. This is why some survivors can stay in therapy for a long time, releasing emotions, without appearing to make progress. Actively directing energy to heal the "opened" wound keeps you from having to relive the same memories again and again. Not long after a session involving work with healing energy, one survivor shared the following:

> I have been in one kind of therapy or another for almost fifteen years. I've rolled around on the floor and screamed, and cried until I thought my heart would break. I've done a lot, but I always felt stuck, like I wasn't finished yet. I'd cry and rage about the same old things over and over again. Doing this energy work has really set me free. I really feel movement and healing inside of me. All that other work I did was good, too, but I wish I had done this healing work earlier. I thought maybe I just wasn't working hard enough, as one of my therapists had told me. Now I know I was working as hard as I could. It was the fact that they didn't know about energy that slowed things down, not my unwillingness to work on myself.

Survivors in this situation know that something is missing from their healing, but they don't know what it is. The crucial missing piece is using energy to "fill" the wound and complete the healing cycle. Unfortunately, survivors often "blame" themselves for "not working hard enough" in their recovery. It isn't your fault if you haven't found all the information you need for complete recovery. As you learn more about using healing energy, your progress will move much more quickly.

For thousands of years, healers and mystics have known about the energy field of the human body. Although generally unseen by the human eye, this field of energy is every bit as real as the physical body itself. Even now, most of Western culture dismisses or ignores the existence of energy fields and the use of energy for healing. Our culture customarily uses a scientific method of thinking. In this view, anything that cannot be readily observed, touched, weighed, or otherwise measured is not considered to exist. Energy does, however, emanate from the body, extending well beyond it. Although this energy field usually cannot be seen, it certainly can be "felt," or sensed intuitively. If you have ever had the experience of feeling good or bad "vibes" around someone, you were sensing their energy field, using that sense to determine whether you wanted to be near them.

It is easy to tell when someone enters your energy field. Hold your hands over your ears, close your eyes, and have a friend begin walking toward you from about ten feet away. Most of the time you will sense your friend's energy before they are standing within a foot of your body. They will have entered your "personal space," your energy field, and you will know it. This energy not only extends outward from your body, it permeates your body completely, pervading each cell and atom. It is within this intricately interwoven energy system that your body holds the memories of your past experiences, including the memory and pain of sexual abuse.

RELEASING THE ENERGY OF HELD PAIN

Whether you are a man or a woman, the pain and trauma of sexual abuse is centralized in your pelvic area (see figure 9). This is your sexual energy center, where your reproductive organs are located. It is also where most of the energy of the sexual abuse experience is stored. No

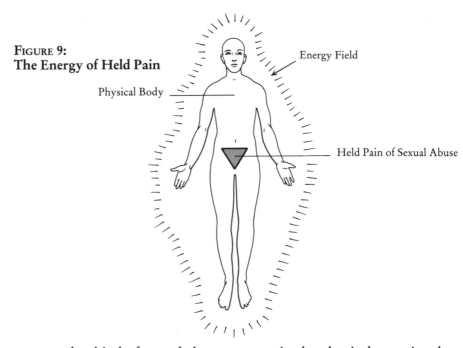

FIGURE 9:
The Energy of Held Pain

Energy Field

Physical Body

Held Pain of Sexual Abuse

matter what kind of sexual abuse you survived—physical, emotional, or both—your pelvic area, your sexual center, will contain most of your held pain.

When you do recovery work to externalize, or release, the energy of held pain, you may feel a sensation of emptiness in your pelvic region. Survivors commonly describe this as a tingling sensation, a hole, or a sense of relaxation and lightness. After doing intense emotional release work, many survivors report feeling as though they have "dropped a heavy rock." You feel relief after emotional release work, and some healing occurs at that time. But when this held energy, or stored pain, is released, it is truly as if a "hole" is left in its place. To maximize your healing, you must focus your awareness and direct your healing energy into this "empty" place. If you do not take the active step of guiding healing energy into the wound after doing emotional release work, the energy hole will reestablish the previous pattern of held pain. This happens because your body has become accustomed to carrying the energy pattern associated with the held pain. If a new energy pattern is not introduced after the pain is released, the original pain pattern will simply reemerge.

In this regard your body is like a sponge. Think of a sponge sitting in a bucket of water. If you reach into the water and squeeze the sponge, it will be emptied of water. But as soon as you release your grip, water will immediately fill the sponge again. There will have been no appreciable change in the sponge except for the brief period of time in which you squeezed the water out of it. If, on the other hand, you squeezed the water from the sponge, removed it from the bucket, and released it in the air, the sponge will fill with air. A significant change would have taken place.

When you externalize your held feelings, your body is similar to the sponge. If you do not take an active step to replace the energy of the emotions soon after releasing them, your inner pain will begin to reassert itself in your body, just as the sponge would fill up with water if it were released again into the environment of the water. So after you do emotional release work, you must change the energy in that part of your body, by directing healing energy into the "empty" spot where the pain was held. In this way, you prevent the pain pattern from being reestablished there.

To release the pain pattern, it is best to have the support of another person, usually a therapist, who can stay with you during the experience. This person can offer encouragement as you encounter intense emotions, help to validate your feelings, and support you in accepting the truth of your sexual abuse experience. Your support person is also there to remind you that, no matter how intense your emotions are, you are experiencing *memories*, things that happened in the past and that are not happening to you now. Having someone with you as you reenter your trauma also breaks the isolation and loneliness you experienced as a sexually abused child.

Externalizing held pain can take a variety of forms: shouting, screaming, hitting pillows, crying, shaking, sobbing, or just being still and staying conscious of your emotions. If for some reason you are unable to join a therapy group or find a suitable therapist, find a trustworthy friend who can hold you while you cry, or who can otherwise support you as you express your feelings. Again, this kind of emotional release work is generally much more effective in a therapeutic setting. Still, many survivors (whether they are in therapy or not) find it helpful to do emotional work by themselves as well, once they have learned the basic techniques of release and healing.

If you do this work alone, it's important to make sure that you have adequate time and privacy to fully honor the release of your emotions. Be aware also that the sounds of your release work can have unexpected consequences. One day one of my clients was screaming angrily, beating upon her bed with a tennis racquet to let go of her rage, when suddenly her next-door neighbors burst into her apartment to save her from her "attacker." My client's experience points up the value of seeking a therapeutic environment in which to do this work. Then, not only will you have the support of a therapist (and possibly a group of other survivors), but you will be much less likely to be interrupted. If you do choose to do anger work by yourself, take care to create a safe place to do it.

While the release is taking place, the held energy is actually "pushed" outward, away from your body (see figures 10 and 11).

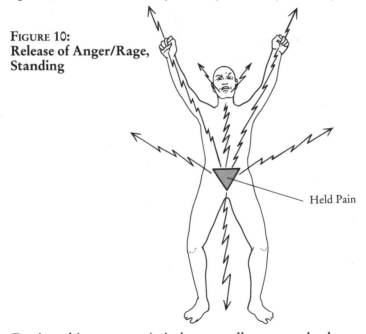

**FIGURE 10:
Release of Anger/Rage,
Standing**

Held Pain

During this process, it is best to allow your body to discover the position that is most effective for letting out the emotional energy. As you begin to release the emotions associated with your sexual abuse experience, your first feeling may be intense fear or terror. Often there will be a "lid of fear" covering more deeply held anger and grief. Conversely, if you first feel anger or grief, you may discover a layer of fear underneath these feelings. When you experience the energy of fear,

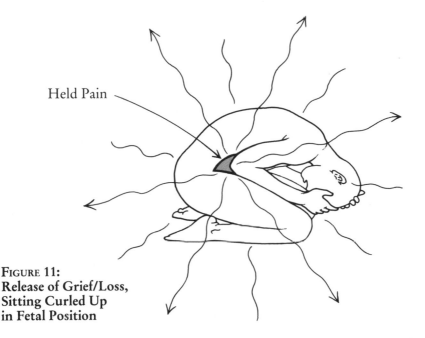

Held Pain

FIGURE 11:
**Release of Grief/Loss,
Sitting Curled Up
in Fetal Position**

your body may shake or tremble, or you may simply be still and feel afraid for a time. Anger or rage can be pushed outward through screaming, yelling, hitting a pillow or couch, or by punching the air with the fists. It can sometimes feel as if the anger is being "thrown" from your body. Grief and loss are often released through curling up the body (as in figure 11), sobbing, crying, and sighing.

The two most common externalization postures (release of anger/ rage and grief/loss) are depicted on the previous page and above. The arrows indicate the energy of these emotions leaving the pelvic region. After the release work is complete, there is a felt sense of release. At this point, you will need to direct healing energy into the "empty space" left by the release of energy associated with your past trauma. To direct this energy by focusing your awareness, it is necessary to understand a bit more about the nature of the energy that has been released, and about the energy that does the healing.

For our purposes, energy can be thought of as manifesting in two primary forms: toxic energy and healing energy. *Toxic energy* is simply energy that is repressed, or held. Since the energy of the pain of sexual abuse has been held in your body for a long time, it can be considered

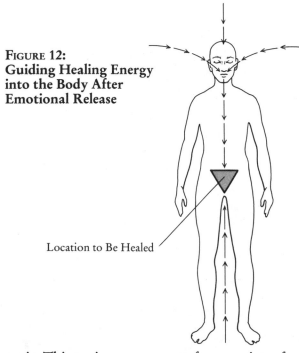

**FIGURE 12:
Guiding Healing Energy
into the Body After
Emotional Release**

Location to Be Healed

toxic. This toxic energy most often consists of unexpressed anger, rage, fear, terror, grief, loss, and sadness, as well as shame and guilt. *It is important to note here that, while you as a child were innocent, not guilty, and therefore had nothing to be ashamed of concerning the sexual abuse, the secrecy surrounding such abuse (whether it was imposed by direct or implied threats) creates feelings of shame and guilt in an innocent child. The toxic energy of these feelings of shame and guilt, as well as the rage, terror, and grief, must be released from your body in order for healing to occur.* When toxic energy is released, it becomes "nontoxic."

Healing energy is unrepressed and free-flowing. It is often experienced as feelings of joy, bliss, peace, happiness, contentment, or "oneness with all things," or simply as the subjective experience of active healing. All these conditions can be "sensed." Energy is the basic building block of everything in our universe—and there is an abundance of healing energy. When you direct healing into your wound, it is helpful to visualize or "sense" this abundant energy in the form of a color or image that represents healing to you. (See figures 12 and 13. The arrows show how you can guide healing energy into your body.)

CREATING A SEXUAL SELF-PORTRAIT

Three women have allowed me to use both their sexual self-portrait and their accompanying journal entries for this book. All of the self-portraits were done in color, and I regret that they could not be reproduced in color here. As you look at each of the drawings, imagine royal purples, bright and soft oranges and pinks, blues and golds, in many hues and shades. Each drawing is alive with color. When you do your own self-portrait, using color, you will experience the dynamic, nurturing, and colorful energy of your sexual self.

LOGAN'S JOURNAL ENTRY

#1 "When I drew this picture of My Sexual Self, I was feeling strong in my solar plexus. Making this picture brought up images of being four- or five-years-old and running around yelling and playing in the dirt. I wanted to dance around a fire and shake rattles. Energies were pulsing up through my body, and I wanted to express unbridled power without shame or guilt. It's good to be a strong young boy."

LOGAN'S JOURNAL ENTRY

#2 *"When I worked with this picture of My Sexual Self, I felt the peace and contentment of being truly connected to myself. In this drawing I re-created my own birth and gave myself what I really wanted. I felt loved and cared for by both a mother and a father—and by Spirit. I was set free to love myself. I embraced my feminine as well as masculine self. I felt soft, very open, and complete."*

LOGAN'S JOURNAL ENTRY

#3 "Glorious, Glorious explosion. I AM ALIVE! This picture of My Sexual Self unfolded in front of me. When this drawing was happening, I felt full of love and aware of the awesome ability that I have to re-create life. I was bursting with love and sexual energy. I wanted to embrace the universe and create. I cried."

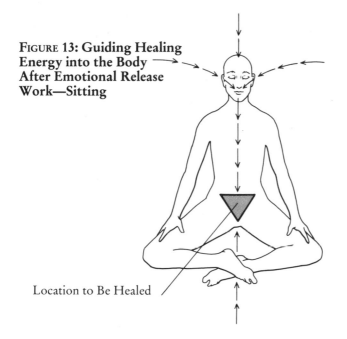

FIGURE 13: Guiding Healing Energy into the Body After Emotional Release Work—Sitting

Location to Be Healed

The following account of a therapy session illustrates how a survivor released her held emotions, then directly guided healing energy into her wound.

Sharyl was twenty-seven years old when she joined one of my survivors' therapy groups. She was also a recovering alcoholic with four years of sobriety and was actively involved in Alcoholics Anonymous. When she began therapy, Sharyl had an "intuition" that she had been sexually abused. During her first year in group, she retrieved some of the memories of that abuse: Sharyl's father had begun to abuse her when she was four years old. The abuse consisted of fondling and oral sex, which continued until Sharyl was nine.

Whenever Sharyl tried to talk about this sexual abuse, she experienced a sensation in her pelvic area, just above her pubic bone. She described this sensation sometimes as a "cold black knot," and other times as a "white-hot burning feeling." Sharyl also occasionally had extreme nausea, and that year she vomited several times while attempting to talk about the abuse. During one group session (conducted sitting on the floor), Sharyl stated that she wanted to work on her inability to express her feelings about being sexually abused. The five other group members moved back slightly, to give Sharyl extra room. I asked her, "What are you experiencing right now?"

SHARYL: I have that same old cold, black knot.

WAYNE: Are you having any emotional experiences?

SHARYL: No . . . uh . . . Yes, fear I think. I'm starting to feel sick to my stomach.

WAYNE: Can you focus on the knot?

SHARYL: Yes, I'm getting scared. (*Her body begins to shake.*)

WAYNE: Do you want to stop? It's okay if you do.

SHARYL: No, I want to keep going.

WAYNE: Okay, keep focusing on the knot and tell me what you experience.

SHARYL: I feel cold and scared. (*Her hands are balled into fists.*)

WAYNE: What would your hands like to do?

SHARYL: Hit him, rip him apart, punch his face. I'm scared. (*Small voice, like a child's. She clutches her belly with her hands, rolls over onto her side, and begins to sob and cry. This lasts several moments, then subsides.*)

WAYNE: Sharyl, do you want to continue?

SHARYL: Yes. The knot feels like it's on fire.

WAYNE: What is that knot trying to say?

SHARYL: No! It's trying to say, "No! Stop, you're hurting me. *No! No!*" (*She screams "No!" over and over again. A group member places a pillow in front of her and she begins to hit the pillow with her fists. This lasts for about ten minutes, and then she begins to sob and cry again. After a few minutes, Sharyl stops crying and asks to be covered with a blanket. Her shaking has stopped, and her breathing is deep and even.*) The knot's gone. I feel empty, and peaceful at the same time. Does anyone have a Kleenex? (*Someone offers a tissue.*)

WAYNE: Is there a color that represents healing to you?

SHARYL: Yes, purple. (*She sits up in a cross-legged position and closes her eyes.*)

WAYNE: Use your inner vision to draw purple energy into the place in your body where you experienced the knot, and

where you now feel "empty." Draw the purple energy
up from the earth and fill your pelvic region with that
purple energy of healing.

SHARYL: I feel light, and powerful. I can feel the energy in my
body. It tingles. . . . I keep getting fuller and fuller. I
feel great! I've never felt like this before. . . . I feel
warm and open. . . . I think I'm done for now.

For the next week, Sharyl agreed to continue to visualize drawing
the purple energy up from the earth into her body. She did this
visualization three times every day. The next week when Sharyl came
to group, she said she had been feeling very relaxed and powerful. She
told the group that her body felt different and that she felt she had had
a major healing experience. Sharyl had enjoyed doing the visualization,
and she continued doing it once a day throughout the year. When she
left therapy, Sharyl told the group that she felt this was the most
important and lasting piece of work she had done.

HEALING ENERGY MEDITATIONS

Using healing energy does not have to be confined to the therapist's
office. You can create your own images for using healing energy. As
you work in your journal or in other support groups, you can access
this energy to facilitate your healing. Creating your own healing
images is quite empowering for survivors. It places the control of your
healing where it belongs—with you. When you become able to focus
your awareness, using energy to heal yourself, you are well on your
way to stage three of recovery: integration.

The following are two healing meditations that I often teach to my
clients. One meditation is for women; one is for men. These Earth
Healing meditations work extremely well. Try doing the meditation
for a week. Twice a day is best (once in the morning and again at night).

In these meditations, you will draw on the healing power of the
earth. The image of the earth as the Great Mother and Healer has been
with us in various forms throughout recorded history. From ancient
times, healers and mystics have drawn on the Earth Mother's power to
heal and to nurture. This nurturing earth energy is real. Just as you have
an energy field within and around your body, the earth's energy

permeates and surrounds her as well. The earth's energy field is powerful beyond our imagination. You can tap into this energy and invite it into your body to assist your healing. Remember that the Earth Mother is an archetype. Though she is an integral part of our human experience, she also transcends it. The Earth Mother is not your human mother (who may have abused you) but the transcendent Mother of us all.

Because the wound of sexual abuse resides in the pelvic area, this is where you will focus the earth energy as you draw it into your body. Although these two exercises begin and end in the same way, the specific focusing of energy in the sexual center is different.

Earth Healing
Women's Meditation

Do this exercise with your back straight but comfortable and relaxed, sitting either cross-legged on the floor or upright in a chair, with your legs slightly apart and your feet flat on the floor. It is good to use soft music during the meditation and to have a friend read it aloud to you. Or you could tape-record the imagery, then play it back until you have memorized it and can do it without referring to the instructions. In the text below, an ellipsis (. . .) indicates a pause of approximately three seconds.

Begin this experience by becoming aware of your breath . . . Watch your breath as it moves in and out of your body . . . Feel the movement of your body as you breathe in . . . Be aware of the expansion of your chest as you inhale . . . When you breathe out, feel the letting go of the air in your lungs . . . Continue to focus on your breath . . . the cycle of breath . . . in and out . . . This is a natural cycle of receiving and letting go . . . Breathe without forcing your breath . . . Breathe slowly and deeply . . .

As you sit becoming aware of your breath . . . also become aware of your body . . . Feel the force that the earth exerts on your body . . . Feel the nurturing pressure of the earth's gravity as it supports and holds you . . . Be aware of where your body touches the floor or the chair . . . Focus your attention on where your buttocks are touching the floor or the chair. Be aware of the pressure of your weight on the base of your spine . . .

Begin to think of a color that represents healing to you . . . Let the color come to you . . . gently, without forcing it . . . Any color you choose can be the color of healing for you . . . If you cannot think of a color, try a rich green or any earthy color . . . This is your healing color . . .

As you sit and breathe, open your body to the earth's healing power . . . Sense the strength of the Earth Mother . . . Breathe in, drawing the color of healing up from the earth into your body . . . Each time you breathe in, draw the healing energy up, filling your pelvic area . . . Feel the color of healing entering your body through your vagina . . . Use your inner vision to see the healing color filling your vagina . . . Feel the healing warmth spread through your vagina and up into your uterus . . . Fill your uterus with the healing power of the earth . . . Sense the healing warmth of the Great Mother as it spreads across your pelvic area . . . Feel it entering into your body through your anus . . . filling you with healing . . . With each inhalation, draw the healing deeper into your body . . . Sense the warmth and power of the healing earth . . . Fill your lower body with the healing . . . Each fallopian tube is filled with healing . . . Each ovary is filled with healing . . . Each breath pulls in the energy of healing . . .

Each time you breathe out, let the pain leave your body . . . Send it out and down into the earth . . . The earth can heal and transform your pain . . . Send the pain downward with each outgoing breath . . . Let your pain fall away . . . Give it to the Earth Mother . . . With each in-breath, draw in the healing, and with each out-breath, send out your pain . . . Do this for a few minutes . . . (*Pause*) . . .

Feel the warmth of the healing energy . . . Invite the healing energy to enter deeply into your body . . . Open each organ and each cell to the healing color . . . Sense the healing spreading across your pelvic area . . . Every woman has two hearts . . . The heart of creation is your womb . . . The heart of your soul is in your chest . . . As you breathe in, draw the healing color up from the heart of your womb and into the heart of your soul . . . You have been wounded in both hearts . . . Feel the power of the earth filling your heart with healing . . . With each in-breath, draw the color of healing from the earth up into your pelvis, filling it, then drawing the energy up into your heart . . . Fill your whole body with healing energy from the earth . . . Feel your whole body healing . . . With each out-breath, breathe your pain and sorrow down into the earth . . . Healing . . . Healing . . . Float gently in the healing presence of the Great Mother . . .

Become aware of your breath as it moves in and out of your body . . . Be aware of the rise and fall of your chest as you breathe in and out . . . Become aware of the clothes you are wearing . . . Feel your clothes against your body . . . Become gradually aware of your surroundings . . . Breathe deeply and fully, then slowly open your eyes.

Earth Healing
Men's Meditation

Do this exercise with your back straight but comfortable and relaxed, sitting either cross-legged on the floor or upright in a chair, with your legs slightly apart and your feet flat on the floor. It is good to use soft music during the meditation and to have a friend read it aloud to you. Or you could tape-record the imagery, then play it back until you have memorized it and can do it without referring to the instructions. In the text below, an ellipsis (. . .) indicates a pause of approximately three seconds.

Begin this experience by becoming aware of your breath . . . Watch your breathe as it moves in and out of your body . . . Feel the movement of your body as you breathe in . . . Be aware of the expansion of your chest as you inhale . . . When you breathe out, feel the letting go of the air in your lungs . . . Continue to focus on your breath . . . the cycle of breath . . . in and out . . . This is a natural cycle of receiving and letting go . . . Breathe without forcing your breath . . . Breathe slowly and deeply . . .

As you sit becoming aware of your breath . . . also become aware of your body . . . Feel the force that the earth exerts on your body . . . Feel the nurturing pressure of the earth's gravity as it supports and holds you . . . Be aware of where your body touches the floor or the chair . . . Focus your attention on where your buttocks are touching the floor or the chair. Be aware of the pressure of your weight on the base of your spine . . .

Begin to think of a color that represents healing to you . . . Let the color come to you . . . gently, without forcing it . . . Any color you choose can be the color of healing for you . . . If you cannot think of a color, try a rich green or any earthy color . . . This is your healing color . . .

As you sit and breathe, open your body to the earth's healing power . . . Sense the strength of the Earth Mother . . . Breathe in, drawing the color of healing up from the earth into your body . . . Each time you breathe in, draw the healing up, filling your pelvic area . . . Feel the color of healing enter your body at the base of your spine . . . Use your inner vision to see the healing color spreading out and filling your pelvic area . . . Feel the healing warmth spreading through your testicles and penis . . . Fill your prostate gland with the healing power of the earth . . . Sense the healing warmth of the Great Mother spreading across your pelvic area . . . Feel it entering into your body through your anus . . . filling you with healing . . . With each inhalation, draw the healing deeper into your body . . . Sense the warmth and power of the healing earth . . . Fill your lower body with the healing . . . Each testicle is filled with healing . . . Your prostate gland is filled with healing . . . Each breath pulls in the energy of healing . . .

Each time you breathe out, let the pain leave your body . . . Send it out and down into the earth . . . The earth can heal and transform your pain . . . Send the pain downward with each outgoing breath . . . Let your pain fall away . . . Give it to the Earth Mother . . . With each in-breath, draw in the healing, and with each out-breath, send out your pain . . . Do this for a few minutes . . . (*Pause*) . . .

Feel the warmth of the healing energy . . . Invite the healing energy to enter deeply into your body . . . Open each organ and each cell to the healing color . . . Sense the healing spreading across your pelvic area . . . Your wound extends to your heart as well as being in your sexual center . . . As you breathe in, draw the healing color up from your pelvis and into your heart . . .

You have been wounded in both places . . . Feel the power of the earth filling your heart with healing . . . With each in-breath, draw the color of healing from the earth up into your pelvis, filling it, then drawing the energy up into your heart . . . Fill your whole body with healing energy from the earth . . . Feel your whole body healing . . . With each out-breath, breathe your pain and sorrow down into the earth . . . Healing . . . Healing . . . Float gently in the healing presence of the Great Mother . . .

Become aware of your breath as it moves in and out of your

body . . . Be aware of the rise and fall of your chest as you breathe
in and out . . . Become aware of the clothes you are
wearing . . . Feel your clothes against your body . . . Become
gradually aware of your surroundings . . . Breathe deeply and
fully, then slowly open your eyes.

The Earth Healing meditation has worked well for many survivors.
The more often you use it, the better it will work for you. After you
have done the Earth Healing a number of times, you will be able to do
it easily by yourself. Many people find the meditation most effective if
it is done in the morning for several minutes, then again in the evening
for several minutes. This really works, but you will have to do it to find
that out.

The Blue Sphere

Another healing meditation I teach to my clients is called the Blue
Sphere. The meditation focuses on healing your heart. The betrayal
you experienced has wounded your heart deeply. This wound has
affected your ability to be vulnerable and compassionate with yourself
and others. When your heart is restricted this way, your ability to give
love freely, without expectation, becomes limited. Healing your
wounded heart will free you from your abandonment and betrayal,
allowing you to love yourself and others. In this meditation, the color
blue is used to represent healing, but feel free to choose any color that
you associate with healing.

Again, do the exercise with your back straight and comfortably
relaxed, sitting cross-legged on the floor or upright in a chair with your
legs slightly apart and your feet flat on the floor. Play soft music during
the meditation, and have a friend read the meditation to you. Or
memorize the instructions so that you can do the visualization without
referring to them.

Begin this experience by becoming aware of your breath . . .
Watch your breath as it moves in and out of your body . . . Feel
the movement of your body as you breathe in . . . Be aware of the
expansion of your chest as you inhale . . . When you breathe out,

feel the letting go of the air in your lungs . . . Continue to focus
on your breath . . . the cycle of breath . . . in, and out . . .
This is a natural cycle of receiving and letting go . . . Breathe
without forcing your breath . . . Breathe slowly and deeply . . .

Using the power of your active imagination, visualize a blue
sphere of energy floating in front of you . . . Watch this blue
sphere as it floats in the air before you . . . This sphere has an
endless supply of healing energy . . . It can never be
depleted . . .

Reach out with your senses and experience the blue sphere of
healing . . . Feel its warmth and healing . . .

Continue to breathe deeply and fully . . . Now, with every
intake of breath, begin to draw energy from the blue sphere into
your heart . . . With every intake of breath, visualize a line of blue
energy coming out from the blue sphere into your heart . . .
Create a path of blue energy from the blue sphere to your
heart . . . Breathe deeply and fully . . . With each breath, bring
more and more healing energy into your heart . . . Experience
the unlimited healing power of the blue sphere . . .

As you continue to breathe the blue healing energy into your
heart, experience your heart filling with healing energy . . .
Allow your heart to fill . . . All parts of your heart are filled with
the light of healing . . . There is no place in your heart that is
untouched by the healing energy of the blue sphere . . . When
your heart is full, that energy will begin to overflow from your
heart, spilling out into your entire body . . . With each breath,
more healing energy enters in through your heart and overflows
into every part of your body . . .

Your body is filling with healing energy . . . The blue healing
energy fills your legs and feet . . . your pelvic region is filled . . .
Your belly area is filled . . . Your chest is filled with healing . . .
Your arms and hands are filled with healing energy . . . Your
neck and throat are filled with the blue healing energy . . .
Experience the energy filling your head . . . Your whole body is
filled with the healing energy of the blue sphere . . .

Allow your body to overflow with healing energy . . . There is
energy and healing without limit . . . You can never run out of
healing energy . . . This energy will heal the wounds of your
heart and the wounds of your body . . . Allow it to flow freely
from the blue sphere into your heart and body . . . Know that
this energy of healing is always available to you . . . Whenever
you need love and energy, you can reconnect with the blue sphere

by taking several deep breaths and opening your heart to its presence . . .

Become aware of your breath as it moves in and out of your body . . . Be aware of the rise and fall of your chest as you breathe in and out . . . Become aware of the clothes you are wearing . . . Feel your clothes against your body . . . Become gradually aware of your surroundings . . . Breathe deeply and fully, then slowly open your eyes.

Learning both the Earth Healing meditation and the Blue Sphere meditation gives you an active role in a major portion of your healing. No one will be doing the healing to you, or for you. You will be inviting it yourself; you are in charge of the process. Even if you are also working with a therapist, you can feel confident that, by actively practicing this and other kinds of healing work (such as writing in the Healing Journal), you are taking responsibility for your recovery. You are at the center of your healing. Even the best therapist can only guide and assist you.

DIRECTING HEALING ENERGY
TO OTHER PARTS OF YOUR BODY

Although the pain of sexual trauma is located primarily in the pelvic area, other trauma associated with the abuse can be held in other places throughout your body. If, for instance, you were choked or orally raped, the memory of this experience may be energetically located in your throat and neck. Jeff, a client of mine, had been violently orally raped at the age of nine by several older boys. Although Jeff remembered what had happened to him, he had no access to his emotions about the experience (an instance of dissociation). When Jeff began to remember his feelings of terror, he would choke and become unable to speak. He reported that it felt as though something were lodged in his throat and that he had difficulty breathing.

Mary, another survivor, was vaginally penetrated with objects (sticks and nails) by her female babysitter at the age of six. The babysitter (age fifteen) told Mary that if she told anyone what had happened, she—Mary—would be killed. At age twenty-nine, Mary remembered this sexual abuse, but each time she tried to tell what had happened, she would feel overwhelming fear and become unable to talk. Mary said, "It feels like a lump in my throat every time I try to tell what happened to me."

Both Jeff and Mary experienced trauma to the throat area. Jeff's trauma was based on his actual physical experience of oral rape, and Mary's was based on the threat of death if she told anyone what had happened to her. Though the causes were different, the result was the same in both cases: Both Jeff and Mary felt as though they were choking whenever they tried to talk about how they had been abused. It happened that both clients were in the same survivors' therapy group. During one group session, Jeff was trying to express his feelings about the sexual abuse he had experienced when, as before, he began to choke and could no longer talk. This time, his breath also became ragged and shallow.

With a great deal of effort, Jeff was able to whisper, "I hate them. I really hate them." This was a real triumph for Jeff, and the group encouraged and complimented him on his effort. Mary told Jeff how difficult it was for her to express her feelings and acknowledged how hard he was working.

The Energy Chalice

I asked Jeff what kind of a healing image he could create to use at home. He said that he had once had an image of a silver chalice filled with blue water and that the water was energy. Jeff agreed that, once every morning and evening, he would imagine drinking the healing blue water from the silver chalice.

When he returned to group the following week, Jeff reported that he had been doing the healing image with the silver chalice and was eager to see if it was working. That day, although he experienced some choking sensations, Jeff was able to describe in detail how he had been sexually abused. While telling his story, he freely expressed his anger and sadness. Over the next few weeks Jeff was able to express what had happened to him with less and less of the choking sensation. After a month of using his healing image, Jeff could relate the story of the abuse without any choking at all.

Mary did not say much in group during that month, but she did report at one point that she had created her own image of a golden chalice filled with silver energy. Mary told the group that she would imagine drinking from her golden chalice twice a day, as Jeff had done. In one session not long after Jeff had talked about his experience, Mary began to talk about hers. She told, in detail, about one of the incidents in which her babysitter had abused her. Even though Mary reported having a feeling of choking, she was able to tell the entire story. Over the next several weeks, Mary continued to break the silence she had kept for so many years.

Both Jeff and Mary successfully used healing imagery as part of their recovery process. Since that time several years ago, I have encouraged many clients who were feeling choked or extremely afraid to talk to use that same image. Provided with the initial idea, they could then adapt the image in their own way. Some clients changed the chalice into a cup or bowl; sometimes they changed the color of the energy. However they changed it, the imagery always worked to help remove the choking sensation that prevented them from telling their stories.

You may have been frightened into silence, or you may have had a physical trauma to your throat. If you have had either, or have difficulty talking about your experience, create your own healing image. Use the image twice a day for a week and see what happens.

HEALING TOUCH

Some nurses, doctors, physical therapists and other health care providers have now recognized and begun to use what "primitive" healers have known for centuries: that touch can provide healing. One of our first instincts, when someone is hurt, is to touch them. The loving touch of a parent can soothe and heal a child's emotional and physical pain. (This may account for the custom of mothers and fathers "kissing the hurt.") When you touch someone *with love and respect*, you are transmitting healing energy to them. When you are touched by others with love and respect, you also receive healing energy. Hugs heal.

Healing Touch and Your Boundaries

As a survivor, you have been touched in ways that violated you emotionally and physically. Although healing is available in hugging, touching, and holding, this healing will only take place if you have invited or welcomed the touching. You have the *absolute right* to determine who touches you, when you are touched, and how you are touched—without exception. This right of refusal extends to therapists, lovers, friends, doctors, strangers, and anyone else. When someone wants to hug you or touch you, you always have the right to say no.

In group therapy I encourage my clients to discover the healing benefits of nonsexual hugging and touching. During and after grief work, a member of the group will often request that someone hold or cradle them. On the other hand, I also encourage clients to practice making the choice not to be touched: "If you have any doubts or reservations about being touched, say no!" Although I sometimes touch my clients during sessions, I always ask their permission or wait to be invited. If you are working with a therapist or group that encourages touching, practice stopping sometimes to ask yourself whether you really want to be touched. Some days you may answer, "Yes, I do." Other days you may feel, "No, I don't want to be touched today." Whatever your response is—and it is likely to change frequently—be sure that you are the one choosing whether you will be touched.

Julia, a former client of mine, told her therapy group that she resented people who came up to hug her without first asking permission. She said, "I have a lot of fear about saying no. I let people hug me when I don't want them to. Then I get resentful." The other group members supported Julia in telling people not to hug or touch her. Besides her group therapy, Julia was also attending a twelve-step support group where people often hugged each other after meetings. Julia had been leaving immediately after the meetings were over to avoid facing people who might want to hug her.

During one twelve-step meeting, Julia raised her hand to talk. She told the group that she did not want to be hugged or touched after the meeting. That day, for the first time, Julia was able to stay after the meeting to talk and make friends. Julia told her therapy group, "I feel more in control now, and when I ask someone to hug me, it really means something to me. I can feel the difference."

Hugs can heal, and the power of healing inherent in a human touch can be extremely profound. The kind of healing is available to you, if you invite it into your life. But it will only work if you feel comfortable with touching. Remember that you are in charge. You decide whom you hug or touch, and who hugs or touches you. There is never anything wrong with saying no or "Not now." When you set the limits on your interactions with others, you will probably find that you feel freer to explore the healing aspect of touch.

Healing Touch and Energy in a Group Setting

Bob was both neglected and sexually abused as a child. He never remembered his mother or father hugging or touching him in a loving way. During one group session Bob told the group (which was all men), "The only thing I remember being picked up as a child was when I was being carried somewhere. I never remember being held or rocked as a child. When I was eight, our live-in nanny began to fondle me, and shortly after that we began to have intercourse. It felt good—not only the physical touching, but the attention. The abuse lasted until I was around ten or eleven. The only time I hold, or am held, today is when I'm having sex. I know I'm missing out on something important, but I don't really know what." As he spoke, Bob began to cry. "I feel so lonely, like no one was ever there for me."

I asked Bob if he would like to explore his feeling of loneliness, and he agreed. I then asked, "Where do you experience the loneliness in your body?"

BOB: In my belly. It feels like a cold, hard rock.

WAYNE: Focus your attention on that cold rock in your belly.

BOB: Okay, now it feels like a black hole, a cold black hole.

WAYNE: Can you remember when you first felt that cold black hole?

BOB: I was around three. I can see myself lying on a bed. I'm so lonely. I wish someone would be with me. (*He begins to cry.*) Nobody ever cared about me. I was a thing. It hurt so much.

WAYNE: That little boy now has permission to cry. Let the tears go. (*He continues to sob and cry for a time.*)

WAYNE: Is it okay for you to continue?

BOB: Yes, but I feel so lonely.

WAYNE: What does your little boy want?

BOB: He wants to be held and rocked. But there is no one to hold him.

WAYNE: Would it be okay if this group rocks you and holds you?

BOB: I guess so. (*He is now lying on the floor, curled up on his side. He has stopped sobbing, but the tears are still falling.*)

WAYNE: Please gently roll over on your back now. (*While he turns onto his back, the men gather around him. One holds Bob's head, and the others carefully slip their hands underneath his body. The group then lifts Bob up off the floor and, all standing, hold him in a "human cradle." Slowly and gently, Bob is rocked back and forth.*)

BOB: This is great. I feel like I'm floating. I've never felt like this. (*He is silent for a time, and one of the men begins to hum a lullaby. The rest of the group joins in, continuing to rock him back and forth. They are humming "Rock-a-Bye Baby."*) I think you guys better stop now; this feels too good. (*The group gently lowers Bob back down to the floor.*)

WAYNE: Would you like to continue?

BOB: Yes, but it can't get any better than this, can it? I've never felt so much love. (*The group is still gathered on the floor near him.*)

WAYNE: Is it okay for the group to touch you again?

BOB: Yes.

WAYNE: I would like each member of the group to lightly place your hands on Bob and direct healing energy and love to him through your hands. (*The men in the group do this for a while as Bob lies quietly on the floor. After about five minutes, the group sits backs and Bob sits up.*)

BOB: I have never in my life felt so loved and cared for. My whole body is tingling. I feel so relaxed and peaceful.

This account shows how easily and naturally a group of survivors can direct love and healing energy. After this experience, Bob began to seek out nurturing touch by asking people he trusted to hug him. He also began to experiment with hugging and holding his lover without continuing into active sex. He reported that he felt a little bit "strange" just holding and hugging without having sex, but once he got used to it, he really liked the experience.

This healing experience can be done with any healing group. There are only two requirements needed for the "human cradle" to work well. First, there have to be enough people in the group to safely hold the person to be rocked (generally six to eight, depending on the size of the person to be cradled). And second, all participants have to be willing to do the exercise. If you are working with a group, suggest this exercise to them and then try it yourself. If your group is too small to hold you and rock you, consider doing only the second part of the experience. Have the group direct healing and love to you by gently and respectfully placing their hands on your body. You may tell the group members where to place their hands, or you may allow them to intuit where to place their hands—it is entirely up to you.

Everyone in the group benefits from this experience. The person being held and rocked receives the focused attention of the group and the experience of healing touch. The group members are given the opportunity to offer their nurturing and love to another, which is often a powerful healing experience for each of them as well.

A HEALING CIRCLE

Yet another group healing experience involves having your group sit in a circle, holding hands. Ask the members to close their eyes and take five or six deep breaths. Then, starting with you or the facilitator and moving to the right, each member of the group says his or her name. As the name is spoken, the whole group directs healing energy to that person for approximately one minute. Then the next person's name is called out, and the process is repeated until the healing circle is complete.

There are countless ways to do focused energy healing. Create your own exercises, and try them out with trusted friends or with your therapist or therapy group. Your imagination and creativity are limitless. Use them to explore this wonderful and necessary aspect of healing your wounds, and you will begin to experience what it is to feel fully alive.

CHAPTER 8

A Safe Place

During your time of active healing, it is imperative that you find a safe place to heal. As a sexually abused child, you experienced your environment as an unsafe place. If you survived incest, your home and family were not safe. If you were molested outside your family, the world became a dangerous place for you. Further, for any number of reasons, you were unable to recover from your experience of sexual abuse. In short, through no fault of your own, you did not experience the safety you needed as a child. Now that you are an adult, however, it is up to you to find and maintain a safe place where you (and your inner child) can recover. To feel the pain and to experience the healing of recovery requires an environment you can trust.

Trying to heal in an unsafe environment will only cause you more pain. There are ways to find or create the safe place you need. Although I will start with suggestions for choosing a therapist and a discussion of styles of treatment for survivors, your safe place must extend beyond the therapist's office or the treatment program. Creating a safe place also includes developing trustworthy support groups and healthy sexual relationships, as well as creating a safe place for your own children. In an ideal "safe place," you would feel safe enough to confront (if you wanted to) the person or persons who abused you, or who allowed the abuse to occur.

FINDING A THERAPIST

Finding a qualified therapist could be one of the most important steps in your recovery. A good therapist will lead you to the places inside yourself where you need to go to release your pain, guiding you beyond your defenses and providing support as you experience the wounds of your childhood. Your therapist should be someone whom you trust and who *respects you.*

One of the most effective ways of finding a therapist is to ask other survivors about their experiences with therapy and therapists. If you don't know any other survivors to ask, begin attending survivors' support groups. Listen to people at these meetings, and when you hear people who seem to speak your language or who seem to be well into recovery, ask whether they've ever been in therapy and, if they have, which therapist(s) they would recommend. Most recovering survivors are quite willing to share information about therapy and therapists. Hearing their experiences will help you narrow down your list of prospective therapists.

If you cannot find a survivors' group in your area, try going to an Adult Children of Alcoholics (ACOA), Al-Anon, or Co-dependents Anonymous meeting. The people who attend these meetings often know where the survivors' meetings are; some of them will be survivors themselves. They, too, may be able to share their therapy experiences with you. Getting a personal referral to a particular therapist is much better than blindly picking someone out of the phone book.

After you have the name of a therapist, call to set up an interview. Many therapists will give a brief consultation without charge or at a reduced rate. During your first visit, be prepared to ask your prospective therapist a number of questions. Remember that you are there to get help for the abuse you suffered; you deserve the best and most competent help you can get. An unqualified therapist could delay your recovery or even harm you. During the interview, it may be hard to remember all the questions you need to ask. Below is a list of some of the most important questions. You may want to copy these and take them with you. If your prospective therapist makes fun of you for having a list or does not want to answer your questions, leave immediately and find someone else to work with.

Here are some questions you might ask:

How many of your current clients are survivors of childhood sexual abuse?

What specific training do you have in working with survivors?

Are you a survivor? If so, how did you heal?

How much do you charge per session?

What do you do during a typical session?

Which books have you read about incest and sexual trauma?

Will I be able to reach you if I am in crisis?

If you are unavailable, who else would I be able to call during a crisis?

Do you have a process for termination of therapy?

How can I be sure that what I tell you will remain confidential?

These general questions will help you to keep focused during your interview. You may feel you do not know enough to evaluate the answers to your questions concerning the therapist's training; but the answers given are actually less important than *how you feel when you hear them.* A therapist who becomes defensive when asked a few questions about how he or she works probably will not be able to provide a safe place for you to recover (regardless of his or her level of training). Your best bet is to listen closely to your own feelings as your prospective therapist answers you. Take a note pad and jot down the answers so you can refer to them later. Add any other questions that come to you during the interview. Later, go over the answers in private. This will give you a general idea of the therapist's overall attitude and training. Then ask yourself:

Do I like this person?

Did I feel safe with this person?

Was this a nonjudgmental atmosphere?

Was this a healing atmosphere?

Did the therapist appear calm and relaxed?

Was I respectfully heard?

Will I be able to say anything I want to this person?

Will I get what I need here?

Does my gut reaction say yes to this interview?

If you answered with a definite, strong "no" to any of the above questions, keep shopping around. The most important part of the therapeutic process is your relationship to your therapist. If you find someone whom you can trust, who will treat you with dignity and respect, and who has good training, you will do well. After you start therapy, reserve the first four or five sessions to get to know one another. You may find out after a few sessions that you don't want to stay with your first choice. If that is the case, simply leave. You've wasted very little time. After you have been with a therapist for a while, it is good to continue to reassess your relationship. Sometimes people find that, though they have made good progress with a particular therapist, it's time to move on.

Whether you decide to pick a same-sex therapist is entirely up to you. Many female therapists work successfully with male survivors as well as female survivors. Likewise, many male therapists work well with both women and men. The gender of your therapist is less important than how you feel about him or her. Some survivors begin therapy with a same-sex therapist, then switch to an opposite-sex therapist, while for others the process is reversed. You must do what is right for you. There are no clear guidelines for you to follow. Your best test of a therapist is simple: If you feel that you can trust that person and if they have the skills to assist your healing, then you're probably in the right place.

Like many survivors, you may have entered therapy for reasons other than having been sexually abused. Many survivors, unaware of their sexual abuse history, enter therapy to address the secondary consequences described in Part One of this book. If, during the course of therapy, you begin to retrieve memories, then realize the deep pain you are carrying, it is a good time to reassess your therapy situation. Your therapist may have been great at helping you sort out your ambivalence about your career but may not be able to help you heal your childhood sexual trauma. In fact, a therapist can even hinder your healing by downplaying your memories or by telling you to ignore your past and focus on the reasons you entered therapy. Be candid with your therapist. Ask the questions listed above, and if you do not receive satisfactory answers, look elsewhere.

A survivor named Irene had arranged to have a series of ten massages by a reputable massage therapist. During the fifth massage, Irene remembered being sexually abused: "I was lying face down on the table. My massage therapist was doing my lower back, and suddenly I remembered being abused. I felt so terrified that I started shouting, 'Get off of me!' over and over. Then I just broke down and cried really hard. After I calmed down, we talked about what had just happened. My massage therapist confirmed that I was having a memory of sexual abuse, and he said that traumatic memories frequently surface during massage. Then he explained that, even though he had a good deal of experience doing massage with survivors and would like to continue with our series, it was important for me to find another therapist who specialized in working with survivors. He was very supportive and offered to help me find a good person to work with. I was so confused and scared about what was happening to me, I was ready to do just about anything. He really helped me."

Irene's experience is fairly common. Fortunately, her massage therapist knew what to do to support her. Larry, on the other hand, was not as lucky. He was in an inpatient treatment program for alcoholism and drug abuse when he remembered being sexually abused. "I was told to focus on staying sober for a year and not to think about being abused," he said. "Shit, I couldn't think of anything else! When I tried to talk about it, I was told, 'We don't deal with that here.' I wish I had walked out, but I stayed there. I was miserable the whole time. It felt like I was being shamed because of what happened to me." Eventually, after several relapses, Larry received treatment for sexual trauma: "After I started working on these sexual abuse issues, staying sober was easy."

Remember that, just because you have a good relationship with a particular therapist, you are not bound to that therapist permanently. You must do what is best for you. Don't stay with a therapist just because you are used to him or her. You may discover that your therapist is quite well-trained and capable of working with you. Still, you need to find that out by assessing their skills in light of knowing that you're a sexual abuse survivor.

Some time ago, a friend gave me a quote by Hermann Hesse that sums up my thoughts about therapy and therapists:

I can give you nothing
that has not already
its origins within yourself,

I can throw open no
picture gallery
but your own,

I can help make
your own world visible—
that is all.

No matter how good and talented your therapist is, you are the one who is doing the work and feeling the pain. The best therapists lead you to your feelings and stand by you during your experience of recovery. They provide a safe place for you to heal, while treating you with honor and dignity. When it is time for you to move on, they support your decision without judgment. (My personal goal as a therapist is to put myself out of business, one client at a time.)

TREATMENT OPTIONS

Whatever the type of treatment you seek for healing your childhood wounds, you must feel safe there. Without a safe place, you cannot heal. Some of the treatment options available to survivors are described below.

Individual Therapy

In individual therapy, you have the undivided attention of an individual therapist. In this setting (traditionally one or two hour-long sessions per week), you can explore your past with one other person. Sometimes this setting is the only one in which you will feel comfortable and safe talking about your past. For some survivors, the relationship they build with a therapist is the first trusting relationship they have ever had with another human being.

Every therapist has a personal style and has developed an individual way of conducting therapy. The person you choose, however, should have had some training in treating survivors of sexual abuse. Use the above guidelines for choosing a therapist. There is no set amount of time that you should spend in individual therapy. Some survivors spend years in therapy with the same person, and some move from therapist to therapist, depending on their needs.

Group Therapy

In a group therapy setting you are one of a group of survivors who meet together to heal their past, along with a therapist who facilitates the group. Most therapy groups range in size from six to eight members, and some groups have two facilitators. Some therapy groups last for a specific length of time and do not admit new members once the group has started. Open-ended groups may continue for years, admitting a new person to the group whenever there is an opening.

Being part of a small group focused on healing is an exciting, frequently transformative experience. Within this framework you can create a "safe family" where you will be able to freely vent your anger and cry your tears. Here you can show your fear and sorrow and get support from survivors who share a common experience of sexual abuse. The small group is one of the most powerful mediums for healing, and I recommend trying group therapy at least once. When choosing a group therapist, use the same guidelines given earlier in this chapter.

Treatment Programs

Inpatient treatment programs generally last from two to six weeks. During this time you will live at the treatment program and focus on memory recall and processing your feelings as they arise. It can be a powerful healing experience to devote a large block of time exclusively to your recovery. Of course, even after two to six weeks of nearly continuous treatment, you will still have a lot more recovery work to do. Don't expect to "finish" recovery in that short a period of time.

Good inpatient programs have "after care" built into their total treatment plan, are thorough in screening clients for other compulsions and addictions, and take into account diet and nutrition. Before you invest your time and money in inpatient treatment, try to find out all that you can about the program. Ask the director to give you a list of "alumni" who live in your area, and ask if there are after-care groups you could visit in your area. Listening to the experiences of other survivors who have gone through treatment is invaluable to your search.

Before I began writing this book, I interviewed six women who had gone through an inpatient treatment program designed for survivors of sexual abuse. Two of the women told me that a male doctor had examined their breasts without another woman present in the room. One woman revealed that she had had sex with a male counselor there. Another told me that her female roommate in treatment had had an affair with a woman who worked in the kitchen. Needless to say, I would not recommend this treatment program to anyone.

When you call an inpatient program for information, ask if they have a program specifically designed for sexual abuse survivors, and ask how many people are currently enrolled in it. I called one program that had been advertised in a national magazine, and when I pressed for additional information, I was reluctantly told that only one person was enrolled for treatment there! Some programs that specialize in treating alcohol and drug abuse will place sexual abuse survivors together with their alcohol and drug clients, without offering any specific treatment for the sexual abuse. This is not a good idea.

Still, some very good inpatient programs do exist. If you feel you need inpatient treatment, search around for a good program. If you are in therapy, your therapist will be able to assist you in finding one. If you go to treatment and are not getting what you need or expect, simply leave.

Outpatient programs are generally designed so that you may attend treatment in the evening, leaving your days free to work or do other things. Outpatient treatment is also effective and can give you a lot of information and support. Most outpatient programs last for a fixed time period. A good outpatient treatment plan will include an after-care program that you can attend for long-term support. Again, when you are seeking outpatient treatment, talk to someone who has attended the program to find out (from a more personal point of view) about the quality of the program.

Treatment Intensives

Treatment intensives focus on short-term treatment; the time period may vary from a weekend retreat to two weeks of intensive work. Most intensives require you to live at or near the place where the intensive is being held. Intensive programs offer an alternative to inpatient treatment. They are much less expensive and don't require the time commitment involved in inpatient treatment. Although you can do a lot of personal work in intensives, some programs are so short that you may not have time to fully recover from the intense work you have done there before it is time to go home.

If you plan to go to intensive treatment, be sure you have an ongoing support group at home to go back to. It also helps to have a therapist to help you process the feelings and memories you are likely to uncover at the intensive. Like other treatment programs, some intensive programs are good, and some are not so good. Try to find someone who has attended the intensive you are planning to attend; you can ask them about how it contributed (or didn't contribute) to their recovery.

Psychiatric Drugs

In your recovery, you will find no shortage of opinions about the benefit (or harm) of taking psychiatric drugs. Someone may tell you, "Taking any drug, prescribed or not, will block your true feelings and hinder your healing." Someone else may say with conviction, "Antidepressants saved my life. You should take them." Of course, both statements contain an element of truth. With proper supervision by a qualified therapist, psychiatric drugs can stabilize mood swings, relieve depression, and induce sleep. Such medications, prescribed wisely, are intended to create an internal environment where you are free to work on the abuse you suffered in childhood.

In some cases, however, taking drugs does interfere with the healing process. If you are too heavily medicated, you may become unable to participate in your recovery. With the help of a psychiatrist, you must evaluate what is best for you. In my own practice, I have worked with survivors who healed while taking medication, and with some who healed without the help of drugs. You are an individual; your treatment must be designed with that fact in mind.

Here are three general guidelines concerning medication:

1. Never begin taking psychiatric drugs without appropriate medical supervision.

2. When taking medication, continue to monitor its effects. What is effective for two weeks may not be effective after a month or two.

3. Never stop taking a prescribed medication without medical supervision.

Support Groups

Support groups, which are free of charge, are generally run by other sexual abuse survivors. These groups offer companionship, direction, and the experience of other survivors who have been in recovery for some time. Most support groups are open to all survivors. Support groups are places where much healing occurs and where lifetime friendships often begin. I strongly advise all my clients to attend survivors' support groups, because I've noticed that those who do move through the stages of recovery faster than those who don't. Many people who cannot afford therapy use support groups as their primary path to healing. I have a personal bias in favor of survivors' support groups that are based on the Twelve Steps of Alcoholics Anonymous (AA). Such groups are usually also conducted according to the format of an AA meeting.

You will find a different kind of support and encouragement in twelve-step groups than you receive in therapy. On the other hand, the work you will be able to do in therapy would often be out of place in a twelve-step support group. A combination of the two is ideal. But if I had to choose between a good twelve-step support group and a mediocre therapist, I would pick the support group every time.

YOUR SEXUAL RELATIONSHIP

For purposes of this section, a sexual relationship is defined as any long-term relationship involving commitment. It may be a same-sex relationship or a heterosexual relationship. Lesbian women, gay men, and heterosexuals all face the same challenges in relationships when one or both partners have a history of sexual trauma. In the process of healing from childhood sexual abuse, the same essential recovery issues emerge, regardless of a survivor's sexual preference.

It is possible that your sexual relationship may not be able to be transformed into a safe place for you. If you are just starting your recovery, you entered into your current relationship while you were still reacting to your past pain. For this reason, you must reassess your sexual relationship by asking yourself, "Is this relationship a safe place for me now?" Has your partner physically assaulted you? Is your partner holding you hostage with emotional threats? Do you think your partner could erupt into physical violence? Are you being raped instead of making love? The first thing you must do in recovery is ensure your physical safety. It will do you little good to recover from your childhood abuse if, in the meantime, your spouse kills you. Don't think it can't happen.

If you believe you are in danger, get help immediately and remove yourself (and your children, if you have them) to a safe place. Call the police and the local battered women's shelter (even if you are a man), and seek counseling and support. You may be able to work things out with your spouse later, but first you must get to a safe place.

If you are in a relationship with a caring and sensitive person and your relationship is already a safe place for you, then you are very fortunate. Even so, most relationships—even healthy ones—are a mixture of active love and support, with occasional distrust and tension. You and your spouse may love each other, but you may be unable to express that love. Whatever your circumstances are, your relationship will face special challenges as you move into recovery. But a relationship that withstands recovery often takes on great strength and compassion in the process.

Early in the active healing stage, you will experience wide mood swings. One moment you will feel happy, and the next, extremely sad. You may feel angry, then moments later plunge into deep grief. During this period you may experience intense fear states and times when you think you have "made all this up." These quick changes are bound to affect your relationship. Keeping a relationship intact during this time presents a special challenge. You must keep your partner informed about what is happening to you. If you try to keep the abuse a secret, you partner will have no idea why you are behaving and feeling as you are. This does not mean that you must give your partner the graphic details of the abuse or talk specifically about what goes on in your therapy or your survivors' support group. Still, you must give your spouse a general idea about what is happening in your healing process. Creating and maintaining a safe place for yourself will be extremely difficult without the active cooperation of your partner.

In part, healing means exploring and reevaluating your adult sexual boundaries. When you were a child, your sexual boundaries were violated. As an adult in recovery, you will need to redefine what is acceptable and unacceptable sexual behavior for you. At this time, your sex life is very likely to change. The sexual activities you engaged in prior to recovery may become repulsive to you, or you may lose your sexual drive altogether. On the other hand, you may become more sexually active with your partner. You will probably experience a combination of the two: One day you may feel a high level of sexual desire, and the next, you may not be interested at all. However these changes occur, they are sure to affect your partner.

Peg, a former client, had engaged in oral sex as a regular part of sex with her husband. During therapy, she remembered her father abusing her by performing oral sex on her, then forcing her to reciprocate. Peg lost all desire for oral sex while she processed these memories in therapy, and she became furious at her husband whenever he suggested oral sex to her. Although this issue resolved itself after a time, both partners had hurt feelings about it, and they attended several joint therapy sessions to clear their relationship of the resentment they both felt. If frustrations arise due to a change in the frequency or nature of your sexual relations with your partner, talk together about your feelings and consider also talking about it to someone you trust outside the relationship.

It is good for the two of you to discuss the changes taking place in your relationship as a result of your recovery. If you do not talk about why you are on an "emotional roller coaster" and why you are redefining your sexual boundaries, your partner will be left in the dark trying to figure out what's happening. In the same way, you need to know how your partner feels about your recovery and its effect on your life together.

It is essential that each of you *seek support outside the relationship*. Both of you must have a place to vent feelings and express thoughts without having to censor what you say. Whether you go to friends, therapists, clergy, or other people you trust, it is absolutely necessary that you seek outside support if the relationship is to remain a supportive environment. It is wonderful if your partner is your best friend; it will be a disaster if your partner is your only friend. You must find for yourself a safe place where your feelings and memories will be validated by others. Dealing with childhood sexual abuse is painful. A professional therapist trained in the treatment of sexual abuse will be able to offer assistance while your relationship is undergoing the stress of active recovery.

Your recovery will involve emotional upheaval for your partner as well as for you. Loving and living with a recovering survivor of childhood sexual abuse can be quite baffling. The best thing that partners of survivors can do for themselves is to find their own support group where they can share their experience and feelings. Partners of survivors are likely to have their own unresolved issues and family dysfunctions. Anything in your partner's past that remains unhealed will surface in response to your recovery work. This is a natural time for your spouse to begin his or her own work in therapy for unresolved childhood wounds.

It is important to remember that you are not "the sick person" in the relationship. You feel and act the way you do because you were hurt very deeply as a child. It is not your fault that you were abused, and you are now taking steps to heal. You are equal in emotional strength and maturity to your partner, and together you can create an atmosphere that will be safe for both of you.

By itself, the fact that one partner has a history of childhood sexual abuse does not cripple a relationship. The healing of sexual abuse can become a deep bonding experience in which both partners increase their love and trust for each other. But the process takes time and work. The psychological issues arising in response to sexual abuse do not disappear in a week or even in a few months. Begin to develop a realistic view of recovery as a lifelong process. This does not mean that your relationship will be disrupted forever. Healing does occur, but in its own time. The support and understanding of a loving partner and the power of a committed relationship can greatly facilitate your healing process. As you work and grow, you will create a safe place for yourself that will remain constant wherever you are. This safe place will naturally extend to your relationship. The safety will exist because of your courage and willingness to persevere in recovery. Then, regardless of your past experience, you will discover within yourself the natural joy and intimacy from which all healthy relationships emerge.

PARENTING

Most survivors have fears about parenting. In fact, the question adult survivors most often ask is, "What can I do to protect my children from being sexually abused?" The single most important thing you can do for your own children is to heal your own childhood wounds. Through your healing, you will learn to create a safe place for your children. Second, you can learn some tools that can help you become a more effective parent.

The more committed you are to your own healing, the more you will be able to teach your children—by example—healthy attitudes about their bodies and their sexuality. Also, as you heal, your awareness about sexual abuse will expand so that you will be better prepared to protect your children and to insure that they have a safe place to grow up. Before you began recovery, you may have had blind spots surrounding sexual abuse. Your own defenses may not have allowed you to see potentially dangerous situations for your children. If you, like so many others, survived incest, you may need to protect your children from their grandparents or other relatives. This can be difficult; a good therapist can offer guidance in this area. There is nothing you can do to change the past, but you can start now to provide safety for your children in the future. In this regard, attention to your own healing is essential.

If you know or suspect that your children have been sexually abused, provide a safe place for them and seek counseling for them immediately. If your children were sexually abused and are now adults, openly talking to them about your recovery can encourage them to enter their own healing. As a parent, you have a natural responsibility to protect your children. Remember, however, that you are also responsible for continuing your own recovery process. Ultimately this is the best thing you can do for your children, as well as for yourself.

Gather information about effective parenting. For whatever reason, the family you were raised in didn't prepare you to be a healthy and effective parent. You don't yet have all the information you need to be a parent. You may love and try to protect your children, but you may not know how to teach them about boundaries and clear, direct communication. In many communities, parent effectiveness classes are now available, and hundreds of books have been written on the subject of child-rearing. Use these resources to learn about healthy parenting.

Worrying about being a bad parent will not help your children. You have a responsibility to them to learn to be the best parent you can be. Like other survivors, you may be surprised to find that, the more you learn about effective parenting, the more you learn about loving yourself and your own inner child. Ironically, as you teach your children about boundaries and about saying no to what they don't want—as you teach them to assert their independence—you will also be emphasizing these lessons for yourself.

One survivor, Joe, had this comment about parenting:

> I didn't know anything about raising a child. For years I was afraid I would abuse my child just the way I was abused. It was frightening. The only thing I knew about parenting was, "Children should be seen and not heard." In my family, if you didn't obey, you got yelled at or hit. After we had our son, we took parenting classes and read a lot of books. The greatest part of learning to be a father was talking to other parents about their feelings. I knew I wasn't alone. Now I know I don't have to repeat the past. If I feel overwhelmed or get too angry, I go and cool off. When I look at the way I treat my son, sometimes I think, *"Wow, that's the way I want to treat myself!"* I've learned a lot about taking care of myself by taking care of that little guy. We really have a great time together.

Parenting during your active healing can be quite challenging. At that time, you will experience bursts of anger and rage. You will experience grief and the tears that go with it. No matter how hard you try to shield your children from your pain, they will know that something big is happening inside you. If you do not tell your children (at least in general terms) why you are having such strong emotions, they assume that they are somehow at fault. Generally, the younger your children are, the more difficult it will be for them to accept that they are not the cause of your pain. Therefore, you must explain to them that they are not to blame for your strong feelings. Once is not enough: You will have to reassure them of this again and again. Older children may become defiant and angry that you are spending so much time taking care of yourself, or they may be quite supportive and sensitive to your recovery. They may also mirror your feeling states. In any case, the more informed your children are, the less confusing your healing will be for them. It is a delicate undertaking to determine how much of your past to disclose. Consider each child individually when you are deciding how much of your story you will tell them. While children will not benefit from hearing the grim details of your abuse, they will be greatly helped by seeing their parent honestly facing an old hurt with courage and love.

In the midst of your healing it can be tempting to rely heavily on your children for emotional support. You will be particularly vulnerable to this if you are a single parent. *Do not use your children as your confidants.* Go instead to your survivors' support group, your therapist, and your friends for emotional support. You need adult support at this time, and you must go to other adults to get it. With your children, you are still the parent. Your children will continue to look to you for support and nurturing, regardless of the challenges you are facing in recovery. You must beware of your children taking over the job of parenting, both of themselves and of you.

Parenting is often difficult even under the best conditions, and it becomes more complex as you enter active recovery. But believe it or not, in the midst of your healing, you can be an effective and loving (if imperfect) parent. As you learn to love *yourself,* to forgive yourself, and to take care of yourself in recovery, you will demonstrate love to your children. You'll be showing them that it's okay not to be perfect, that sometimes life is messy. In this way, you will create a safe place where both you and your children are free to grow. Intimacy between parents and children occurs very naturally in an atmosphere of non-judgmental support.

The bibliography in the back of this book lists several books designed to educate children about sexual abuse, and about how to say no in potentially abusive situations. Also listed are some of my favorite books about parenting. These books are a starting place for learning protective techniques and parenting skills. Keep in mind, though, that there is no such thing as a perfect parent. You will make mistakes. You will have regrets about what you could have done better. Most parents experience this to some degree. In this regard, you are no different from any other parents struggling to raise their kids in the most effective and loving way.

YOUR FAMILY OF ORIGIN

Ideally, your family of origin (the family you were born or adopted into) would have been a nest of comfort and love where you could learn about the world and prepare for your life as an adult. For incest survivors, however, home was a place of fear and shame. In recovery, you will direct your anger, rage, grief, and loss at the person(s) who abused you. As you experience the pain of your childhood, you may question the way in which you currently relate to your family members. You may have questions about how much information to disclose to your family, and about whether to confront your abuser. You may also wonder whether you should confront the members of your family who did not intervene to protect you.

There are no hard and fast rules of recovery about what to do in your relationship with your family. Some survivors cut off all contact with their families, some have limited contact, and some remain in regular contact with their families. Among my clients who experienced incest, I have observed that, as healing deepens, each individual client evolves a solution about family ties that works for them. Early in my career as a therapist, I asked a survivor of incest why she would want to have a relationship with a father who had sex with her when she was nine, and a mother who knowingly allowed it to happen. I'll never forget her reply: "You don't understand. I hate both of them, but I love them too. They are my family, and I want to be able to see them. If I cut myself off from them, I will lose a part of my history, and I don't want to do that."

My client was right—I hadn't understood. From that point on, I had to put away my judgments about what was "good" and "bad" and allow my clients to work things out for themselves. A few years later, this woman had worked out a way to remain in contact with her family. She said, "I wouldn't leave my children with my father or mother, but I do see them on holidays and other special occasions. Emotionally, I stay at arm's length from them. I confronted them both about the abuse, so they know how much I was hurt. We never talk about it, and that's okay with me. My kids know what happened to me, and so does the rest of my family. It's not an ideal situation, but under the circumstances, it's the best that can be done."

Confrontation

Some people may tell you that confronting your abuser is absolutely necessary, that it is the only way to feel empowered in your recovery. This is not true—survivors do not have to confront in order to heal. Confrontation is a decision that each survivor must make based on the individual situation. One woman I worked with clearly felt that confrontation would physically endanger her: "My older brother is crazy. He has already served time in prison for sexual assault and attempted murder. I am afraid that if I confront him on what he did to me, he will kill me or hurt my family." This woman was able to work out her anger and rage at her brother during group therapy, surrounded by support and safety.

If you decide to confront the person or persons who abused you, it is important to have a safe place and a strong support group as a foundation. When you confront, you must do it for your own inner healing. Bringing the truth out into the open may help you to feel empowered, but it's important to know ahead of time that you probably will be met with denial, anger, and judgment. You will be breaking a family secret, and this will not make you a hero in the eyes of your other family members. In fact, your family may unite against you and side with the abuser. If you decide to confront, you must be prepared for this possibility.

When one client, Sam, confronted her mother about the abuse she experienced from her father (deceased), she was met with outright denial. Her mother stated flatly that it had never happened, nor could it have happened. Sam's brother accused her of "being on drugs," and her younger sister, whom Sam believed had also been sexually abused, said, "I don't remember my childhood, and I don't want to think about it anyway." Her mother went even further, telling Sam that she was going to have her "deprogrammed" from the "antifamily cult" she belonged to and sue her therapist (me) for putting these ideas into her head.

Sam was extremely shaken by the refusal of her family to consider that her father had sexually abused her. She herself began to believe she was "making up" her memories, and she needed a great deal of support from therapy and from other survivors in her support group to help her through this difficult period. Several years later, Sam's younger sister regained her memories of being molested by their father, and she turned to Sam for support. Their mother continued to deny that either Sam or her sister had been sexually abused, and Sam's younger brother steadfastly refused to talk about it.

One of the ways Sam processed her anger at her father was to write a letter to him telling him how he had hurt her (see Chapter 18). She then took the letter to his grave and read it to him. Sam reported feeling a great sense of release and freedom after she had done this. She was never able to express her feelings about the abuse with her mother, so she also wrote letters to her mother and read them during group therapy sessions. Not all confrontations are met with the strong denial that Sam experienced. Still, you must be aware that angry denial is not an uncommon response to such confrontation.

When Derek revealed to his family that he had been repeatedly raped by his maternal grandfather, his mother told him that she had been sexually abused by him also, but she had never told anyone. Later, Derek's younger sister disclosed a history of sexual abuse with the same grandfather. When all three survivors talked about their long-held secret, a new feeling of intimacy developed among them. Together they confronted the grandfather and made sure that the rest of their family knew about the abuse they had experienced. After they had exposed the abuse, several of Derek's cousins told of sexual abuse by this man as well. The survivors in this family became determined that no other children would be harmed by him: The grandfather was criminally charged with sexual abuse of a child. Once the secret was told, Derek's family became a safe place for him, as well as for the young children in the family.

I don't know whether your family of origin will ever become a safe place for you. I do know, however, that your recovery will bring you hope and freedom. Even if your family of origin never feels safe to you, you can still create safety for yourself by surrounding yourself with people whom you trust, who value and respect you.

YOUR FAMILY OF CHOICE

One's family atmosphere should be a fountain of love and support. If you don't have such a family, you must create your own. You deserve caring friends and a safe place to live. Your increasing awareness about your health and your needs will help you begin to make wise choices about whom to avoid and whom to trust. In the process of building your support group for your active work in recovery, healthy friendships will emerge. In the past, you may have abandoned some of your interests (music, art, sailing) due to the difficulty of holding in your pain. Survivors often find that, as they rekindle these interests, they naturally meet others who share those interests. Many survivors find a mentor who "parents" them, and friends who feel like "brothers and sisters."

With the support of your family of choice, you will be able to embrace your past and find strength in your recovery. You'll discover that, no matter what has happened to you, you have always had a safe place. This safe place exists in your heart, and you carry it wherever you go.

The Temple of the Heart

This guided meditation can help you discover the safe place inside yourself. Sit with your back straight but comfortable and relaxed, either cross-legged on the floor or upright in a chair with your feet placed flat on the floor, slightly apart. It is good to use soft music during the meditation, and to have a friend read it aloud to you (or tape-record the imagery, then play it back until you have memorized it and can do it without referring to the instructions). After you do this meditation several times, it will naturally change from its present form. In this way it becomes uniquely yours. This is a great opportunity to create what you need, to find your own safe place. In the text below, an ellipsis (. . .) indicates a pause of approximately three seconds.

Begin this experience by becoming aware of your breath . . . Watch your breath as it moves in and out of your body . . . Feel the movement of your body as you breathe in . . . Be aware of the expansion of your chest as you inhale . . . When you breathe out, feel the letting go of the air in your lungs . . . Continue to focus on your breath . . . the cycle of breath . . . in, and out . . . This is a natural cycle of receiving and letting go . . . Breathe without forcing your breath . . . Breathe slowly and deeply . . .

With the power of your active imagination, envision yourself standing on a pathway in a deep green forest . . . You are surrounded by big, old trees . . . Feel the wisdom of the trees . . . Now begin to walk along the pathway . . . After a time, you come to a clearing . . . As you gaze across this clearing, you see a huge mountain rising in the distance . . . You feel drawn to this beautiful mountain, and you begin to make your way across the clearing toward it . . . As you come closer, you see a stairway going up the mountainside . . .

When you reach the stairway at the foot of the mountain, you look slowly upward . . . The stairway is lost in the clouds that surround the top of the mountain . . . You begin to climb the

stairway . . . With each step upward, you can feel your body
becoming lighter, freer . . . The higher you go, the lighter you
feel . . . Soon you enter the clouds . . . Their soft whiteness
seems to wash away your cares and troubles . . . After a time, you
see that you have passed through the clouds, and you find yourself
at the top of the stairway . . .

   The top of the mountain is a flat plain . . . On the plain, in the
distance, a beautiful temple sits in the sunlight . . . From this temple
you can feel waves of love and peacefulness emanating . . . You step
off of the stairway and go to the temple . . . As you approach, a door
opens and you are welcomed inside . . . From floor to ceiling, the
temple is colorful and richly furnished . . . On a table in the center
of the temple is a small golden box . . . The box is emanating the
waves of love that drew you here . . . You walk over and stand in
front of the box, basking in the love and peace flowing out from
it . . . After a time, you open the box . . . Inside is a wonderful gift
for you . . . You hold the gift to your heart, feeling great warmth,
love, and complete contentment . . . You understand that this wonderful place of peace resides inside your own heart . . .

   Without regret, knowing that you will always have this place of
love and peacefulness inside you, you leave the temple and cross the
plain . . . You reach the top of the stairway . . . Looking back,
you see the beautiful temple standing in the sunlight. The door is
open, awaiting your return . . . You descend the stairway, down
through the soft white clouds . . . Down to the bottom of the
mountain . . . You make your way back across the clearing and
into the forest . . .

   You walk back along the pathway . . . You honor the giant,
wise old trees . . . As you continue walking through the forest,
you begin to notice your breath as it moves in and out of your
body . . . You feel the rhythm of your heartbeat . . . You breathe
deeply and fully . . . You have now returned to the starting place of
this journey . . . Become aware of your body . . . Experience the
love and peacefulness emanating from your heart . . . This beautiful
safe place is always with you, wherever you are . . .

PART THREE

THE
HEALING
JOURNAL

The only time I know that something is true is at the moment I discover it in the act of writing.

—JEAN MALAQUAIS

I do not sit down at my desk to put into verse something that is already clear in my mind. If it were clear in my mind, I should have no incentive or need to write about it. . . . We do not write in order to be understood; we write in order to understand.

—C. DAY LEWIS
The Poetic Image

CHAPTER 9

Keeping a Healing Journal

The Healing Journal is a system of writing designed to assist you in healing the wound of childhood sexual abuse. The techniques described in the following chapters have been successfully used by survivors. Every survivor just beginning recovery has an abundance of emotional pain—fear, terror, shame, rage, anger, deep grief, and other feelings. Because simply living through the abuse requires most survivors to repress the memory of the abuse itself, as well as these painful emotions, writing about the abuse and your childhood can help to bring forth your buried memories and feelings.

Exploring past trauma can be a painful and frightening experience. For this reason, I strongly encourage you to join a survivors' support group or begin therapy (or both) as you write in the Healing Journal. Although your journal is for your eyes alone, any real and complete healing from sexual trauma must include sharing your story with others. The silence and secrecy must be broken for healing to occur. But you are the one who will decide when, where, and how much of your story you will share. While writing in your journal, you can feel confident that you don't have to show what you have written to anyone. Paradoxically, though, at some point you must break the silence and talk about what you have written. As you begin to share your story, remember that you have control over when and to whom you disclose this information.

The Healing Journal is most effective in conjunction with therapy or while you are actively participating in a survivors' support group. Your recovery cannot take place in isolation—you must have a support group. If you simply write about what happened without sharing your story with others, you risk increasing your pain and deepening your wound. Healing does occur when you write in the Healing Journal, but you must make contact with others for it to be truly effective.

On the other hand, you cannot stay in a support group or a therapy group twenty-four hours a day, seven days a week. That would be neither desirable nor healthy. Even in the intensive setting of inpatient therapy, a good program allows survivors time for individual reflection and self-investigation. This is part of the beauty of the Healing Journal: It's there whenever you need it. You can write in it in the middle of the night or in the early morning hours, when others are generally not stirring. A great deal of healing happens during times of solitude. Writing in your journal bridges the gap between the work you must do with others and the healing work you can do only by yourself.

The writing exercises in the Healing Journal are designed to give you access to your buried memories and emotions. If you feel over-whelmed during the process of writing, take a break. Go and have some fun. Recovery is not a "race to the finish"—it is a process. Take as much time as you need to do your journal work. Most survivors want to move quickly in their recovery (for good reason). There is nothing wrong with a deep desire to heal, but recovery does take time. Remember that an important part of recovery is learning to be gentle with yourself—so take time out and have fun. Try not to let the recovery process consume all your free time.

When you write, a sort of magic happens. Writing helps make the past feel real. Validating the (often sketchy) past is very important for people whose healing depends upon giving up denial. As you write, you move your thoughts, memories, and feelings out of your head and heart and onto a piece of paper. Seeing your past written down and reading it helps to validate your pain and destroy the natural denial most survivors develop around the sexual abuse experience and its consequences on their lives. You will also find that writing triggers memories and emotions that were previously unknown to you. This is a part of the wonder of focused journal writing: It opens doors into your past that were once tightly shut. Although it can be intense and sometimes frightening, welcoming your past is an important part of healing the wound of sexual abuse. Releasing your repressed emotions and memories through writing makes room for the energy of healing to flow through your life and your body.

As you write, speak as freely as you can. In this way, you give a voice to your inner child—you become a great advocate for that wounded part of yourself. If you allow yourself the freedom to write whatever comes to you, you may be surprised at your own strength. The following poem, written by one survivor for the "Daily Expressions" section of the journal, is a powerful example of the work and healing that comes from journal writing.

> *No one could say this delicately:*
> *you made me fuck*
> *With you it wasn't delicate*
>
> *I'd call you Brute but I need*
> *a name without any strength*
> *anyone fucking a four-year-old. . . .*
>
> *Brother and I ride in a boat called Lover*
> *We wrap in metallic blankets   We sweat*
> *until we believe we're drowning   pull*
> *the cover higher up   Higher up*
>
> *gravity would be missing   We could float*
> *Brother and be differently loved*
> *How on earth can we know Man?   Woman?*
> *How with this nightly worm?*
>
> *And Mother knew   She knew*
> *and brought her blanket higher up*
>
> *Daddy trembling*
> *Why did you want green fruit?*
> *What ache did my pain appease?*
> *What about it crowned you? And what rage*
> *will match the feel of your stick and stones?*
>
> *Is your hell the same color*
> *I dream and leap up swimming*
> *in my juices? Is this torrent a nausea you know?*
>
> *This dark jar is so cold*
> *now that you've held it in your glove*
> *You think you've seen inside it   Look again*
> *The ghosts you breathed into this jar*
> *made blood pour from it!*
> *What else but disgust could it sing?*

Knock again on this clay
Now a mouth opens   Now a cracked
mirror heals over   Hear the sound of a body
restored to memory   Hear the breath of a power
coming alive in me as I expose you
I *expose* you

SETTING UP THE JOURNAL

The Healing Journal is divided into twelve main sections, each with a particular purpose. Because you will be making entries in the various sections of the journal on an ongoing basis, I suggest you keep the journal in a loose-leaf book, preferably a three-ring binder. This gives you the flexibility to add pages to different sections as needed. A bound journal, with a fixed number of pages, does not provide this option.

Select a loose-leaf binder that is both durable and pleasing to you. You will be spending a lot of time writing in the journal—an ugly or dreary cover may discourage you from writing, so please choose one that you like. Some of my clients have used painting, drawing, and collage to personalize their journal covers. Do what feels best to you.

One of the most important differences between the Healing Journal and other journals or diaries is its flexibility. Each journal section has a specific purpose and is separated from the other sections by a labeled divider. As you learn more about your past, you will be adding new information to the appropriate sections. This gives you the ability to move around in the journal in your own way, consistent with your individual recovery.

Each of the journal's twelve sections is marked by a divider showing the title of the section. As with the loose-leaf binder, choose strong, high-quality dividers. This will prevent the frustration of your journal falling apart later on. The dividers should be placed in your journal in the sequence given below.

1. Daily Expressions
2. Family History
3. Family Members
4. Personal History
5. My Body

6. Self-Discovery
7. Welcoming the Inner Child
8. Dreams
9. The Abuser(s)
10. Affirmations for Healing
11. Spiritual Reflections
12. Integration

Your completely assembled journal will be a simple loose-leaf book, both durable and attractive, divided into twelve sections arranged in this order. All you need now is plenty of paper and a writing instrument, and you will be ready to begin your journal work.

Before you actually begin writing in your journal, take some time to look through the different journal sections described in Chapters 10 through 21. This will give you a clearer idea of the type of work you will be doing in the journal. Once you have familiarized yourself with the instructions for each of the journal sections, begin in the first section, "Daily Expressions."

In the beginning, you will probably spend the most time writing in the first five sections of the journal. Over time, you will find that, although the sections seem to follow a certain progression, it is not necessary to "complete" one section before moving on to the next. Once you become familiar with each section of the journal, you can move from one section to another without bothering at all about the sequence. Jumping from section to section is a much more natural way to work than trying to fit yourself into a rigid structure. Working in this way keeps the focus on the *process* of recovery rather than the product.

The following chapters describe in detail how to use each section of the Healing Journal. As you become more familiar with your journal, you may wish to add sections of your own creation, incorporating your own techniques. Please feel free to do so. This is *your* journal and *your* recovery. Anything you do to enhance your recovery is wonderful. Much of the information that is contained here, I learned from survivors who were my clients. They would work with the tools that I gave them, and using their creativity, they changed and adapted those tools to fit their own special needs. I invite you to do the same. Create and change; all that is needed for your healing is already contained within you. It is my hope that the Healing Journal will contribute clarity and insight to your journey.

CHAPTER 10

Daily Expressions

This section of the journal is similar to a personal diary. In it you can record your daily activities, your thoughts, and your feelings. Any aspect of your life or your recovery can be included here. The "Daily Expressions" section serves two important functions. First, it is a "stepping-off place" into the other sections of the journal. As you write about the day-to-day events of your life, you may find that memories, feelings, and images of your abuse begin to surface. When this happens, you can move to the appropriate section in your journal and write about the experience there. Second, the "Daily Expressions" section serves as a chronological record of your recovery. After you have made journal entries in this section for a while, look back over them to see the flow and continuity of your healing. It is easy to get caught up in the immediacy of life's details and the intense emotional experience of recovery, thereby losing sight of what you have accomplished. Reviewing the "Daily Expressions" section will remind you that your previous efforts in recovery have not been wasted.

This "Daily Expressions" entry was written by Elena, who was a member of one of my therapy groups for two years:

2/8/90

It seems like I have been doing this forever. All I do is work, go to therapy, go to meetings, work, and go back to therapy, talk about my abuse, again and again and again. I am so sick of it. It feels like I am not making any progress in my recovery. When will I be over this? I am so tired of this. I had a nightmare again last night, I woke up sweating and crying. I don't remember much about the dream, but I remember being scared and trying to run. I really wish this would be over. I hate that son of a bitch for doing this to me. If he had just let me alone I would not have these nightmares.

I did have some fun today. Donna and I went to the park and took a walk on the trail around the lake. We talked and got real silly. We laughed at each other and at the people who were jogging. Everyone must have thought we were crazy. Donna was doing an impression of our therapist. It was so funny, I laughed so hard my sides hurt. Another day gone by.

There are two things to note about Elena's entry. First, the date is written at the top. This is *very* important. Date every entry you make in your journal (not only in this section, but in all the sections). Because you move from section to section in the journal, dating all the entries lets you keep track of the last time you worked in a particular part of the journal.

After Elena wrote this entry, she reviewed her earlier journal entries to see how long she had actually been working on her sexual abuse issues and how much difficult work she had already done. She used the information about her nightmare to begin an entry in the "Dreams" section of the journal. If she had chosen to, Elena also could have made an entry in the "Abuser(s)" section since she mentioned the person who sexually abused her.

I suggest that you write in the "Daily Expressions" section every day for the first thirty days you work in the Healing Journal. Doing this gives you a sense of what it's like to work in your journal regularly, and it supplies you with plenty of information to use in the other sections. After you've used the journal for a while, you may find that you go directly to the sections you wish to work in, making fewer entries in the "Daily Expressions" section. Some people who have used this journal have gone for long periods of time without ever writing in this section, but later on they went back to making daily entries. Stay flexible, and you'll discover what you need to do.

The more often you write in your journal, the easier it is to use. As you become skilled at using the Healing Journal, you will find that you intuitively know where to write the entries that will facilitate your healing process. There will be times when the journal almost seems to "write itself." This is part of the fun and mystery of using this effective instrument in your recovery.

CHAPTER 11

Family History

THE FAMILY TREE

Here you will create your family tree, an overview of your family of origin. It is simple to do and easy to read. When it is done correctly, the family tree shows at least three generations of your family on one sheet of paper. This makes it easier for you to see the patterns in your family relationships. You may not know much about your family history, or your information may be distorted or muddled. If this is the case, the family tree can assist you in clarifying your family history. Many survivors have memory loss of their childhood years; doing a family tree often helps them recover some of the lost memories.

Most sexual abuse happens within families. If you are an incest survivor, creating a family tree will give you an opportunity to see, on paper, your connection to the abuser. In many incest family systems, sexual abuse is passed down through the family for generations. When you map out your family tree, you may be able to identify both the survivors and the offenders (some will fit both categories), in this way depicting the extent of the sexual abuse in your family. Even if you were sexually abused by someone outside your family, creating a family tree is still quite beneficial. Because you are dealing with your trauma now, as an adult, it is likely that your family did not protect you in childhood or were not able to support your healing from the abuse. The family tree can also reveal dysfunctions in your family that may have prevented your healing (such as alcoholism, gambling, and mental illness): You will enter each person's addiction or disease below their name on the tree. When such dysfunctions exist in a family, the members are unable to adequately protect or help a child who is being sexually abused. The more you know about the environment in which you were raised, the more material you will have to assist your recovery.

Ann is an incest survivor who was sexually abused by both her maternal uncle and her maternal grandfather. Until she reached her mid-thirties, Ann had completely repressed her memories of the incest. When Ann drew up her family tree, she realized that her sister, Kim, might also have been abused. When Ann asked her about it, Kim revealed that she had survived abuse by the same uncle. The two sisters then approached their mother, who told them that she herself had been sexually abused by her father, their grandfather.

Ann's family tree is shown in figure 14.

FIGURE 14: Ann's Family Tree

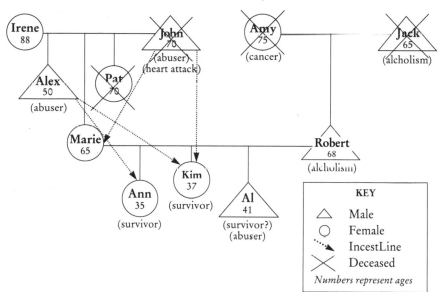

The broken lines represent relationships between perpetrators and survivors of child sexual abuse, in Ann's family's case showing that intergenerational incest existed. As Ann became more aware of the extent of her family's sexual abuse history, she tried to talk to her brother, Lou, about the incest she had experienced. He refused to discuss the topic. Lou, who was married and had two children, had recently been arrested for molesting a neighbor's child.

When you draw up your own family tree, use circles to represent women and triangles for men. To indicate deceased relatives, draw an X through the circle or triangle. Use a broken line to represent the connection between you and the abuser, and write the word *Abuser* under the name(s) of the person(s) who sexually abused you or others in your family. Write each person's age in the center of the circle or triangle. (For those who are deceased, enter their age at the time of death.) Next to each name, write down any addictions or mental illnesses the person had. Write the cause of death below the names of family members who have died.

Try to complete your family tree back through your grandparents. Go farther back if you can. You may have to do some investigative work to get all the information you need, but this is important work and well worth the trouble. It will help fill in the blank spots in your memory and will give you a visual picture of your relationships with your family members. If you have a large family or have had several stepparents and extended stepfamilies, it will be useful to make more than one family tree. Be creative in your approach.

After you have worked on your family tree, complete the following open-ended sentences in your journal. Remember to date this and all other journal entries. Each time you add information to your family tree, you will experience subtle changes in your perspective. At those times, come back to this exercise and finish the sentences again.

I learned my family was . . .

I was surprised by . . .

I now know . . .

I would like to find out . . .

My next step is to . . .

My family is . . .

Right now I want to . . .

FAMILY ENVIRONMENT

The "Family History" section is also where you can set down your thoughts and feelings about your family as a whole. The most important place for any child is the family. Like all children, you looked to your family for the love and support you needed to establish security for yourself in the world. What was your family like? Did they help or hinder your growth? Answering the questions below will help you clarify how your family influenced your growth and development.

Feel free to make your answers as long or as short as you like. Also, you don't have to complete the entire list of questions at one sitting. You may want to answer a few, then move on to another journal section and return to this section later. It isn't so important how long it takes you to finish the questions, but it is important to attempt to answer each one. As always, include the date at the top of each entry.

How were you punished as a child?

How were your siblings punished?

Could you express your emotions?

Describe a typical family dinner.

What were holidays like in your family?

Did your family discuss sex?

What was the overall atmosphere of your family (raging, silent, cynical, joyful, vindictive)?

How did your family members communicate with one another?

Did your parents divorce? If so, what was your reaction?

Was there violence in your family? If so, what kind (physical, emotional, both)? How did you respond to the violence?

How did your family respond to you being sexually abused?

Did your family know about the abuse and not talk about it?

Who, if any, were your allies in your family?

How would your family appear to an outsider?

Did your family members shame or blame one another?

Did you have friends?

What was school like for you?

Who was your best friend?

Was there any hugging in your family?

Did your family have a motto? What was it?

Were you sexually abused by a family member? If so, by whom?

What was the thing you liked least about your family?

What was the thing you liked most about your family?

Add any questions or remarks about your family that these questions do not cover. It is sometimes helpful to copy these questions into your journal. Each section of the journal is open-ended—you can use as much or as little space as you need. As you write, you may "go blank," or suddenly feel that you don't remember anything. If this happens, simply move on to the next question. You can always come back and complete this section later.

Remember always that *you* control the journal-writing process. You can stop and take a break whenever you like. As you write, maintain contact with others: Talk about the feelings you have as a result of doing this writing. The writing itself is healing. When you write, you are releasing long-held pain and freeing repressed memories.

CHAPTER 12

Family Members

Using your family tree as a guide, this section can help you learn more about your family members. Each person on your family tree has had some impact on you and your development. Apply the questions below to each person on the tree. Pay special attention to stepfamily members—it's often easy to lose sight of your stepfamily's influence on you. If the sex offender is a family member, complete the questions, then enter their name in the "Abuser(s)" section. Later, using the instructions in that section, you'll be writing to the abuser.

At this point, you may ask, "Why am I doing all this work about my family?" My experience is that the more survivors know about their family background, the easier it is for them to release their core defenses (memory repression, dissociation, and denial). As the defenses gradually diminish, feelings and information about the sexual abuse will surface, and healing will begin to take place.

Father

If he is deceased, what was your age and his age at the time of his death?

What was his occupation?

How was his health (past and present)?

What kind of personality did he have?

What was his attitude toward you?

What was his attitude toward your brothers and sisters?

What was his attitude toward your mother?

What was his attitude toward his parents?

What was his attitude regarding sex?

Was he sexually abused as a child?

What would you like to say to him that you have not said?

What kind of a relationship did you have with him?

What could he have done to protect you from being sexually abused?

If your father sexually abused you, enter his name in the "Abuser(s)" section of your journal.

Mother

If she is deceased, what was your age and her age at the time of her death?

What was her occupation?

How was her health (past and present)?

What kind of personality did she have?

What was her attitude toward you?

What was her attitude toward your brothers and sisters?

What was her attitude toward your father?

What was her attitude toward her parents?

What was her attitude regarding sex?

Was she sexually abused as a child?

What would you like to say to her that you have not said?

What kind of a relationship did you have with her?

What could she have done to protect you from being sexually abused?

If your mother sexually abused you, enter her name in the "Abuser(s)" section of your journal.

Siblings

List your siblings by birth order, starting with the oldest first (indicate your own position in the birth order). Leaving adequate space beneath each name, answer each of the following questions for each of your siblings.

If they are deceased, what was your age and their age at the time of their death?

What was their occupation?

How was their health (past and present)?

What kind of personality did they have?

What was their attitude toward you?

What was their attitude toward your other brothers and sisters?

What was their attitude toward your father?

What was their attitude toward your mother?

What was their attitude regarding sex?

What would you like to say to them that you have not said?

What kind of a relationship did you have with them?

Were they sexually abused?

What, if anything, could they have done to protect you from being sexually abused?

If a sibling sexually abused you, enter his or her name in the "Abuser(s)" section of your journal.

Other Family Members

Apply the same questions to all members of your family: cousins, uncles, aunts, grandparents, and any others.

Stepfamily Members

Apply the same questions to all your stepfamily members.

LETTER WRITING

Writing "unsent" letters to family members is a powerful method of externalizing emotions, while establishing a feeling of safety about communicating those emotions. Many survivors are unable or unwilling to communicate with family members, and their family members may be unable or unwilling to communicate with them. Whatever the case, writing a letter *that remains unmailed* is an excellent way for you to say things that you would not be likely to say otherwise.

Again, the letters written in this journal section are for your eyes only—they are not to be mailed. This privacy will give you the freedom to write whatever you want or need to write, without having to explain or defend what you have written. This will allow you to tap into previously repressed emotions and to spontaneously express those feelings in writing.

Letter writing is simple. As with all journal entries, begin by writing the date at the top of the page. Then just begin writing to the person as if you were writing them an actual letter. Allow yourself to write down all the things you have never said to them that you would like to say. If you are angry at a member of your family, write an angry letter to them; if you were hurt, write a hurt letter to them. Most letters, however, involve a variety of emotions. You may write to any of the people on your family tree—including those who are no longer living. This was written by a survivor to her deceased mother:

January 30, 1990

Dear Mama,

I miss you. I wish you were still alive and here to talk to me. I'd love to ask you questions about yourself. There are so many things I don't understand. I needed you so much when I was a little girl. You were there sometimes. And those times were wonderful for me. I remember you cooking beans and cornbread and meat loaf. But all those times were when you lived with Jerry.

Did you love him? Why did you have babies with him? Is he my father? Is he June's father? How did you decide to get a divorce? What led you to it? Did he help you? When did you first start to drink? Were you drinking when you were pregnant? How did you feel about your mother? Oh, I know the answer to that one. Was she really mean to you? Is that why you married so young?

Did you always need a man? Did you feel that you couldn't make it without one? I guess I really see how hard it would be for you with two kids and no education and no hope. Alcoholism diseased you out of hope for anything better.

So when Big Bud came along he was a harmless, nonthreatening provider for you and your children. No, you didn't really love him, did you? You needed someone to care for us. He must certainly have seemed safe enough. I admit he was basically a very good man. You chose well—except he sexually abused your two young daughters. One was about nine and one about seven. Did you ever know? Did you ever wonder? Or was your denial too strong to see the possibility of his "perverted" sexuality extended to June and me? I remember your talking about how perverted he was—how he wanted you to suck his penis and how he wanted to lick you. Poor Mama. That wasn't perverted. It was probably the only normal sex he had. Perverted was sexually touching your two young daughters. They didn't fight—they complied. They didn't register disgust as you did. They didn't register anything. I'm angry at you for letting him hurt us. Somewhere deep down I blame you. If you hadn't been so screwed up sexually, maybe you could have provided him with sex instead of us. But wait a minute. He abused us the first time he met us. It wasn't your fault. It wasn't my fault. It wasn't June's fault. It was *his* fault!

I'm tired. I hope you can answer some of these questions someday. Maybe someday they won't matter. I want to be close to you again.

I love you mama.

This letter speaks for itself. Saying things that need to be said, in the atmosphere of safety provided by the journal, is very effective. Try writing a letter to every person in your family. (The letter does not have to be long or intense.) Doing this will connect you with each person in your family. You may find that you have more to say to them than you thought.

DIALOGUING

Dialoguing is like writing a script for two people. Quite simply, first one person speaks, then the other person replies. As the conversation continues, the dialogue between the two people begins to flow more naturally. The conversation continues until one or both people agree to stop. The same thing happens when you practice dialoguing in your journal. You write down a conversation with one of your family members. The dialogue process, like any good conversation, involves an exchange of feelings, ideas, and information.

When you first attempt to write a dialogue, it may feel awkward. You may even feel you are forcing the conversation, but don't worry about this—and don't quit. If you continue to practice this technique, you will find that your "conversations" become more spontaneous. You will also find that the dialogue will begin to "write itself." At this point, the dialogue will often take off in directions that you never dreamed of. This can be quite surprising, even exciting. You will be able to express your anger and hurt to someone who is unavailable, and get a response! Many survivors have found this technique useful to resolve unfinished business with people who are unavailable, and to gain access to repressed information about family relationships. The following dialogue was written by a survivor named Louise. Here Louise dialogues with her alcoholic mother, who had died eight years earlier.

June 16, 1986

LOUISE: Tonight I screamed "I hate you." I really don't hate you, but I'm very angry at you. When I was little, I wanted you to hold me and take care of me, but you were either gone or too drunk. Why did you do that? I needed you and wound up taking care of you. It should have been the other way around. My life was so goddamn shitty because of you.

MOTHER: What do you mean?

LOUISE: You know damn well what I mean. You were drunk so much, and when you weren't, I was fucking afraid you were going to start again.

MOTHER: But you didn't understand how hard it was for me. All the trouble I had.

LOUISE: Bullshit! Other people had it hard too. You got drunk and got married three times. All of the men were weaselly, weak wimps. The third one sexually molested me. You just needed them and used them. You didn't care about them. Bitch, you and your fucking men. I learned from you to find weak men.

MOTHER: Yes, and you married one just like them.

LOUISE: You always made comments like that to me when you were drinking.

MOTHER: Yes, but it was usually the truth.

LOUISE: Yeah, but that's the only time you had the guts to say how you felt. You're right, I did marry a man like my three fathers. But I'm doing something about that now.

MOTHER: You always seemed so smart, and as a little girl you seldom asked for anything and were so strong.

LOUISE: But I wasn't. I went off by myself and cried and worried. I couldn't tell you anything.

MOTHER: I always loved you. I loved you very much.

LOUISE: Well, a lot of fucking good your love did me. I know you loved me, but I could never understand why you hurt me so much. I wanted to tell you, but now you're dead.

MOTHER: I can help you now. I love you. I'll give you my love in many ways and through many people. Especially through yourself. You will love yourself, something I could never do. You will break the patterns and become healthier and healthier.

LOUISE: Thank you. Thank you for all of my experiences. Thank you for holding me as much as you could. I'm still pissed that it wasn't different, but I'm learning to get through my feelings and release them, and I'm starting to ask for what I want and need in my life. I'll talk to you soon.

MOTHER: Okay. Good-bye for now.

Dialoguing adds an invaluable dimension to your journal work—it enables you to receive feedback about your innermost questions and feelings. I'm often asked, "But I'm making this up. And if I am, what purpose will it serve?" If you are able to become spontaneous in writing your replies, you will be answering from a place deep within you that contains information of which your conscious mind is not usually aware. When you tap into this inner knowledge, healing is the result.

Writing dialogues is hard work, so take your time. Remember that you can always go on to another section and work in this section later. As you continue working in the "Family Members" section, you will discover new information and old repressed feelings. Dialogue with all the members of your family, living or dead. All this work will contribute to your healing. No effort is ever wasted.

CHAPTER 13

Personal History

Often, survivors do not have a clear sense of their own personal history or life story. For some, the trauma of their sexual abuse has forced them to repress their past. Other survivors remember the details of their past vividly but without its emotional content. However you remember your past, writing in this section can assist you in clarifying what happened to you and how you felt about it.

The exercises here are designed to help you fill in those blank spots in your life history. Blank spots exist in your memory because you were sexually abused. Using the techniques given here (writing about your life milestones and answering questions about your sexual history and the incidents of your sexual abuse) will cause painful memories to surface. You will then have the opportunity to experience and "process" these memories. At these times, you will find it helpful to call someone in your support group to talk about your discoveries. Remember that emotional trauma, as well as physical sexual trauma, can cause memory loss, dissociation, and denial. Using the writing exercises in this "Personal History" section will help you let go of these tired defenses in order to recover your past and your health.

Like the other sections of your journal, the "Personal History" section is not meant to be completed in one, two, or even three or four writing sessions. Writing here is a continual process. As you update your personal history by adding new information and insights and expressing your feelings about your discoveries, you will fill in the blank spots in your past.

182

MILESTONES

A milestone is an important event in your life. It might be an event that would seem insignificant to someone else, but if it is important to you, it is a milestone. Milestones are "life shapers"—events that mark the passage of something significant in your personal history. Milestones may also be apparently minor events that you intuitively feel are important. Such a milestone is often the tip of the iceberg: It points to important information hidden below your ordinary awareness. When you write about a milestone, you may be surprised at how much information about your past surfaces. These are repressed memories and feelings waiting to be released.

Writing about a milestone causes your defenses to weaken, so that more memories will come to you. This begins a kind of "domino effect": One memory triggers the recall of another, and so on. The domino effect continues, allowing you to feel and experience some of the events of sexual abuse that caused you to develop your defenses and self-destructive patterns. When you reach through your defenses toward the truth of your past, you will begin to discover how much of your memory you had lost. You may feel deep grief as a result. If you have very little memory of your childhood, then each memory is a milestone. In turn, each milestone is the starting point for a journal entry exploring that milestone. Ed, a former client of mine, could remember only the address of a house he had lived in from age seven until he was nine. Using nothing but that address as an entry point into his past, Ed began writing and was flooded with childhood memories.

When making your milestones list, it is important to keep the list manageable. To do this, start with five-year intervals. List three to six milestones for each five-year period. Below is a list of milestones written by Ralph, a recovering survivor of childhood sexual abuse.

> *January 15, 1990*
> **Life Milestones**
>
> **0 to 5 years old.**
> *Being born*
> *Living on Tenth Street*
> *Dad being drunk*
> *Playing in the woods*

6 to 10 years old:
Mr. Burns, my fourth grade teacher
Moving to Eastwood
Mom and Dad fighting and yelling
Sister being born (Kim)
Masturbating, afraid someone would catch me
Dad beating me

11 to 15 years old:
Hitchhiking with Don
Dating Julia
Starting high school
Getting a new bike

15 to 20 years old:
Joining the army
Graduation from high school
Starting to drink heavily in the army
Breaking my leg in a car accident (I was drunk)

20 to 25 years old:
Getting sober in AA
Marrying Julia
Getting into therapy
Ralph Jr. born
Starting night school

Ralph's milestones stop at his current age, twenty-five. The first milestone Ralph chose to write about was "Playing in the woods." Here is an excerpt from Ralph's journal:

January 15, 1990

I remember playing in the woods. I was about five. I wonder why I chose this to write about. I remember I was with someone else. It was a girl. I don't remember her name, but she was much bigger than I was. She was about ten or eleven. I remember being by this big tree, it was summer and I had on shorts. She was next to me. Then I remember I was crying and had my shorts off. She stuck a stick up into my rectum. I feel sick, like I am going to throw up. I remember crying, she told me we were playing doctor and she was the doctor and I was the patient. I was ashamed. Wanted to play with her but the stick hurt. She held me down. I was scared someone would find out. I remember that this was not the only time this happened with her. I remember my dad beating me. I was naked and he hit me with a strap. Then he took off his clothes and lay down on top of me. Shit. Did that really happen? I feel real pissed off right now. I feel like hurting both of them.

At first glance, "playing in the woods" may not have seemed a likely milestone in Ralph's life, but his discoveries while writing about this milestone show how important it was in helping him to recover the memories of being sexually abused by a playmate and by his father. Up until this time Ralph, like many survivors, had an intuition that he had been sexually abused, but he had no memory of the experience itself. He had entered therapy because he felt intense shame during sexual intercourse. The new information that came to him as a result of writing about "playing in the woods" began a period of active healing in which he was able to recover further memories and to express the emotions he had repressed at the time of the sexual abuse.

When you list your own milestones and write about them, they will change as you gain new information and clearer memories of your past. I encourage my clients to write a new list of milestones every six months—sometimes even more frequently. Each milestone is a valuable entry point into your past; write about each one. As Ralph did, you may find that your milestones lead you to key memories, often giving you more information than you expected.

Another of my clients had a similar experience, in which she suddenly discovered a number of repressed memories. Speaking about her writing experience in group, she said she had "hit the jackpot." Each time you write about a milestone, your work will pay off by revealing parts of your past that need to be felt and expressed. You may not always "hit the jackpot," but your writing will always take you closer to your healing.

The three exercises here are lists of questions about your sexual, physical, and emotional abuse history. Although these events usually overlap, as you answer the questions simply write down the answer as it comes to you, without worrying too much about being precise. Nothing is very precise about childhood memories. But be assured that whatever has had the strongest effect on you, whatever carries the greatest emotional weight, will come through in your writing about your history. Also, as you write, remember that these answers are for *you*, for *your* healing. You choose how much of your history you want to share with those in your support group.

YOUR SEXUAL HISTORY

This list of questions about your sexual history is designed to jog your memory. Answer each one as best you can. As you write, try to expand on the answer to any question that has an emotional charge or seems to make you uncomfortable. Such questions are most likely to hold the information needed for your recovery.

Where did you get your first information about sex?

How old were you?

When did you become aware of your sexual feelings?

Who told you about sex?

What was it like to reach puberty?

Who told you about the changes that would happen to you when you reached puberty?

For Women

What was it like to begin your period?

What was it like to develop breasts?

What was it like to grow pubic hair?

For Men

What was it like to have your voice change?

What was it like to ejaculate?

What was it like to grow pubic hair?

For Both Women and Men

Have you ever had an orgasm?

Describe your first nonabusive sexual experience.

When did you first become aware of having been sexually abused?

Who was the first person you told (that you had been sexually abused)?

Have you ever masturbated?

How old were you when you first masturbated?

How often did you masturbate?

Do you have orgasms during masturbation?

What kind of fantasies do you have during masturbation?

Do you have orgasms during sex with another person?

Are you easily sexually aroused?

Is it difficult for you to become sexually aroused?

How often do you have sex with another person?

What kind of behavior do you find erotic?

What kind of fantasies do you have during sex?

Do you use sexual aids (vibrators, pictures, and the like)?

What is your sexual preference (opposite-sex partner, same-sex partner, either)?

Add and answer any other questions you think are important that were not included above.

WRITING ABOUT THE SEXUAL ABUSE INCIDENT(S)

The most effective way to come to grips with your experience of being abused is to write or talk about it in very specific, direct terms. When you state, "I am a survivor of childhood sexual abuse," an important level of healing and acceptance takes place. When you go further by stating, "I am a survivor of childhood sexual abuse, and this is what I experienced," a much deeper level of healing opens up to you.

If the abuse happened frequently over a long period of time, pick one single incident to write about. When you have finished writing about that incident, pick another to write about. Do this until you have written about all the abusive incidents you can remember. The following questions are very specific and, like the other journal exercises, are designed to assist you in retrieving repressed memories and feelings. Remember that you must have the support of a therapist and/or a survivors' support group where you can share the details of your experience and express your feelings about what happened. This is essential. Don't try to do all of this by yourself, and don't try to do it all at once.

Physical Sexual Abuse Incident

Who was the perpetrator?

How old was the perpetrator?

How old were you?

Where did the abuse happen?

When did it happen (time of day, time of year)?

What kind of sexual abuse was it?

Were your eyes open or closed?

If your eyes were open, what did you see?

What did you hear during the abuse (TV in another room, sound of breathing)?

What did you physically feel (weight of body on you, pain of penetration)?

Did you smell anything (body odor, breath, cooking in other room)?

Do you remember tasting anything (forced kissing, semen)?

What was your emotional state (numbness, fear, shame, pleasure, anger, excitement)?

What was your mental state (confusion, disbelief, surprise, thoughts of other things)?

Did you experience pleasure, pain, or both, during the incident?

What did you do immediately after the abuse?

Add and answer any additional questions about your specific experience that were not covered above.

Emotional Sexual Abuse Incident

Most emotional abuse occurs over a long period of time. To answer the following questions, try to select just one incident that stands out in your mind, then answer about that particular incident. If, while you write, you remember another incident, you might make a brief note about it in the page margin. This way, you won't be distracted by it, and you can write about it later if you choose to do so.

Did either parent (or other adult caretaker) ever talk to you about their sexual behavior?

Did either parent or other adult caretaker ever talk to you about their sexual difficulties?

Did you ever feel like your father's "wife" or your mother's "husband"?

Were you consistently asked to act as a parent to younger brothers or sisters?

Did either parent (or other adult) buy you sexy underwear or clothing that was inappropriate for your age?

Were you asked intrusive questions about your sexual thoughts or behavior?

Were you allowed privacy when bathing or going to the toilet?

Did anyone consistently walk in on you while you were dressing?

Were you forced or asked to dress in clothes that were too "adult" for you?

Were you the target of sexual jokes and sexual humiliation?

Were you included in adult conversations about sex?

Add and answer any additional questions about your specific experience that were not covered above.

The work you do in the "Personal History" section of the Healing Journal is an integral part of your recovery. As your understanding of these events in your childhood becomes more complete, so does the personal history. This section is never really finished; throughout your recovery, you will continue adding to and reviewing your personal history. Later, you will use your personal history information to begin working in the other sections of the journal. You will be able to use the information here in those sections. The writing itself is a healing act. When you write, you are letting go of fear, rage, and pain that have been buried within you for a long time. Writing your personal history allows parts of your pain to escape, to dissolve. Still, as powerful and effective as the journal writing exercises are, it is vital that you make contact with others who can support and nurture you during your recovery.

CHAPTER 14

My Body

Childhood sexual abuse has serious effects on the relationship you have with your physical body. Some survivors have learned to hate their physical bodies. This self-hate causes some survivors to treat their bodies as objects to be bartered, or to be hurt and abused. Some survivors blame their physical bodies for what happened to them, believing that "if only I were not a girl" or "if only I were ugly, it would not have happened to me." Over the years I have heard various forms of this statement hundreds of times. Your body did not betray you. You were betrayed by the person who abused you. But the trauma of your past has probably left you feeling "disconnected" from your body; you may have lost the ability to listen to its natural signals. In this section of your journal you will learn how to reestablish communication with your physical body. Though it may sound strange at first, getting to know your body, reconnecting with your physical self, is a fascinating—and essential—part of recovery from childhood sexual abuse.

Your physical body has been with you from the very beginning. All the experiences you have had have also been experienced by your physical body. Even if you remember very little of your past or have only partial or distorted memories, your body remembers clearly. A vast wealth of information and wisdom about your past is contained within your physical body. This "body wisdom" can guide you through the physical aspect of your recovery. Healing your relationship with your physical self is a major milestone in recovery. It is a great homecoming.

DIALOGUING WITH YOUR BODY

When you began the "Family Members" section of your Healing Journal (Chapter 12), you learned the fundamentals of dialoguing. As you dialogue with your body, however, you will be using an additional step: the focusing statement. A focusing statement briefly and generally describes your present relationship with your physical self—your current attitude or feeling about your body. The focusing statement can help you connect with your body before you start writing the dialogue. Many survivors who have used this journal successfully have reported that they do not use focusing statements. I would suggest that you begin by using them, then drop them if you decide that you don't need them.

The following examples of dialogues with the body begin with focusing statements. They were written by a woman who had recently joined a survivors' therapy group and who had just started her Healing Journal. The dialogues were written approximately five weeks apart. The significant differences between the two dialogues points up the value of continuing to dialogue with the body over time, rather than doing the exercise only once.

January 14

Focusing Statement

I have abused my body so much, first with alcohol and then with overeating. Now I am trying to take better care of it. No sugar for over ninety days, and most of my overeating is under control. I am walking two to four days a week and feeling better about my body. I'm starting to feel hope and pride. I'm somewhat upset that my belly is so big. I want to treat my body better and pay more attention to it.

Dialogue

JOETTA: Well, I guess you're sad about how I've treated you and how I've felt about you. I have been very abusive to you in the past, and I'm sorry.

BODY: Yeah, you have. Where the hell has your mind been?

JOETTA: Well, I just get lax. I know the stuff I have to do to be healthy, but I don't do it. Thank you for not shutting down on me. I've been afraid you would get sick.

BODY: You've done this for so long! I'm exhausted and disgusted with you.

JOETTA: Please don't give up on me. I have the time now, and I'm taking care of us. I've really been working hard the past few months.

BODY: You have to make me a priority—no matter what!

JOETTA: That's what I have been doing. I have started to take real good care of you. All that walking I've been doing is getting us in good shape. I've stopped the sugar too. How about that?

BODY: I'm afraid you'll just take care of me when it's convenient. If your mood changes or there's a crisis, I'm afraid you'll quit. You have to keep at it. It's the little things you do for me on a day-to-day basis that really count. That's when I stay healthy. Do you understand that?

JOETTA: God, you are really angry with me. I can't trust I'll do this forever—that's why I need the support of my twelve-step group and friends. We can do it. I know it.

BODY: That's true, we can. Over the years we've been a good team. I'll still let you know when you're not treating me well. That's when I get headaches, fatigue, sick, and other things.

JOETTA: We're getting better all the time. I'm falling in love with myself. Good-bye for now.

BODY: It's okay to love yourself. Keep it up.

Joetta did the following dialogue a few weeks later:

February 21

Focusing Statement

This morning I stayed in bed late. I didn't want to get up. I'm afraid about not making the right choices, and I'm resistant to giving up the easy way of life, like lying around watching TV, sleeping late all the time, and overindulging myself. I'm not happy when I do that. My body gets lazy and fat when I do that, and I begin to hate my body.

Dialogue

JOETTA: I'm still overeating, but no sugar or desserts. I'm watching TV a lot. I'm afraid I won't change.

BODY: Whoa! Slow down! Look what you've accomplished—no sugar or desserts for four months. That's a major victory. And twenty pounds off! Great. You're walking, exercising, and working very hard in your therapy. You have a lot to be proud of. Your best chance at lifelong success is to take small steps and keep looking at what you have accomplished.

JOETTA: You've been angry at me when I've written you in the past. Now you're a cheerleader. What gives?

BODY: We're a team. We help each other. You've done a lot. There is still a way to go, but that's life. I want to support you so we can continue to go forward. That's the best we can do. There's been a lot of abuse that needs to be healed, and we're doing it. "Progress, not perfection." That's what got us in trouble—trying to be perfect.

JOETTA: I've been aware of us working together, and it feels good. I like it when we feel good.

BODY: We are okay, you and I. We have a workable plan, and it's okay if we don't do it perfectly. We're not only going to survive, but we will continue to be happier and happier.

As you work in your own journal, becoming more familiar with the journaling process and more skilled in the writing, you will find that dialoguing with your body is a great source of "inner information," a way into feelings and memories that were previously difficult to gain access to. Continuing work in this "My Body" section will give you a deeper look at your attitudes, feelings, and beliefs about your body. Still, a gentle perseverance is required in order to benefit fully from dialoguing with your body. Keep communicating with it. The two of you have been out of touch for a while, but it's a friendship well worth renewing.

CREATIVE COLORING AND ARTWORK

Many of the recovery methods described in this book were techniques shared with me by clients. It was during a survivors' group I facilitated that I learned the following powerful healing technique: I had given the group an assignment to get a coloring book of the human anatomy, different colored pens, and then to color the sexual organs pictured in the book. When they met again, the group members talked about how it felt to do the coloring. One woman brought in a book: *The Dinner Party*, containing photographs of feminist sculpture and artwork by Judy Chicago. The woman who had brought the book suggested that each group member do an abstract painting or drawing of her vagina, or her sexual self (all the members of this particular group were women), and bring the artwork to the next group meeting.

The following week, each of the women brought in her painting. Then each one spoke about her experience of doing a "sexual self-portrait." Everyone in the group reported a positive healing experience. One woman said, "For the first time in my life, I love my sexuality." Another told the group, "As I drew and painted, I could feel a healing power well up in me. I felt proud and joyful to be a woman."

When I asked male survivors to do this same exercise, their response was equally enthusiastic. One man shared, "I never thought about what my sexuality would look like. But when I did the drawings, I was amazed by the bright colors and the sensitivity in the pictures. I could feel my sexual wholeness." Another man explained that, while doing the drawing, he had realized that "my sexual self was alive and well at four years old! He was the little guy who would *hug* piles of dirt, and would run around the house clapping his hands and yelling at the top of his lungs!"

I encourage you to try this exercise yourself. Using colored pencils, pens, or paint, create a picture of your sexuality. Let the colors represent your self-love and your sexual passion. Be bold and adventurous with your picture. All the pictures in the photo insert between pages 122 and 123 were painted by men and women survivors of childhood sexual abuse.

Try experimenting in this section of your journal. Your healing is strongly linked to your creative energy. The more you listen to your inner self, allowing it to guide your healing, the deeper your recovery will become.

CHAPTER 15

Self-discovery

Survivors of childhood sexual abuse often say that they feel they have "lost themselves," that others have stolen a part of them, and that they are not sure who they are anymore. This section includes a series of general exercises to help you get to know yourself better. By completing these self-descriptive statements, you will be describing what you think and feel about yourself at this time. This will give you a clearer sense of how you view yourself. As you heal from your painful past experiences, your responses to the questions will change. For this reason, it is best to do the exercises several times during your recovery, keeping your written responses in your journal so that you can observe how your self-image changes over time.

SELF-DESCRIPTION

Each of the following statements allows for five answers. This is because we rarely think of ourselves as being just one way or having only one feeling. When you write down five responses to each statement, you are encouraged to expand your evaluation of yourself. If you are not able to complete all five statements, there is no cause for alarm. All this means is that, at this time in your life, this is your most complete response. If you like, you can always come back later to fill in the blanks.

Sometimes survivors write degrading descriptions of themselves. If this happens, know that you are only reflecting the pain of the abuse. During recovery, your self-concept will become more positive. At the conclusion of this exercise, you will have a word picture of yourself. This information can help you understand how much your past has affected what you think and feel about yourself.

Complete each of the following statements:

I am . . .

I am . . .

I am . . .

I am . . .

I am . . .

I feel . . .

I feel . . .

I feel . . .

I feel . . .

I feel . . .

I think . . .

I think . . .

I think . . .

I think . . .

I think . . .

I do . . .

I do . . .

I do . . .

I do . . .

I do . . .

I wish . . .

I wish . . .

I wish . . .

I wish . . .

I wish . . .

THROUGH THE EYES OF OTHERS . . .

Describe yourself from the point of view of each of the people listed below. Add the perspectives of any other people you would like to include. In this exercise you are describing how you believe other people see you. Remember that these people may not really think of you in the way that you describe; still, this is the way *you* believe they would respond to these questions. Doing this can help you see yourself from a broader perspective and from different points of view.

My best friend would describe me as . . .

My lover would describe me as . . .

The person(s) who sexually abused me would describe me as . . .

My employer would describe me as . . .

Someone who dislikes me would describe me as . . .

My mother would describe me as . . .

My father would describe me as . . .

My brothers and sisters would describe me as . . .

FEELINGS RESPONSES

Complete the following sentences, listing your fears, joys, and so on in order of their importance. This exercise will assist you in identifying some of the situations and experiences that produce particular emotional states. Gathering this kind of information often helps survivors discover more childhood memories and learn more about their abuse history.

I feel most afraid when:

1.

2.

3.

4.

5.

I feel the most joy when:

1.

2.

3.

4.

5.

I feel angriest when:

1.

2.

3.

4.

5.

I feel saddest when:

1.

2.

3.

4.

5.

I feel the most hurt when:

1.

2.

3.

4.

5.

I feel the most ashamed when:

1.

2.

3.

4.

5.

I feel the most stressed-out when:

1.

2.

3.

4.

5.

FEELINGS STATEMENTS

Most survivors have difficulty identifying and expressing feelings. The open-ended statements that follow can help you practice recognizing and naming feeling states. If you "draw a blank" when you consider any of the statements, check to see if you are feeling any tension or stress in your body. If you are, then the question has triggered a repressed memory. At this point, you can go to the journal section "My Body" and dialogue with your body about what you are experiencing physically. Your body may be able to tell you more than you think. One of the great strengths of the journal is the ability to move freely from one section to another.

I feel okay when . . .

I feel sad when . . .

I feel affectionate when . . .

I feel hurt when . . .

I feel loving when . . .

I feel shy when . . .

I feel excited when . . .

I feel anxious when . . .

I feel joyful when . . .

I feel ashamed when . . .

I feel angry when . . .

I feel confused when . . .

I feel happy when . . .

I feel frustrated when . . .

I feel blissful when . . .

I feel jealous when . . .

I feel secure when . . .

I feel worried when . . .

I feel delighted when . . .

I feel resentful when . . .

I feel hopeful when . . .

I feel grief when . . .

I feel loss when . . .

I feel exhilarated when . . .

I feel embarrassed when . . .

I feel afraid when . . .

I feel tender when . . .

I feel desperate when . . .

I feel peaceful when . . .

I feel playful when . . .

I feel loved when . . .

I feel rage when . . .

I feel helpless when . . .

I feel powerful when . . .

I feel wonderful when . . .

Add any feelings you experience that are not listed in the preceding list.

Tina had been working at her journal for several years when she redid the self-discovery section. She was astounded at the difference between the entries and the change in herself.

"I did this section when I began my recovery, then three years later I redid it. It was amazing. In my first entries I had written very negative self-descriptions."

I think I am a piece of garbage.

I think no one likes me.

I feel hopeless.

I feel sick all the time.

I am never going to get better.

I am a bad mother.

I do need to work on myself.

I do not like myself.

I wish I was done with this.

I wish I was dead.

"When I wrote in this section three years later, my answers were much more positive."

I think I'm beautiful.

I think I am a child of God.

I do contribute to life in a positive way.

I do have good relationships now.

I am a wonderful woman and a good mother.

I feel satisfied with my life.

I feel hopeful and happy most of the time.

"When I redid the feelings statements, I wrote about feeling states I hadn't been able to write about before, like *powerful,* or *joyful.* After three years of recovery, I realized that now I've experienced all these feelings, even the positive ones! My life has gotten so much better and richer. I do have bad days sometimes but not anything like the depression I felt before. I wonder what my answers will be like in another three years. I can hardly wait!"

As in the other Healing Journal sections, the exercises in this section are not meant to be completed in one sitting. You may want to do parts of it, then move to another section. As you complete certain statements, you may discover information for a new entry in a different section of the journal.

CHAPTER 16

Welcoming the Inner Child

Working in this section of the journal can be deeply serious at times. It can also be a *lot* of fun. When you welcome your inner child back into your life, you welcome the most scared, angry, and grief-stricken part of you there is—but at the same time, you open the door to the most spontaneously playful, beautiful, and wise part of you. As you become more and more intimate with your inner child, everything (even your recovery itself) will begin to feel lighter, simpler, and better.

To establish a healing relationship with your inner child is to welcome the wounded child who lives within you, holding the pain of your past. Allowing your inner child to release that pain is essential if you are to have lasting recovery from childhood sexual abuse. In Chapter 6, I described the inner child in detail and suggested a guided imagery exercise ("The Gift of the Star") to help you get in touch with your own inner child. Here in your journal, you will be using writing techniques to make contact with your inner child.

Working with your inner child quickly cuts through the repressive defenses of memories, dissociation, and denial. When you communicate with your wounded inner child, you are in direct contact with the part of you who experienced the abuse. As this wounded child is healed, a great inner teacher will emerge: the magical child. The magical child is also part of you but remains unaffected by all that has happened to you physically, emotionally, and mentally. When these two aspects of your inner self emerge from hiding, you will experience profound healing. The single most important thing you can experience in recovery is the healing of your inner child.

Letter writing is one of the most effective techniques for contacting your inner child. It's also simple: All you need to do is write a letter to your inner child, then have the child write back to you. (I'll give more detailed instructions shortly.) Recovering survivors have often told me that this powerful experience connects them with their childhood in a way that few other experiences can. Once you make initial connection with your inner child, you'll be writing to each other on a regular basis. But the letter writing doesn't have to be an even exchange. You may write letters to your inner child without the child writing back immediately, and your inner child may write to you without getting a return letter. What is most important is the letter-writing *process,* not the form it takes.

There are several things you can do to create an atmosphere conducive to communication between you and your inner child. If you have photographs of yourself as a child, looking at them as you write can be very beneficial. Put some of the childhood photographs in your journal. Carry one of them with you in your wallet or purse—take it out and look at it often. Put a photograph—or several—on your desk or dresser at home and in your workplace. The pictures will keep open your connection with your inner child during the times when you are not writing, and they will serve to jog your memory when you write in the journal. If you have any childhood toys, get them out and place them around your living area. Buy a teddy bear or another cuddly child's toy. Make a special trip to a children's toy store and pick out a toy that you think your inner child would like. Using these props will enhance the process of writing to (and from) your inner child.

If you don't have any childhood pictures of yourself, that's fine. You can use your list of early childhood milestones (see Chapter 13) to get in closer contact with your past. Don't hesitate to be creative, to use your own ideas. Your relationship with your inner child is extremely important to your recovery; it deserves your time and effort. Anything you do to enhance this phase of your healing will give you back much more than you ever expected.

LETTER WRITING

As you prepare to write to your inner child, remember to use words and phrases that a child would be able to understand. In the beginning, it helps to be brief; try not to overwhelm your inner child with a flurry of words. Below are four general guidelines for writing letters to your inner child.

1. Before you start, take several deep breaths. Become quiet for a few minutes.

2. Think about your childhood. Use your childhood picture or your list of early childhood milestones to help you remember.

3. Write a letter to your inner child. Ask for a return letter if it's the first time you have written.

4. Write a letter from your inner child to your adult self, *using the hand you do not normally write with*. If you are right-handed, have the inner child write the return letter with the left hand, and vice versa.

Step four will feel awkward, but try it anyway. You may be quite amazed at the result. If you find you cannot write at all with your nondominant hand, switch back to the hand you normally write with, but write very slowly and deliberately (as you did when you were first learning to use a pencil). The letter below was written by a survivor named Bill to his inner child, Little Bill. Following it is another letter, from Little Bill to "Big Bill."

March 14

Dear Little Bill,

I don't really know you very well. When I try to think about being little, I don't remember very much. I'm not even sure you're there. Are you? I am now trying to find out what really happened to me when I was little, and I hope you can help me. I am in therapy, and I remember a little about how frightened I was all the time. I think I stopped crying when I was a little boy like you. Now I am starting to cry again. I don't like it much. But it also feels good.

I'm supposed to get in contact with you and learn about you. This is supposed to help me get better from what happened. Will you help me? I know we don't know each other very well, but I'd like to get to know you better. It's really hard to write this letter, and I am feeling a lot of sadness. I want to love you and protect you from what happened. It wasn't your fault—you couldn't do anything to stop it. I know you're ashamed and afraid. Maybe together we can help each other to get better. I love you. Please write back.

Love,
Big Bill

DeaR BiG Bill,

I am hiding. WheRE have you Been?

I want to come out AND PLAY But
I'M scared. I'M alone, sometime
Its DARK. will you play with me? Don't
Be afraid of me. I Love to RUN. Im hurt
INSiDE out I am your FRIeND to. I want
you to help me. PLeaee.

Little
Bill

Bill's letters marked the beginning of a deeply healing relationship. It took time for Bill to become comfortable with his inner child and for Little Bill to really begin to confide in "Big Bill." Establishing this contact was an important start in a new kind of recovery for Bill. As you can see, Little Bill's letter looks as if a child had written it—if you read it aloud, it also sounds as though a child wrote it (which is true, of course).

DIALOGUING WITH THE INNER CHILD

Dialoguing, as it is described in the "Family Members" section of the journal (Chapter 12), is another effective way to communicate with your inner child. When you dialogue in this way, you write a conversation between yourself and your inner child. As you write the dialogue, a natural exchange begins to take place between you and your inner child. This experience is often quite informative and very touching. The more often you dialogue with your inner child, the more spontaneous the exchange will become. Remember, as you dialogue, that you are speaking with the child who was sexually abused. Information you may not have remembered previously is likely to surface during the dialoguing process.

Preparing to write the dialogue is a lot like preparing to write a letter to your inner child:

1. Before you start, take several deep breaths. Become quiet for a few minutes.
2. Think about your childhood. Use your childhood pictures or your list of early childhood milestones to help you remember.
3. Write a focusing statement about the nature of your relationship with your inner child.
4. Begin writing the dialogue.

Like the other dialogues in your journal, continue this one until it subsides naturally. When neither you nor your inner child has anything left to say, simply stop writing.

Sue had been sexually abused by her maternal grandmother, who abused her with enemas and by inserting her fingers into her rectum. Sue used both dialoguing and letter writing to get information about her childhood. Doing this writing also allowed her inner child to express her fear and hurt. In her journal, Sue wrote the following dialogue with her inner child, Little Sue.

March 16

Focusing Statement

I am both happy and afraid of the relationship I am developing with my inner child, Little Sue. I am afraid because I know that she knows things about my past that I don't want to know, and I'm happy because Little Sue is helping me learn to play.

Dialogue

SUE: Hi, Little Sue.
LITTLE SUE: Hi, Big Sue.
SUE: I wish I could remember everything that happened to me.

LITTLE SUE: Why? I don't like to think of what happened.

SUE: I think I need to so I can stop being so afraid and embarrassed.

LITTLE SUE: Why don't you just forget about it? Let's have some fun.

SUE: I can't. Every time I go to the bathroom to have a BM [bowel movement] I get scared. Sometimes I don't go for days—I just hold back.

LITTLE SUE: I was always afraid to go too. I hate going. Peeing is not so bad, but I hate number two.

SUE: Will you help me remember when Gramma abused me? I remember some things, but not all of it.

LITTLE SUE: Well, okay. I was real young, a baby. I was on the table being changed. I could see her face over me. She knows she is doing something bad. I think she is drunk. Do we have to do this?

SUE: Yes, please go on.

LITTLE SUE: She has on her old dress. The walls are pale. There is a sharp pain in my bottom. It hurts so bad. I cry and try to get away. She is holding me with one hand and has her other up inside me. It hurts. I am helpless. I remember drifting away. I am still crying but I'm not there anymore. I don't remember any more.

SUE: I am so pissed off. What fucking right did she have to do that? I hate her.

LITTLE SUE: Me too. I was so afraid. Every time she would babysit the same thing happened. I can't remember it all. Then she started to give me the enemas. Sometimes two or three times a day. It hurt so much. I want to stop now.

SUE: Okay, let's stop. I'm really sorry that happened to you. She can't hurt us anymore, she's dead.

LITTLE SUE: Good. I think she was a witch.

SUE: I wish she was alive so I could tell her how much I hate her.

LITTLE SUE: Yeah, me too. I didn't like remembering. Let's go outside and play.

SUE: Okay. We can play tomorrow. It's the middle of the night now. But tomorrow we'll go fly kites.

LITTLE SUE: That sounds like fun. Good night.

SUE: Good night. I love you and I'll take care of you and keep you safe. Thanks for helping me.

Sue was able to get more detailed information about the abuse she had suffered from this dialogue. More important, her inner child was able to express her hurt, anger, and fear about what happened. For the next few months, Sue continued writing letters and dialoguing with her inner child. As a result, she began to lose her fear of having bowel movements and her chronic constipation ceased. After months of work Sue received this letter from her inner child.

June

Dear Sue,
I love you too. I always have. It's okay now that you didn't know how to be with me. I was lonely, but now you see me, really see me. I want to be your friend and love you + play with you. You can't are care of me and I'll show you how to be with me and have fun.
See you soon.
Love,
Sue

When you work in your journal to establish contact with your inner child, surprising things can happen. If you spoke a language other than English when you were young, your inner child may write back to you in that language. You may also be amazed at the level of honesty and love your inner child shows. This child truly exists within you, and once you make contact with this part of yourself you will never be alone.

CHAPTER 17

Dreams

Here is a place to record your dreams. Dreams are one way in which your unconscious gives you information about material from your past that is usually hidden behind your defenses. All of us dream, but not everyone remembers their dreams. Some dreams are so vivid that they are held in memory for a long time; most dreams, however, are quickly forgotten. Even dreams that you recall vividly on waking up in the morning are often forgotten by mid-afternoon. In order to remember your dreams better, write them down as soon as possible after you wake up. If you keep an ongoing log of your dreams, you will increase the likelihood of discovering what your dreams are trying to tell you.

Dreams are personal. No one can interpret your dreams better than you yourself. Because the language of dreams is highly symbolic, dreams can be difficult to understand at times. If you keep a steady record, you will be much more likely to identify a common theme in your dreams, and their meaning will become clearer over time. There are as many different kinds of dreams as there are dreamers. Some dreams are readily understood, while others seem impossible to interpet.

You may have terrifying nightmares, as many survivors do. Writing down the nightmares may help you learn about their source. Handle these bad dreams just as you would any other emotional experience that is linked to the sexual abuse. Express your feelings about what happened in the nightmare, and then direct healing energy to the wound (see Chapter 6). Tell others in your support group about the nightmares—sharing them will often cause the fear to dissipate.

Having frequent nightmares was one of the reasons that Hope began therapy. When I asked her to describe her nightmares, all she could remember was her terror, not the dream itself.

> I woke up filled with fear, I was so afraid that I couldn't move. My bed was soaked with sweat and my body was so tense that it hurt. I can't recall the dream, but I know I was being hurt.

I asked Hope to write about the dream in her journal immediately upon waking.

> When I began to write about the dream, I started to remember it. I think I'm having the same dream every time. I was trapped in a black room, like a big box. It had no windows or doors. I was terrified that something outside was going to get me. I ran around the room, bashing into walls, trying to get out. Each time I ran into a wall, some part of my body started to bleed. Soon I was covered with blood. Then suddenly I sensed something in the room with me. I would scream and then wake up.

After Hope had written in her journal and talked to her group about the dream, she began to recover her memories. At the age of four or five, she had been sexually abused by her mother's boyfriend. Hope would attempt to hide from him in a dark closet. He would find her there, beat her and rape her. Hope stopped having this nightmare after she remembered the abuse she experienced. As happens with so many survivors, Hope's dream was trying to tell her what had happened to her in childhood. Through her willingness to begin writing, she discovered its message. Their purpose fulfilled, the nightmares simply stopped.

Some dreams that many survivors have are *freedom dreams*. These dreams generally take place in the early phase of the active healing stage of recovery. Although the symbology in "freedom dreams" varies from person to person, the feeling that accompanies the dreams is very similar.

Marian had been sexually molested by a girlfriend's older sister when she was nine years old. Part of the abuse included having a dog lick her genitals. Marian vividly remembered the abuse, but was never able to talk about it with anyone. She felt deep shame about what had happened to her and kept her "secret" for over twenty years. When Marian first told the story of her abuse during group, she had a freedom dream that she recorded in her journal:

March 14

    I was standing on a ledge, high up on the side of a cliff. I was
so afraid of falling, I knew if I did I would die. At the same time
I felt excited and wanted to jump. All of a sudden I opened my
arms and leaped out into the air. I didn't fall, instead I flew. It
was wonderful! I glided and soared. Suddenly I was in a giant
domed building. I could see others flying and gliding. Every
once in a while someone would land on a ledge and then take off
again. As I flew, I could see other people standing on ledges and
knew that they were standing there waiting to fly for the first
time. Then I would fly real close to one of these people and yell,
"Jump! You can fly too!" It was great. I felt so light and free.
Part of me knew I was dreaming, but I didn't care and I wanted
this dream to go on forever.

Marian interpreted her dream as a reflection of her becoming free of
her secret, and healing the pain that went with it. She felt she would
soon be encouraging others to share the freedom she had found by
telling her story.
    Survivors in recovery also have *resolution dreams*. These dreams
occur when a significant part of your wound has been healed.
    Daniel is a recovering alcoholic whose father sexually abused him in
childhood. Throughout his adult life, Daniel had had a recurring
nightmare about being chased. Five months after joining a survivors'
therapy group, Daniel wrote the following resolution dream in his
journal:

January 17

    I was a little boy and I was being chased. I didn't know who
was chasing me but I was very frightened. I ran all around my
house locking doors and closing windows. I would get to a
window or a door just in time to prevent someone from getting
in. I was so scared. I had this dream over and over. Then one
night I had it again. Only this time I let the person outside in the
house. It was my father. When he came in I just stood there
looking at him. I got bigger and bigger, and he got smaller and
smaller. I was no longer afraid of him. I turned away from him,
and walked away.

Daniel reported to his therapy group that he felt he had come to a deep kind of completion with this dream. "I know I'm not done with my work yet," he said, "but there was a healing. I can feel it."

By writing down your dreams regularly over a period of time, you may discover that they are a great source of information for your healing. Often while recording dreams, you may tap into feelings that lead you to begin writing in another section of the journal, sparking even further helpful discoveries. Our dreams are a rich resource. Using this section of the journal will greatly enhance your healing, introducing you to parts of yourself that you've only dreamed about.

CHAPTER 18

The Abuser(s)

You will use this section to tell the person (or persons) who abused you how their behavior affected you. In the safety of your journal, you can tell them exactly what you think and feel about them. You don't need to hold back anything at all.

As I discussed in Chapter 8, it is not necessary to have a face-to-face confrontation with your abuser in order to heal. Some survivors do directly confront the person who abused them, and they receive a great deal of healing and empowerment from that experience. Other survivors, however, choose not to confront their abuser—but they, too, heal and experience empowerment in their recovery. One survivor I worked with feared that the man who had sexually abused her in childhood would rape her again if she confronted him face to face. Instead, she confronted him by writing in her journal, and was quite satisfied with the result.

Some survivors cannot remember who abused them. Sometimes the abuser is dead or has disappeared. Whatever the case, you can effectively use the journal to vent your emotions toward the abuser. Even if you have already had a direct confrontation with the abuser, using this section will still be beneficial to you. Venting your rage, disgust, terror, contempt, and other strong feelings is an ongoing process, not a one-time event. You have held in these strong emotions for a long time, and it will take a while to express everything you want and need to say. As your feelings about the abuser continue to surface, use this section of your journal to vent those emotions, to reclaim your strength.

LETTER WRITING

Letter writing is a powerful way to tell the abuser what you want to say. (You may want to refer to the instructions for letter writing in Chapter 12.) Here are two examples of survivors' letters, written to the offender concerning how they felt about being sexually abused. When you write your own letter to the abuser, you may be surprised at the strength of your emotions.

The first letter was written by Marjorie, an incest survivor, to the stepfather who sexually abused her.

January 14

Dear Daddy,

Here I am writing to you again. I didn't think I would be doing this again. I'm glad I got to talk to you before you died and tell you how much your crazy, sick touching of my genitals hurt me and filled me with terror and disgust.

I'm still angry as hell at you. The little girl in me is, anyway. I have power now. You and your memory can't hurt me anymore. The little girl in me is still frightened of the memory. She was so terrified she could not move. Now she would like to scream at you. How could you put your hand between her legs and touch her genitals? You had no right to do that. I was not your possession. What pisses me off is you got away with it. No one ever knew.

I want to forgive you, but I can't. I just can't. I don't understand. How can I forgive an adult for hurting a child? I am going to have to have help. I can't forgive you myself. I want to for my own good, not yours.

I want to forgive my stepfather for sexually abusing me. I ask my Higher Power, I ask my Higher Self to give me the grace and the power to forgive him. Give me guidance. Show me how to do it.

Marjorie

The second letter was written by Paul, a man of thirty-six who was molested by his father from the age of five until he was eleven years old.

October 12

Dear sick son-of-a-bitch,

Why did you do that to me? Why didn't you just go jack off? Why did I have to be a part of it? I hate you for that. I hate myself for letting you. I didn't even say a word. I didn't even move. Did you ever wonder what I was thinking or feeling? Did you care? I wish I could have spit on you and kicked you. I wanted to run away. Why didn't I? I don't care how you feel. You shouldn't have done that to me. I shouldn't have had to cope with that. I wanted a father, not a sick person like you. Do you have any idea how what you did affected me? It really fucked up my life. I get sick when I think of you. I want to punch you in the face and kick you in the balls. God, I hate you. I love you too. I don't understand why. I guess because you worked and bought food. You were better than nothing, I guess. Fuck! I would rather have had nothing than live with what you did to me. I hate you. You stole my childhood. I lived in fear and terror because of you. I feel you are still stealing my life because I have to live with what you did to me. All I seem to do is work on my sexual abuse stuff. Shit, you are still in my life. But I will get rid of you. I will.

Paul

Writing to the person or persons who sexually abused you can be a deeply cleansing experience. It provides a release for the intense emotions trapped inside you, so that you can be free of them. Remember, as you do this writing exercise, that you are in control of the experience. If, at any point, you feel too frightened to continue—stop. Put your pencil down and do something else. It is not uncommon to feel frightened while writing this kind of letter, even though the abuser may be far away or even deceased. Your fear does not have to make sense. So stop if you need to. You can always come back to this exercise later. Part of the beauty of the journal is that you are the one in control.

CHAPTER 19

Affirmations for Healing

Affirmations are positive thoughts which you deliberately introduce into your consciousness. They serve two important healing functions: They support and validate your recovery, and they assist you in discovering a positive image of yourself. Using affirmations, you can neutralize and replace the negative internal messages you acquired as a sexually abused child. Children are open and vulnerable; they believe what adults and others tell them about themselves. To replace this negative "self-talk," you can create affirmations which will support a more accurate self-image, taking into account your innate beauty and strength.

Children who are sexually abused always receive negative messages (whether directly or indirectly) from the perpetrator of the abuse. Some of these messages are, "Your body is not your own," "You are an object," and "You are no good." You may have developed still other self-destructive beliefs as a result of your sexual trauma: "I hate myself," "Sex is frightening and painful," or "I exist to please others." Buried in the unconscious mind of every survivor of child sexual abuse is a long list of such messages. When you use affirmations you are, in a sense, "reprogramming" your mind. You are replacing the old, inaccurate beliefs with new, truthful ones that create a positive thought pattern. Many survivors find that, as they begin telling the secret of their sexual abuse, their negative inner messages seem to become "louder" or stronger.

CREATING AND USING AFFIRMATIONS

Writing or saying affirmations is a gentle and positive response to this onslaught of negative self-talk. This way, instead of feeling bullied by your internal nagging, you can take action, repeating these affirmative statements to yourself. Below are five general guidelines for creating and using affirmations.

1. Affirmations are *positive statements.* ("My body is beautiful," **not** "My body is not ugly.")

2. Affirmations are worded in the present tense ("I love myself").

3. Affirmations are most effective when they are short and simple.

4. Affirmations take time to produce results.

5. Affirmations must be repeated to be effective.

There are many different ways to do affirmations. In the Healing Journal, you will be writing them down. Other methods include saying the affirmations silently to yourself or to another person, and repeating the affirmations out loud.

Writing is the most effective way to use affirmations. Writing an affirmation works so well because, while you write, you experience the statement on three levels: you see the affirmation, you say the affirmation to yourself, and you "feel" the affirmation through the act of writing it down. In this way, writing helps to establish the affirmation more firmly in your mind. The more often you write the affirmation, the more quickly it moves from your conscious into your unconscious mind, positively influencing your feelings about yourself.

Affirmations are powerful and effective, but too much of a good thing can render them useless. Use affirmations sparingly—only one or two statements at a time. When you write them, repeat them only ten times at a sitting. If you do more, you may begin to resent doing the affirmations, and resentment really interferes with the process. More than anything else, it is the *positive feeling* you have as you write or say the affirmations that makes them work best for you.

Maggie was forty pounds overweight when she began therapy for childhood sexual abuse. She described herself as a slender, pretty child until she was ten years old (the time when her older brother began to sexually abuse her). After the abuse started, Maggie rapidly began to gain weight: "I hated myself for being attractive and pretty. I thought that if I were fat and ugly, he would leave me alone."

In addition to entering therapy, Maggie joined Overeaters Anonymous to help with her eating disorder. She discovered that when she began to lose weight, she felt disgust and hatred toward her body. Along with the courageous work of expressing and externalizing her emotions in the therapy group, Maggie used affirmations to help her change her hatred of her body. The affirmation she created was short and to the point: "I love my body." Maggie wrote this affirmation ten times in the morning and ten times in the evening. She continued to do this for several months.

Over time, Maggie began to be excited about the prospect of losing weight and feeling more attractive, rather than dreading the change in her looks. She told her therapy group, "I never thought I would be able to look into a mirror and like what I saw. Now, most of the time, I really do love myself and my body."

Below are some suggested affirmations. Try using one or two of them to see how they work. As you become more familiar with using affirmations, you may want to create your own. Self-created affirmations generally have the most lasting impact. You may also be inspired to try a variety of creative approaches to using your affirmations. You could try writing them down and taping them to the bathroom mirror or to the refrigerator, where you will see them often. Some of my clients tape their affirmations so they can literally play back the new messages to themselves rather than listening to the "old tapes." Here are some sample affirmations:

I love myself.

I love my body.

My body is beautiful.

I am free from guilt and shame.

Every day I am healthier and healthier.

My emotions are natural and healthy.

I believe in myself.

My memories are valid and real.

I am innocent.

My body is my own.

I am sexually fulfilled.

I love my genitals.

My inner child is healed.

I am the right sex.

I am healed and whole.

CHAPTER 20

Spiritual Reflections

"Why did this happen to me?"

"I was a child—how could God allow this to happen to a child?"

"I didn't have a choice. I was forced and I was hurt. Why me?"

"I didn't do anything wrong. I was innocent, I didn't deserve it."

"If there is a loving God, how could God let an innocent child be raped?"

"To hell with God!"

I have heard statements like these in one form or another from nearly every survivor I have worked with. I have asked the same questions about my own childhood and after hearing my clients talk about the traumas they have survived. It is not unusual to be angry at God, at life, or at Fate for what happened to you. And sooner or later you will naturally begin to ponder the questions above. It is important to address the "Why me?" question, because without some kind of an acceptable answer, you will experience a continuing discontent in your recovery.

Most of the survivors I have worked with have reached some form of spiritual understanding of their trauma. Some are confused about what they believe, and some are angry at their God. But generally they believe in the existence of some kind of Higher Power at work in the universe. Whatever you believe about the existence of a God or a

Higher Power is strictly your own business. But I am sure of one thing: If you are deeply angry or rageful at God for what happened to you as a child, your anger and rage must be experienced and externalized. As I've said throughout this book, continuing to repress the feelings will keep you stuck in the pain.

LETTER WRITING

A fine technique for expressing your anger and rage is to write a letter to God. In your letter, tell God *exactly* why you are angry. You might feel hesitant about expressing anger at God—most people do. But remember that when you give vent to held anger and rage, relief and freedom will follow. Expressing anger toward God about having been sexually abused is often the first step in developing a philosophy or spiritual path that will help you to come to peace with your past. Time after time, I have seen this technique work quite well for survivors. Try it—it works.

SPIRITUAL EXPLORATION

This section is not only a place for you to express your anger at God or a Higher Power. It is also a place for you to explore or reevaluate your spiritual beliefs. In addition to writing a letter to a Higher Power, or even dialoguing with God, you may use this part of your journal to set down your thoughts and ideas about spirituality. Sometimes as you write you may feel spiritual guidance coming from within. During the course of their recovery, many survivors have had spiritual experiences and life-changing awakenings. This section is a place to record such experiences. In this section, in any number of ways, the "Why me?" question can be answered. Many survivors I have worked with have developed strong spiritual beliefs. Some have returned to the faith of their youth, while others have chosen to follow a guru. Some have become Christian, while others decided to follow the Earth Religions. In recovery, every spiritual door is open. As you recover and heal, your heart will lead you to the place where your questions will be put to rest, and you will find your own peace.

My work in recovery has given a deeper meaning to my spiritual beliefs.

When I was a child I felt very connected to God, then I hated God for what happened to me. Now I have come full circle. I can feel that special connection to God again.

I'm still not sure about my relationship to a Higher Power, but when I share my story with another survivor, I feel something I can only describe as holy or sacred.

I used to think that all of me had been injured when I was abused. Now I know that only a small part of myself was really hurt. The greater part of myself, my spirit, can never be hurt. My recovery proved that to me.

FORGIVENESS

In spite of their suffering and pain, most survivors come to a new, or deeper, understanding of their spirituality during recovery. When this source of inner power and strength is tapped, there is a dramatic acceleration in healing and personal growth. I believe that true forgiveness is a spontaneous and powerful manifestation of this spiritual connection. There is no logical reason to forgive the people who caused you so much suffering and pain, yet time and again I have seen survivors forgive their abusers.

For most, the experience of being sexually abused as a child was truly "hell on earth." To forgive those involved in your abuse requires a spiritual courage and commitment that comes from a deep love of self and of God. Some people are able to experience forgiveness because they have a soul-shaking spiritual awakening that results in a feeling of forgiveness. These rare individuals seem to be touched by the grace of a higher power. For most of us, however, forgiveness is a state that occurs gradually over time. As the work of recovery and healing takes place, anger and hurt are often replaced by forgiveness and deep spiritual understanding. With every tear that is shed and every cry of rage that is released, more room is opened for forgiveness to enter the heart.

Considering what you survived, forgiveness can only be described as a spiritual state. How or when you arrive at this state will be determined by your own individual path in life. But as you do the work of healing, forgiveness will naturally manifest in your life to some degree.

Let me say, however, that I do not believe that forgiveness is the goal of recovery. I would never tell you, or any other survivor of sexual abuse, that forgiveness is necessary for healing. It's not. What is necessary is your commitment to healing. Forgiveness will then take care of itself.

Use this "Spiritual Reflections" section to write about forgiveness and what you think about it. Write down the name of anyone you would like to forgive. Would you like to forgive yourself? The people who hurt you? God? As you write, you will begin to clarify your ideas about forgiveness and the part it will play in your recovery. Be open to whatever comes to you. As you continue to heal, your thoughts and feelings about forgiveness will change and grow.

In this section I have not included examples from other survivors' journals. I feel you have the right to explore your own spiritual beliefs, and to make your own spiritual discoveries, with a minimum of influence from me and others.

CHAPTER 21

Integration

The "Integration" section is a place to write about your healing as it occurs and about the work you have already done. Here you can record your triumphs and successes, documenting the ongoing process of your recovery. As each important breakthrough is made, each time a defense is discarded, each time healing is experienced, you can write here about what happened and how you felt.

It is important to record your healing experiences. At times you will feel that you're not making progress or that you're getting worse instead of better. You may despair and become discouraged. During such dark times, it is extremely helpful to review the healing experiences you've written about here in your journal, where it will be easy to see concrete proof of your progress in recovery.

There will also be times in your recovery when everything is going along smoothly. Write about these experiences in this section too. You may want to use this section to reflect upon your recovery experiences and how they have changed your approach to life. One survivor reads parts of this section of his journal to people who are just beginning their own healing. He says that reading stories of his healing experiences to others gives them hope and encouragement and renews his own feeling of gratitude for his progress in recovery.

This section of the journal is unstructured. As always, write the date on each of your entries. As you heal from the profound childhood wound of sexual abuse, your life and your perspective is certain to change—you will need a special place to write about these changes. Create new journal sections if you like; you are by no means limited to the format presented here. This is only an outline, a way to begin.

Here are several entries from "Integration" sections of childhood sexual abuse survivors.

I never believed that I would be able to look him in the eyes and tell him how horribly he hurt me. I did, and I felt so powerful. He seemed to shrink and become a little insignificant person. He had no power over me. I felt free.

My grandmother is dead. She abused me so many times, I can't count that high. She instilled such fear in me and loathing for my body that I felt I was paralyzed and worthless. The fear and loathing are gone now. It felt so good when I wrote her the letter telling her I hated her for for what she did to me. I felt twenty pounds lighter. I still don't like her much, but I've been able to let go of the pain. I am so excited about being a whole person, a healed person, a complete man, I just want to smile and dance.

February 19

Why recovery? Why go through the process of remembering and feeling? Why spend the time, effort, and money?

My best answer for myself is comparing two images I have experienced. On February 9, 1985, I saw a young girl dressed in white lying bleeding and bruised beside a river. Me. Her body and her spirit were very hurt. The cuts and bruises were real pain. She lay on barren ground beneath a barren tree. Alone— except for me there. I wanted to help her, touch her, heal her. But I didn't know how.

I kept trying, though. I did keep trying. I looked for help in every way I could find. I wanted to heal inside and outside. Then in December 1985 I entered therapy. On December 12, 1985, I wrote: "Being in this group is where I belong now. Reaching into my body for the buried feelings, ridding my body, mind, and spirit of the pain, then filling with energy, light energy, warm energy. It's so good to be in a place with someone who knows what I've been knowing I need for a year or more. It's such a relief."

I had found help, a way I could help myself. Finally, I could

reach the young girl in the white dress and begin to heal her cuts
and bruises.

Many experiences and much work helped me to clear my
mind. I began to find a sense of me. I began to belong in my
body. I began to speak up for myself, to take care of myself. I
began a relationship with ME. I got a divorce, got out of a
relationship that was hurting me. The more healing I did, the
more hope I found. This allowed me the safety to look at the
cuts and bruises: abandonment, neglect, sexual abuse, and
emotional abuse. With the group's help, I found courage to see
and feel my hurt and pain so I could heal.

One experience of many was April 20, 1986, at a group
intensive. I wrote about the end of the intensive: "Part of this
time was spent with my magical child. I felt a sense of her
presence. I knew she was with me, loving me, giving me
courage, and nurturing me. We comforted the child who had
been hurt and lived with fear, the child who screamed in pain,
the silent child who was terrified, but wouldn't utter a sound,
much less scream. She, the child in white, filled with light, took
us to play, told me we could go into any darkness, because she
would always be there, in me, and the light would also be there
in me. We shared love, comfort, and nurturing. We remembered
the image I had had a year ago of myself, dressed in white,
bruised, bleeding, hurt. We healed her, loved her, took her in.
We all joined in ME. She, the injured one, had gone through
much healing during the past hours, and now I was at peace,
soaking in more and more healing, healing that didn't end when
I opened my eyes."

And the healing hasn't ended. Neither has the work ended.
Right now I cry tears from deep inside when I see the girl in
white who was bleeding and bruised. She is still part of me, a
part I love. But my body and my spirit have healed so much.
My tears are of gratitude. They are from thankfulness for being
able to trust the process of healing, the process that led to the
second image. A few weeks ago, on February 1, 1990, I had a
dream. I saw the outline of my body. Inside, in many different
parts, were what looked like colored lights. They were
pulsating, small circles of different colors. I don't know how

many there were, or exactly what colors, but I experience the feeling of healing in my body and spirit when I see that image.

After this last group on healing sexual abuse, I feel a sense of power and creativity I've never experienced before. I feel assurance about who I am. I know I am a very special person. I have unique, healing gifts to give. I've always known, even as a little girl, that I have a connection with the earth and the universe that is very strong. But I guess the hurts and pain were too strong. The young girl in white now stands on beautiful, lush green grass, beneath a tree that showers glimmering drops of gold and silver. And in place of each cut and bruise is a source of power and energy.

CHAPTER 22

Some Questions and Thoughts

Survivors of childhood sexual abuse have hundreds of unanswered questions. These questions deserve to be answered. Some answers can only come through your individual efforts. Other answers will come from listening to other recovering survivors sharing their experiences of sexual trauma and healing. Still other answers may be found in books such as this one, in news articles, in film documentaries, and in unexpected sources.

As your recovery unfolds, it is likely that your questions will lead to more questions. As you continue to work toward healing, answers will come to you—sometimes suddenly, sometimes gradually. Recovery is a remarkable learning process that brings about a gradual shift in perspective: We trade in our worn-out and unworkable patterns of living for a dynamic, joyful way of life that is true to our experience. To achieve this shift involves perseverance: Keep asking the questions until you find your answers. And keep telling the secret until someone believes you.

Here are some answers to the questions I have been asked most frequently about recovery from childhood sexual trauma.

1. How long will it take for me to recover?

Survivors who are just beginning recovery usually ask this question first. Unfortunately, there is no accurate way to estimate how long your healing will take. Each survivor responds to the trauma of sexual abuse somewhat differently. Although survivors have many feelings and beliefs in common, each survivor holds inside a well of pain unique

231

to his or her experiences and conditioning. After working on recovery issues for a time, most survivors come to feel that recovery is a process rather than an event. In a sense, you will be involved in the process of recovery throughout your life. That isn't as bad as it may sound. In the beginning stages of recovery, the pain of healing can be very intense. As you continue to heal, however, the pain lessens considerably. Recovery will grow lighter as your experience of abuse becomes integrated into the rest of your life experience.

2. Do I have to forgive the person(s) who did this to me?

No. As you heal and your held pain diminishes, you may feel that you would like to forgive the offender(s). This is fine. Remember, however, that you don't have to forgive the abuser in order to experience healing. Another note: Forgiveness does not mean that you in any way *excuse* the offender(s) from responsibility for sexually abusing you. For some survivors, trying to forgive too early on can get in the way of recovery. Like healing, forgiveness usually happens gradually over time. Some survivors are never able to forgive completely, yet they still experience quite remarkable healing. The key is not to rush things.

3. I feel like I'm going crazy. Am I?

No, you are not crazy. You are having very intense emotional experiences that are a direct result of the abuse you suffered as a child. As you experience these powerful emotions from your past you will probably feel "out of control"; the fear of going crazy is common to survivors who are just about to enter (or have just recently entered) recovery. As you build a support group and continue to work on your recovery, the "crazy" feeling will diminish and eventually disappear.

4. Isn't it better just to forget about the past and go on with my life?

Unless you actively enter into the healing process, the pain of the sexual abuse you experienced in childhood will continue to affect your feelings about yourself and your relationships with others. You have been living with the unhealed wound of the abuse ever since it happened. That pain will not simply go away. If you truly want to "go on with your life," you must actively pursue the healing of this wound. Rather than interfering with their lives, many survivors say that being actively involved in the healing process has enhanced and enriched their lives.

5. How can I protect my own children from sexual abuse?

The more committed you are to your own healing, the more you will be able to teach your children—by example—healthy attitudes about their bodies and their sexuality. Several books are available that are designed to educate children about sexual abuse and about how to say no in potentially abusive situations—most abusers will shy away from an informed child who has firm personal boundaries about touching. (See the Bibliography and Resources for some titles of children's books.) As you heal, your awareness about sexual abuse will expand so that you will be better prepared to protect your children, and to insure that they have a safe place to grow up. If you know or suspect that your children have been sexually abused, provide a safe place for them and seek counseling immediately. If your children were sexually abused and are now adults, openly talking to them about your recovery can encourage them to enter their own healing. As a parent, you have a natural responsibility to protect your children. Remember, however, that you are also responsible to continue your own recovery process. Ultimately this is the best thing you can do for your children as well as yourself.

6. Will I need professional help to recover?

Many survivors choose, at some point in their recovery, to seek professional help. Other survivors work on their recovery issues by themselves with the support of family and friends and by attending nonprofessional support groups. My own view is somewhat biased. I'm a therapist, so most of the successful recoveries I have seen have occurred within the context of therapy. Also, a number of the survivors I have worked with did not enter therapy specifically for sexual abuse—they discovered their history of sexual abuse while in the process of working on other issues. Generally speaking, the more severe your sexual trauma, the more likely it is that you will need professional help with your recovery.

7. How can I find a good therapist?

Your best resource is to listen to other survivors who are in therapy. Attend survivors' support groups. Ask other survivors about their experiences with therapists. Most survivors are more than willing to share their feelings and thoughts about their therapists. If you like what you hear about a certain therapist, then make an appointment for an interview. It is helpful to "shop around": Interview more than one therapist before you make a choice. After you have chosen a therapist, make a commitment to see him or her for a set number of sessions— say, five times. Then you can evaluate whether you are getting what you need. If you aren't, find another therapist. Trust your feelings and your intuition. If your internal warning lights go on, leave. The most important aspect of therapy is the rapport between you and your therapist. Granted, rapport usually takes a little time to develop. But if you genuinely feel that you can't trust your therapist or if you dislike your therapist, then it is unlikely that you will get much help from that relationship. (For more guidelines on finding a therapist, see Chapter 8.)

8. It seems that all I have time to do is to work on my recovery; it's all-consuming. Will this ever change? Will I ever have a normal life?

It is "normal" for you to be consumed with your recovery. Many survivors in the first stage of healing give nearly all their available energy to the work of recovery. But this intense focus will last only for a time; as you continue to heal, the recovery process will take less and less of your time and energy. Gradually you will find a balance between your recovery work and the rest of the things you do in your life.

9. I am still afraid of the person who abused me. Will this fear ever go away?

Some survivors report that they never feel completely unafraid of the person who abused them. Others say that they have become totally free of this fear. Among people I have worked with, I've observed that as they become more and more empowered in recovery, their fear level decreases dramatically. Some fear of the offender may remain, but this fear no longer controls the survivor's actions or interferes with their functioning in the world.

10. Do I have to remember everything that happened to me in order to recover?

No. Recovery can begin with only a suspicion that you were sexually abused. As you actively begin the healing process, you may not regain cognitive memories of what happened to you. You may have purely emotional memories (see Chapter 4). Some memories are so deeply repressed that they never become fully conscious. Don't be discouraged if this is the case. You can heal without regaining cognitive memories of the abuse.

11. I have no proof that I was sexually abused, but I think that I was. When I hear survivors talk about how they feel, I really relate to them. It's as if they were reading my inner thoughts. What should I do?

Proceed as if you were sexually abused. Seek counseling and/or attend survivors' support group meetings. Reading this book and writing in the Healing Journal can help to stir your memory. As you continue in recovery, it will probably become apparent to you whether you were sexually abused. If you discover that you were not sexually abused, your time will not have been wasted. For you to relate so closely to sexual abuse survivors, you surely experienced some type of childhood trauma. Your recovery work will facilitate the healing of that trauma, whether it was sexual or not.

12. Can my sexual relationship survive my recovery?

Yes, your relationship can survive, but you and your partner face some difficult challenges. The emotional intensity of your healing process places additional stress on your sexual relationship. Couples who are committed to stay together can survive the stress, discovering a greater intimacy as a result of dealing with the past trauma. Remember that, in this case, *both people* in the relationship must deal with the issues surrounding the sexual abuse, even if only one of you was abused as a child. My book *Healing Together: A Guide to Intimacy and Recovery for Co-Dependent Couples* discusses in more detail what happens to relationships, and what couples can do, when one or both partners are survivors of childhood sexual abuse.

13. Can I really recover?

Yes, you can. Thousands of survivors have already walked this rocky road ahead of you. They have proven that you can heal from your past sexual abuse. Through their determination to become free of the past, these courageous men and women have shown the way for you and other survivors. As awareness grows, more and more survivors of childhood sexual abuse will be joining you on your way to healing. Although recovery involves feeling a lot of old pain, as you release that pain you make room for joy and laughter to enter your life. The peace and wholeness you will experience as a result of your work will inspire others to seek help. It is quite an amazing and rewarding journey.

As you heal and as you encourage other survivors to heal, our society can begin to heal as well. With grace and our continuing perseverence, someday perhaps the sexual abuse of children will be simply a tragic part of human history. No child should have to endure the terror, shame, and loneliness that you have experienced. You are a survivor and a healer, and you can get to "the other side" of your pain.

In Closing . . .

In the years it has taken to write this book, more and more about child sexual abuse has been brought to the public awareness. During this time, hundreds of books and articles have been written on this subject. It is as though the professional community and society at large is waking from a deep sleep. But information alone will not break the cycle of sexual abuse. Knowledge is powerful, but by itself it is simply not enough. Only the individual healing of each survivor can stop these crimes of violence against our children and mend this terrible wound in our society.

In the next few years, I believe we can expect to see many legislative changes designed to make our legal system more responsive to child victims and adult survivors of sexual abuse. Still, we cannot hope to legislate the sexual abuse of children out of existence. Real and lasting change must come from the healed heart of each survivor. You are the one who will make the final difference. Each of us has a different part to play in our collective healing. Some survivors will publicly share their stories of childhood horror; others will organize survivors' groups in their communities to support the constantly growing numbers who seek healing. Having returned to wholeness and awareness yourselves, many of you will give your time and attention to raising children who are aware and whole. Your recovery will affect your family, friends, co-workers, and anyone else who comes in contact with you. However it manifests, your individual healing will make an enormous difference to all those who come after you, for you are helping to create a blueprint for the healing of our world.

It is with great respect and love that I honor your courage and your strength.

Bibliography and Resources

NOTE: Resources for adult survivors of childhood sexual abuse are constantly changing and growing. This is not a fixed or complete list. Please search out additional resources in your area.

THE HEALING JOURNEY

Bass, Ellen, and Laura Davis. *The Courage to Heal: A Guide for Women Survivors of Child Sexual Abuse.* New York: Harper and Row, 1988.

Bear, Euan, with Peter Dimock. *Adults Molested as Children: A Survivor's Manual for Women and Men.* Orwell, VT: Safer Society Press, 1988. (To order, send $12.95 to Safer Society Press, Shoreham Depot Road, RR1, Box 24-B, Orwell, VT 05760-9576.)

Blume, E. Sue. *Secret Survivors: Uncovering Incest and Its Aftereffects on Women.* New York: John Wiley and Sons, 1990.

Bradshaw, John. *Homecoming: Reclaiming and Championing Your Inner Child.* New York: Bantam Books, 1990.

Carnes, Patrick. *Out of the Shadows.* Minneapolis: CompCare Publishers, 1989. (Based on a twelve-step model, this book was the first to identify and define sexual addiction.)

Cohen, Barry, Esther Giller, and Lynn W., eds. *Multiple Personality Disorder From the Inside Out.* Dallas: Sidran Press, 1991. (To order, write to Order Dept., 11271 Russwood Circle, Dallas, TX 75229.)

Covington, Stephanie. *Awakening Your Sexuality: A Recovery Guide for Women.* San Francisco: Harper San Francisco, 1991.

Davis, Laura. *The Courage to Heal Workbook: For Women and Men Survivors of Child Sexual Abuse.* New York: Harper and Row, 1990.

Delaney, Gayle, Ph.D. *Breakthrough Dreaming.* New York: Bantam Books, 1991.

Dodson, Betty. *Sex for One: The Joy of Selfloving.* New York: Harmony Books, 1987.

Gil, Eliana. *Outgrowing the Pain: A Book for and About Adults Abused as Children.* San Francisco: Launch Press, 1983.

————. *United We Stand: A Book for People with Multiple Personalities.* Walnut Creek, CA: Launch Press, 1990. (To order, write to P.O. Box 31493, Walnut Creek, CA 94598. This cartoon-style book explains multiple personalities and dissociation.)

Hunter, Mio. *Abused Boys: The Neglected Victims of Sexual Abuse: Healing for the Man Molested as a Child.* Lexington, MA: Lexington Books, 1990.

Kane, Evangeline. *Recovering from Incest: Imagination and the Healing Process.* Boston: Sigo Press, 1989.

Kapit, Wynn, and Lawrence M. Elson. *The Anatomy Coloring Book.* New York: Harper and Row, 1977.

Kolk, Bessel A. van der, *Psychological Trauma.* Washington, DC: American Psychiatric Press, 1987.

Kritsberg, Wayne. *The Adult Children of Alcoholics Syndrome: A Step-By-Step Guide to Discovery and Recovery.* New York: Bantam Books, 1988. (This book examines the chronic shock state of adults abused as children and gives descriptions of family dysfunction.)

Love, Pat. *The Emotional Incest Syndrome: What to Do When a Parent's Love Rules Your Life.* New York: Bantam Books, 1990.

Nair, Mohan, M.D. *A Step-by-Step Guide to Recovery: For All Adult Survivors and Co-dependents.* Deerfield Beach, FL: Health Communications, Inc., 1990.

Poston, Carol, and Karen Lison. *Reclaiming Our Lives: Hope for Adult Survivors of Incest.* Boston: Little, Brown, 1989.

Progoff, Ira. *At a Journal Workshop.* Revised edition. New York: Dialogue House Library, 1992.

Sonkin, Daniel Jay, Ph.D., and Michael Durphy, M.D. *Learning to Live Without Violence.* San Francisco: Volcano Press, 1989.

Wilmer, Harry, A., M.D. *Practical Jung.* Wilmette, Illinois: Chiron Publications, 1987.

Yudofsky, Stuart, Robert Hales, and Tom Ferguson. *What You Need to Know About Psychiatric Drugs.* New York: Grove Weidenfeld, 1991.

Survivors Tell Their Stories

Bass, Ellen, and Louise Thornton, eds. *I Never Told Anyone: Writings by Women Survivors of Child Sexual Abuse.* New York: Harper and Row, 1983. (Vivid firsthand accounts of child sexual abuse.)

Estrada, Hank. *Recovery for Male Victims of Child Abuse.* Santa Fe: Red Rabbit Press, 1990. (Interview with a male survivor. P.O. Box 6545 Santa Fe, NM 87502-6545. $7 includes tax and shipping; make checks payable to Hank Estrada.)

Evert, Kathy, and Inie Bijkerk. *When You're Ready: A Woman's Healing from Childhood Physical and Sexual Abuse by Her Mother.* Walnut Creek, CA: Launch Press, 1988.

Grubman-Black, Stephen. *Broken Boys/Mending Men: Recovery from Child Sexual Abuse.* Blue Ridge Summit, PA: Tab Books, 1990. (Human Services Institute, Inc., P.O. Box 14610, Brandenton, FL 34280. Written by a male survivor, this book includes many firsthand accounts of men sexually abused as children.)

LeLoo, Mary, *Through the Fire: Personal Recovery Stories.* Freedom, CA, The Crossing Press, 1992.

Smith, Michelle, and Lawrence Pazder. *Michelle Remembers.* New York: Pocket Books, 1987. (A firsthand account of ritual abuse.)

Spencer, Judith. *Suffer the Child.* New York: Pocket Books, 1989. (Personal story of ritual abuse and resulting multiple personalities.)

Healing Music

Bearns and Dexter. *The Golden Voyage,* vol. 2. Awakening Productions, Inc., 4132 Tuller Avenue, Culver City, CA 90230. (213) 659-6238.

Ruth Huber and Kate McLennan. *Trailblazers.* Available on cassette. Send $9.95 (incudes postage) to Trailblazers, 7209 Grover Avenue, Austin, TX 78757.

Daniel Kobialka. *Timeless Motion.* Arkay Records, San Jose, CA. (Includes a beautiful extended version of Pachelbel's Canon.)

Patricia Troth Ricker. *The Magical Child Suite.* Available on cassette. Send $10 to Patricia Troth Ricker, 1709-B Wild Basin Ledge, Austin, TX 78746. (Four heart-healing songs that help listeners get in touch with the magical child within.)

Mike Rowland. *The Fairy Ring.* Sona Gaia Productions, 1845 North Farwell Ave., Milwaukee, WI 53202. (414) 272-6700.

Energy and Healing

Douglas, Nik, and Penny Slinger. *Sexual Secrets: The Alchemy of Ecstasy.* New York: Destiny Books, 1979. (Includes valuable information and exercises centering on energy awareness and sexuality.)

Gordon, Richard. *Your Healing Hands: The Polarity Experience.* Berkeley: Wingbow Press, 1984.

Gunther, Bernard. *Energy Ecstasy and Your Seven Vital Chakras.* North Hollywood, CA: Newcastle Publishing Company, 1983.

Joy, W. Brugh. *Joy's Way: A Map for the Transformational Journey. An Introduction to the Potentials for Healing with Body Energies.* Los Angeles: J. P. Tarcher, 1979.

ABOUT SEXUAL ABUSE

Armstrong, Louise. *Home Front: Notes from the Family War Zone.* New York: McGraw-Hill, 1984.

Burks, Judith Emry. *Helping Children Heal: What School Personnel Need to Know About Child Sexual Abuse.* Bandon-by-the-Sea, OR: Pinesong Cottage Press, 1990.

Burson, Malcolm, et al. *Discerning the Call to Social Ministry. An Alban Case Study in Congregational Outreach.* Washington, DC: The Alban Institute, 1990. (4125 Nebraska Avenue NW, Washington, DC 20016.)

Butler, Sandra. *Conspiracy of Silence: The Trauma of Incest.* Updated. San Francisco: Volcano Press, 1985.

Courtois, Christine A. *Healing the Incest Wound: Adult Survivors in Therapy.* New York: W.W. Norton, 1988.

Crewsdon, John. *By Silence Betrayed: Sexual Abuse of Children in America.* New York: Little, Brown, 1988.

Fortune, Marie. *Sexual Violence: The Unmentionable Sin: An Ethical and Pastoral Perspective.* New York: Pilgrim Press, 1983. (475 Riverside Drive, Room 1140, New York, NY 10115.)

Herman, Judith. *Father-Daughter Incest.* Cambridge: Harvard University Press, 1981.

Kehoe, Patricia. *Helping Abused Children: A Book for Those Who Work with Sexually Abused Children.* Seattle: Parenting Press, 1988.

Klaussner, Mary Ann, and Bobbie Hasselbring. *Aching for Love: The Sexual Drama of the Adult Child.* San Francisco: Harper and Row, 1990.

Lew, Mike. *Victims No Longer: Men Recovering from Incest and Other Sexual Abuse.* New York: Harper and Row, 1986.

Miller, Alice. *Thou Shalt Not Be Aware: Society's Betrayal of the Child.* New York: New American Library, 1986.

Pellauer, Mary, Barbara Chester, and Jane Boyajian. *Sexual Assault and Abuse: A Handbook for Clergy and Religious Professionals.* San Francisco: Harper and Row, 1986.

Rush, Florence. *The Best Kept Secret: Sexual Abuse of Children.* Englewood Cliffs, NJ: Prentice-Hall, 1980.

Westerlund, Elaine. *Responding to Incest: In Memory of Nancy.* Cincinnati, OH: Forward Movement Publications, 1988.

FOR PARTNERS

Anand, Margo. *The Art of Sexual Ecstasy: The Path of Sacred Sexuality for Western Lovers.* Los Angeles: J.P. Tarcher, 1989.

Covington, Stephanie, and Liana Beckett. *Leaving the Enchanted Forest: The Path from Relationship Addiction to Intimacy.* New York: Harper and Row, 1988.

Davis, Laura. *Allies in Healing: When the Person You Love Was Sexually Abused as a Child.* New York: HarperCollins, 1991.

Gil, Eliana. *Outgrowing the Pain Together: A Book for Partners and Spouses of Adults Abused as Children.* New York: Dell, 1991.

Graber, Ken. *Ghosts in the Bedroom: A Guide for Partners of Incest Survivors.* Deerfield Beach, FL: Health Communications, 1991.

Hansen, Paul. *Survivors and Partners: Healing the Relationships of Adult Survivors of Child Sexual Abuse.* (Self-published; to order, send $11.00 to: Paul Hansen, 7548 Cresthill Drive, Longmont, CO 80501.)

Kritsberg, Wayne. *Healing Together.* Deerfield Beach, FL: Health Communications, 1990.

Maltz, Wendy, and Beverly Holman. *Incest and Sexuality: A Guide to Understanding and Healing.* Lexington, MA: Lexington Books, 1987.

Maltz, Wendy. *The Sexual Healing Journey.* New York: HarperCollins, 1991.

FOR PARENTS

Adams, Caren, and Jennifer Fay. *No More Secrets: Protecting Your Child From Sexual Assault.* San Luis Obispo, CA: Impact, 1981.

Ames, Louise Bates. *Your One-Year-Old* through *Your Ten- to Fourteen-Year-Old.* Ten-book series. New York: Dell, 1980.

Balter, Lawrence. *Who's in Control? Dr. Balter's Guide to Discipline Without Combat.* New York: Poseidon Press, 1989.

Briggs, Dorothy Corkille. *Your Child's Self-Esteem: The Key to Life.* New York: Dolphin Books, 1975.

Hagans, Kathryn B., and Joyce Case. *When Your Child Has Been Molested: A Parent's Guide to Healing and Recovery.* Lexington, MA: Lexington Books, 1988.

Nelsen, Jane. *Positive Discipline.* New York: Ballantine Books, 1987.

Planned Parenthood. *How to Talk with Your Child About Sexuality: A Parent's Guide.* New York: Doubleday, 1986.

Shiff, Eileen. *Experts Advise Parents: A Guide to Raising Loving, Responsible Children.* New York: Delacorte Press, 1987.

Smith, Shauna. *Making Peace with Your Adult Children.* New York: Plenum, 1991.

SOME HEALING ORGANIZATIONS AND NEWSLETTERS

Believe the Children, P.O. Box 1358, Manhattan Beach, CA 90266.

An organization providing a variety of resources and a newsletter, as well as support for children who are victims of ritual abuse, and for their families.

Families of Crimes of Silence, P.O. Box 2338, Canoga Park, CA 91306. (805) 298-8768.

Provides resource information and support for families of abused children, clinical training, and speakers on ritual abuse.

First Class Male, 50 N. Arlington Avenue, Indianapolis, IN 46219.

Quarterly newsletter for sexually abused boys and men and the people who support them. Church-sponsored.

Healing Hearts, c/o Bay Area Women Against Rape, 1515 Webster Street, Oakland, CA 94612.

Offers an annotated bibliography, audiotapes of training conferences, and referrals for both professionals and ritual abuse survivors.

Incest Resources, 46 Pleasant Street, Cambridge, MA 02139. (617) 492-1818.

Looking Up, P.O. Box K, Augusta, ME 04332. (207) 626-3402.

A national support organization for incest survivors. Provides referrals, resources, excellent publications, regional gatherings, and an outdoor adventure program.

Many Voices: A National Bi-monthly Self-Help Publication for Persons with Multiple Personalities or a Dissociative Process.

Yearly subscriptions are $30. Write to: Many Voices, P.O. Box 2639, Cincinnati, OH 45201-2639. Subscriptions outside the U.S. are $36.

The National Child Abuse Help/IOF Foresters Hotline: (800) 422-4453.

Provides twenty-four-hour crisis intervention and referrals. Call this number to report child abuse.

PLEA, P.O. Box 6545, Santa Fe, NM 87502-6545. (505) 982-9184.

The national organization for nonoffending male survivors. Provides resources, a bibliography, referrals, and a newsletter.

The Safer Society Program, Shoreham Depot Road, RR1, Box 24-B, Orwell, VT 05760. (802) 897-7541.

National referrals and literature for both youth and adult victim and offender populations. Write for a list of publications.

Survivors of Incest Anonymous, P.O. Box 21817, Baltimore, MD 21222-6817.
Provides free, confidential support meetings for survivors around the country. Based on the twelve-step model. To locate meetings in your area, call a local social service agency, or request a directory of meetings from the above address. Send a self-addressed stamped envelope with two stamps.

VOICES in Action, P.O. Box 148309, Chicago, IL 60614. (312) 327-1500.
International organization for survivors and partners (called "pro-survivors"). Annual conferences, trainings, and a newsletter.

Index

A

AA. *See* Alcoholics Anonymous.
"Abuser(s)" section, in Healing Journal, 167, 169, 216–18
letter writing, 217–18
Accidents, 68–69
Accomplice, to child sexual abuse, 21–22
ACOA. *See* Adult Children of Alcoholics.
Acquaintances, 16–19, 21
Active healing stage, of recovery, 77, 79–80, 82, 89, 92, 93, 149
Addictions, 65. *See* Compulsive-addictive diseases.
Adult Children of Alcoholics (ACOA), 140
twelve-step groups, 82
"Affirmations for Healing" section, in Healing Journal, 167, 219–22
creating and using affirmations, 220–22
After-care groups, 145, 146

Age
and memory repression, 49–50
and wounded inner child, 105–6
Al-Anon, 140
Alcoholics Anonymous (AA), 67, 123
Twelve Steps of, 148
Alcoholism, 13, 65, 67, 81, 114, 123, 143, 146, 192
in families, 15, 18–19, 47, 170, 179
Anal abuse, 25, 26
Anal rape, 32–33, 64
Anal soreness or swelling, 64
Anger, 94, 96, 120–21, 200. *See also* Rage; Release of anger/rage, standing.
at God, 223–26
Animals
ritual killing of, 31
sex with, 25, 27–28, 31
Anorectic problem, 67
Antidepressants, 147

Artwork, 95. *See also* Creative coloring and artwork.
Attention span, shortened, 56, 60
Authority, misuse of, 17–18

B
Babysitter, 16, 17, 18, 132, 134
Backaches, 42
Back pain, lower, 68
Bathing, 6, 27, 189
Beating, 50. *See also* Sexual beating.
Betrayal, 130
    of child sexual abuse, 4, 21–22
    and incest, 10–11
Biting, 30
Blame, and seductive physical abuse, 35
Blank spots, in "Personal History" section, 182
Blue Sphere meditation, 130–32
Body, 84, 85–86, 91. *See also* "My Body" section.
    and Blue Sphere meditation, 131
    dialoguing with, 192–93, 201
    directing healing energy to other parts of, 132–34
    as sponge, 119
Body awareness, 93–94
Bodybuilding, compulsive, 67
Body image, 39
Body memories, 56, 64, 65, 85–86
Body objectification, 57, 65–66
"Body wisdom," 191
Boundaries, 27, 79
    abused, 69
    and saying no, 152–53

and sexual relationship, 149–50
    for touching, 134–36
Boys, 3, 7, 96
    and seductive physical abuse, 35
    See also Older boys
Breathing, 99–100, 124
    and Blue Sphere meditation, 130–32
    and Earth Healing men's meditation, 128–30
    and Earth Healing women's meditation, 126–28
    and "Gift of the Star" exercise, 110–12
    in panic attacks, 65
    and Temple of the Heart meditation, 158–59
Brothers, 10, 155–56, 189
Buying things, compulsively, 67

C
Caregivers, 7, 14, 16, 17, 35
Caretaker, and emotional sexual abuse incident, 189
Catharsis, 95–96
Ceremonies, sadistic or satanic, 31
Chest, tightness in, 65
Chicago, Judy, 195
Child-to-child sexual abuse, 15
Children. *See also* Inner child; Magical inner child; Parenting; Wounded inner child
    protecting, 233
    sexual curiosity of, 6–8
    and traumatization process, 45–46

younger and older, 153
Child sexual abuse, 3–22. *See
    also* Emotional sexual abuse;
    Physical sexual abuse, Sex-
    ual abuse incident.
    accomplice to, 21–22
    and acquaintances, 16–19, 21
    as betrayal, 4, 21–22
    categories of, 23–42,
    definition of, 5
    and family members, 10–16,
        21–22, 35, 38, 47
    myths vs. realities, 8–9
    secondary consequences of,
        56–72, 87
    and strangers, 19–21, 52
    survivors of, 4–5, 15–16, 19–20
    victims of, 4
    who commits?, 9–21
    wound of, 3–4
Choking, 30, 64, 132–34
Cigarette smoking, 114–15
Clergy, 16, 150. *See also* Minis-
    ters; Priests.
Co-dependents Anonymous, 140
Coercion, 50
Coercion/intimidation, 30
Cognitive memory, 85, 88, 89–90
    and recovery, 235
Color, 130. *See also* Creative col-
    oring and artwork.
    and Earth Healing men's med-
        itation, 128–29
    and Earth Healing women's
        meditation, 127
    and healing, 122, 124–25
Communication, 60, 152, 205–6
    and letter writing, 178
Compassion, 101, 103

Compulsive-addictive diseases,
    47, 57, 67
Concentration, and communica-
    tion, 60
Confrontation
    with abuser(s), 216–18
    in family of origin, 155–57
Constipation, 64, 86, 211
Conversation. *See* Dialoguing.
Core defenses, in traumatization
    process, 48–54, 93, 175
    denial, 48, 52–53
    dissociation, 48, 51–52
    memory repression, 48, 49–51
    vs. pain, 54–56
    in sleep, 63
Counseling, 149, 152, 233, 235
Cousins, 10, 177
"Cradle, human," 135, 137–38
Creating and using affirmations,
    220–22
Creative coloring and artwork,
    195–96
Creativity, 138, 167
    and mind, 88
"Cross-dressing," 28
Crying, 95, 101, 116, 119, 121,
    124, 136. *See also* Sobbing.
Cursing, 100

D
"Daily Expressions" section, of
    Healing Journal, 165–66,
    167, 168–69
Dates, in Healing Journal, 168,
    169, 172, 173, 178
Dating, 40
Death, 47, 65, 90, 115, 172

Denial, 20, 24, 36, 48, 52–53, 63, 78, 79, 93, 175, 179, 182, 205
  after confrontation, 156–57
  by minimization, 53
Depression, 62, 147
Desserts. *See* Overeating.
"Deviants," 8
Dialoguing, 179–81
  with your body, 192–94, 201
  with inner child, 208–11
  with mother, 180–81
Diapers, changing, 6
Diet, 115, 145
Digestive problems, 86
Dinner Party, The, 195
Discipline, 30
  gentle, 113
Disconnecting from body, 51, 65–66, 191
Discovery stage, of recovery, 77–78, 81–82, 89, 93
Dissociation, 48, 51–52, 93, 132, 175, 182, 205
Divorce, 47
Doctors, 16, 17–18
  and medical procedures, unnecessary, 29
Douches. *See* Vaginal douches.
Drawing. *See* Creative coloring and artwork.
Dreams, 63, 77
"Dreams" section, in Healing Journal, 167, 169, 212–15
  recording, 212–15
Dressed in adult sexual clothing, 25, 28
Dressing, 6, 27, 189
Drinking. *See* Alcoholism.
Drug abuse and addiction, 65, 67, 143, 146. *See also* Psychiatric drugs.
Drunk driver, 71
Dysfunctional families, 18–19, 45–46
  and Family Tree, 170–71
  parents in, 47–48

E
Earth, energy of, 125–26
Earth Healing meditations, 125–30
  for men, 125, 128–30, 132
  for women, 125, 126–28, 132
Earth Mother, 125–26
  in meditations, 127–28, 129
Eating disorders, 67, 221
Emotional experiences
  "feel good," 107–8
  narrow range of, 56, 58
Emotional flooding, 56, 58–59
Emotional memories, 85, 87–88
  repression of, 93–96
Emotional pain. *See* Pain.
Emotional release work, guiding healing energy into wound after, 116–25, *122*
"Emotional roller coaster," 150. *See also* "Roller-coaster rides."
Emotional sexual abuse, 24, 38–42, 85, 107
  combined with physical sexual abuse, 42
  seductive, 24, 40–42, 50, 52
  violent, 39–40
Emotional sexual abuse incident, 189–90

Emotional state, during physical sexual abuse incident, 189
Emotional unavailability, 70–71
Emotions, 84, 86–88, 91. *See also* Feeling responses.
  "switching off," 46
Enemas, 6, 29, 86, 210–11
Energy, of earth, 125–26. *See also* Healing energy; Toxic energy.
Energy chalice, 133–34
Energy field, 117
Environment, family, 173–74
Exercising, 194
Exhaustion. *See* Fatigue, chronic.

F
Falls, 68
Family. *See also* Dysfunctional families.
  of choice, 157–58
  friend of, 16, 18
  and intimacy dysfunction, 70–71
  nudity in, 27
  of origin, 157–58
  questions about, 173–74
"Family History" section, of Healing Journal, 166, 170–74
  environment, family, 173–74
Family Tree, 170–72, 175
Family members, 10–16, 21–22, 35, 38, 47
"Family Members" section, in Healing Journal, 166, 175–81
  dialoguing, 179–81
  letter writing, 178–79

Family Tree, 170–72, *171*, 175
Fantasies, 187
Father, 10, 15, 21, 22, 50, 70, 102, 106, 123, 150, 156, 214
  of friend, 32–33
  letter to, 214–15
  questions on, 175–76
  and violent emotional sexual abuse, 39–40
Father/daughter incest, 11–12
Fatigue, chronic, 57, 66–67, 86, 193
Fear, 95, 200, 234
  energy of, 120–21
Feedback, and dialoguing, 181
"Feel good" emotional experiences, 107–8
Feelings responses, 199–201
Feelings, 21. *See also* Emotions.
  "switching off," 51
Feelings statements, 201–204
Female therapists, 142
Fights, 70
Flashbacks, 56, 63–64, 65, 72, 77
Flu, 68
Focus, lack of, 60
Focusing statements, 192, 193–94, 209
Food, 65
Forgetting about past, 232. *See also* Memory repression; Repressed memories.
Forgiveness, 225–26, 232
Freedom, in integration stage, 80
French kissing, 26
Friend(s), 79, 119, 135, 138, 148, 157, 233
  as abusers, 16, 18
  of family, 16, 18

father of, 32–33
and meditations, 130, 158
partner as, 150

G
Gambling, 170
  compulsive, 67
Gang rape, 18–19
Gastrointestinal disorders, 68
Gay men, 148
Gender, identification by, 3
Gender-specific behavior, 96
Genital pain, 86
Genitals, washing of, 6
"Gift of the Star, The" exercise,
  110–12
Girls, 3, 7, 96
  and seductive physical abuse,
  35
God, 91
  anger and rage at, 223–26
  forgiveness toward, 225–26
"Going crazy," 56, 63, 232
"Gone blank," 46
Grandfather, 10, 157, 171
Grandfather/grandson incest,
  12–13
Grandmother, 10, 50, 65, 86, 228
Grandparents, 152, 177
Great-grandfather, 10
Great-grandmother, 10
Grief, 96, 101, 120, 122
Grief/loss, release of, 121
"Grooming," 17
Group setting, touch (healing)
  in, 136–38
Group sex, 69
  forced, 31

Group therapy, 135, 145, 156.
  See also Therapy group.
Guiding healing energy into
  wound after emotional release work, 116–25
Guilt, 39, 122
  and seductive physical abuse,
  34

H
Handcuffing, 30
Headaches, 42, 86, 193. *See also*
  Migraine headaches.
Healing, cycle of, 92–103
  exposing wound, 92, 93–95,
  99–100
  externalizing pain, 92, 95–96,
  100–101
  healing wound, 92, 96–97, 101
  reexperiencing trauma, 92, 95,
  100
  working with, 102–3
Healing circle, 138
Healing energy, 116–38
  circle, healing, 138
  directing to other parts of
  body, 132–34
  guiding into wound after emotional release work, 116–25,
  122
  meditations, 125–32
  and touch, healing, 101,
  134–38
Healing inner child, 104–15, 164
Healing Journal, 163–236
  "Abuser(s)" section, 167, 169,
  216–18
  "Affirmations for Healing"
  section, 167, 219–22

"My Body" section, 166, 191–96, 201

"Daily Expressions" section, 165–66, 167, 168–69

dates in, 168, 169, 172, 173, 178

"Dreams" section, 167, 169, 212–15

"Family History" section, 166, 170–74

"Family Members" section, 166, 175–81

"Integration" section, 167, 227–30

"Personal History" section, 166, 182–90

"Self-Discovery" section, 167, 197–204

"Spiritual Reflections" section, 167, 223–26

"Welcoming the Inner Child" section, 167, 205–11

writing exercises in, 164–65

Healing Together: A Guide to Intimacy and Recovery for Co-Dependent Couples (Kritsberg), 235

Healing circle, 138

Healing wound, 92, 96–97, 101

Health procedures, inappropriate, 26, 29

Heart, and Blue Sphere meditation, 130–32

Heartbeat, 65

Heart conditions, 114–15

Held pain, *55*, 61, 105

releasing energy of, 117–25, *118*

Helplessness, 56, 61–62, 65, 80, 88

Hesse, Hermann, quoted, 143–44

Heterosexual relationship, 148

Heterosexuals, 148

Higher Power, 103, 217. *See also* God.

High-risk behavior, 113–15

Hitting, 30

pillow, 95, 100, 101, 119, 121, 124

Holding, 30, 134–38

Home, as safety net, 10–11

Homosexuality, 44

Hopelessness, 56, 61–62, 80

Hugging, 6, 134–37, 174

Hurt, as feeling, 201

I

Illness, life threatening, 47. *See also* Minor illnesses, chronic.

Images, 110, 122, 125, 134, 158

and meditations, 126, 128

in nightmares, 62

Imagination, 138

Inbreeding, 8

Incest, 8, 10–16, 155

father/daughter, 11–12

grandfather/grandson, 12–13

intergenerational, 170, 171

multigenerational, 15, 23

seductive, 17

survivors of, 15–16

Individual therapy, 144

Inner child, 104–15, 164

dialoguing with, 208–11

finding, 110–13

letter writing to, 206–8

magical, 107–10, *108,* 205
parenting, 113–15
wounded, 104–7, *105,* 109, 205
Inner vision, 110, 124
Inpatient treatment programs, 145–46, 164
Insanity, 65
"Integration" section, in Healing Journal, 167, 227–30
Integration stage, of recovery, 77, 80–81, 82, 90, 125
Intensive treatment programs, 146–47
Interests, 157
Intergenerational incest, 170, 171
Internalization, of feelings, 39, 40
Intimacy, strength in, 154, 157, 235
Intimacy dysfunction, 57, 70–71
Intimidation, 50. *See also* Coercion/intimidation.

J
Jokes, sexual, 39–40, 189
Joy, 199
  and magical inner child, 108, 109–10

K
Kicking, 30
Kissing, 6, 26
"Kissing the hurt," 134

L
Lesbian women, 148
Letter writing, 178–79, 224
  to abuser(s), 217–15
  to inner child, 206–8

Lifestyles, self-destructive, 113–15
Lighting, for "Gift of the Star" exercise, 110
Loneliness, 86, 119, 136
Loss. *See* Grief/loss, release of.
Love, 149
  in group setting, 137–38
  and inner child, 113
  of self, 154

M
Magical inner child, 107–10, *108,* 205
Male/male child sexual abuse, 13
Male therapists, 142
Massage therapists, 142–43
Masturbation, 28, 37, 44, 97, 98, 187
Medical procedures, unnecessary, 26, 28–29
Medical professional, 16
Medication. *See* Psychiatric drugs.
Meditation
  Temple of the Heart, 158–59
Meditations, healing energy, 125–32
  Blue Sphere meditation, 130–32
  Earth Healing meditation for men, 125, 128–30, 132
  Earth Healing meditation for women, 125, 126–28, 132
Memories. *See* Body memories; Cognitive memory; Emotional memories; Spontaneous memories.
Memory repression (MR), 48,

49–51, 93, 175
  and age, 49–50. *See also*
  Repressed memories.
Men, 96, 142
  Earth Healing meditation for,
    125, 128–30, 132
  questions on sexual history,
    186–87
Mental illness, 170
Mental "jumps," 60
"Mentally undressing," 27
Mental pictures. *See* Images.
Mental state, during physical
    sexual abuse incident, 188
Messages, negative inner, 219
Migraine headaches, 68
Milestones, 182, 183–86, 206,
    207, 209
Mind, 84, 88–90, 91. *See also*
    Conscious mind; Uncon-
    scious mind.
Minimization, denial by, 53
Ministers, 43–44. *See also*
    Clergy; Priests.
Minor illnesses, chronic, 57,
    68–69
Mood swings, 147, 149
Mother, 10, 14, 21, 22, 59, 102,
    156. *See also* Earth Mother.
  dialoguing with, 180–81
  letter to deceased, 178–79
Mouth-to-mouth sexual kissing,
    26
MPD. *See* Multiple personality
    disorder.
MR. *See* Memory repression.
Multigenerational incest, 15, 23
Multiple personality disorder
    (MPD), 57, 67–68

Music, for meditations and exer-
    cises, 110, 126, 128, 130, 158
"My Body" section, of Healing
    Journal, 166, 191–96
  dialoguing with your body,
    192–94, 201

N
Nanny, 16, 136
Nausea, 86, 123
Negative self-talk, replaced by
    affirmations for healing,
    219–22
Newspaper carrier, 18
Nightmares, 56, 62–63, 212
Nudity, 27, 28
Numbness, emotional, 46, 51, 56,
    59–60, 93
Nutrition, 145

O
Objects, 26, 88, 132
Offender behavior, 57, 71–72
Older boys, 132
One-time violent abusive inci-
    dent, 20
Open-ended groups, 145
Opposite-sex therapist, 142
Oral abuse, 25, 26
Oral rape, 64, 132, 133
Oral sex, 20, 33, 43–44, 69, 106,
    123, 150
Orgasmlike experiences, 36
Orgasms, 187
Out-of-body experiences, 51
Outpatient programs, 146
Overeaters Anonymous, 221
Overeating, 192, 194

P

Pain. *See also* Held pain.
vs. core defenses, 54–56
and denial, 52
externalizing, 92, 95–96, 100–101
measuring, 20–21
in recovery, 75–76
Painting. *See* Creative coloring and artwork.
Panic attacks, 42, 57, 65
Parent/child sexual equalization, 40, 41
Parent effectiveness classes, 152
Parenting, 151–54
inner child, 113–15
Parent(s), 233
in dysfunctional family, 47–48
and emotional sexual abuse incident, 189
and nudity, 27
Past. *See also* Milestones.
forgetting about, 232
validating, 164
Pelvic area, 121, 123, 125, 126, 127, 129
and held pain, 117–18
"Personal History" section, of Healing Journal, 166, 182–90
milestones, 183–86
sexual abuse incident, writing about, 187–90
sexual history, 186–87
Personalities, 68
"Personal space," 117
Perverted activity, 179
Photographs, 206
sexually explicit, 28

Physical force, 30
Physical sexual abuse, 24, 25–38, 39, 64, 85
anal abuse, 25, 26
animal, sexual behavior with, 25, 27–28
combined with emotional sexual abuse, 42
dressed in adult sexual clothing, 25, 28
health procedures, inappropriate, 26, 29
medical procedures, unnecessary, 26, 28–29
oral abuse, 25, 26
pornography, made to participate in, 25, 28
privacy violations, 25, 27
seductive, 34–38
touching or rubbing, inappropriate, 25, 27
vaginal/penis abuse, 25, 26
violent, 29–33
watching or hearing someone else being sexually abused, 25
Physical sexual abuse incident, 188
Physicians. *See* Doctors.
Pictures, childhood, 207, 209
Pillow, hitting, 95, 100, 101, 119, 121, 124
Playing doctor, 7, 184–85
"Playing in the woods" milestone, 184–85
Pneumonia, 57
Police officer, 20
Pornographic magazines, 18

Pornography made to participate in, 25, 28
Positive statements, affirmations as, 220
Presents, and seductive physical abuse, 35
Priests, 18. *See also* Clergy; Ministers.
Privacy, 120
  violations, 25, 27
Professional help, 76, 233
  and offender behavior, 71–72
Psychiatric drugs, 147
Puberty, 186
Punching, 30
  air, 121
Punishment, 30

Q
Quality relationships, 81

R
Rage, 95, 101, 116, 122. *See also* Anger; Release of anger/rage, standing.
  at accomplice, 21–22
  in discovery stage, 78
  at God, 223–26
  pushing outward, 120–21
  writing about, 13–14
Rape, 11, 25. *See also* Anal rape; Gang rape; Oral rape.
Recovery, 75–91, 155, 234
  active healing stage, 77, 79–80, 82, 89, 92, 93, 149
  beginning, 76, 232
  discovery stage, 77–78, 81–82, 89, 93
  and Healing Journal, 163–64

integration stage, 77, 80–81, 82, 90, 125
  pain in, 75–76
  possibilities of, 231–32
  as process, not event, 232
  reviewing, in "Integration" section, 227–30
  and sexual relationships, 149–51, 235
  stages of, 75–77, *77*, 232
  time needed for, 231–32
  and whole person, 84–91, *84*
Rectal bleeding, 64, 86
Rectal temperature-taking, 29
Regressing, 106
Relatives, 152, 172
Release of anger/rage, standing, 121
Release of grief/loss, sitting curled up in fetal position, 121, *121*
Repressed memories, 19, 84–85, 182, 205. *See also* Memory repression.
  in discovery stage, 77–78
  and fatigue, chronic, 66–67
  and integration stage, 80–81
  and minor illnesses, chronic, 68
Reproduction, questions about, 7
Reproductive organs, 68, 117
"Reprogramming" mind, 219
Resistance, and healing process, 78
Risk taking, 62. *See also* High-risk behavior.
Resolution dreams, 214
Restraining, 30

Ritual sexual abuse, 30, 31, 68
Rocking, 136–38
"Roller-coaster rides," in recovery, 78, 80
Rubbing. *See* Touching or rubbing, inappropriate.

S
Sad feelings, 200
Sadistic ceremonies, 31
Safe place, 120, 139–59, 233
    family of choice, 157–58
    family of origin, 154–57
    parenting, 151–54
    sexual relationship, 148–51
    Temple of the Heart meditation, 158–59
    therapist, 140–44
    treatment options, 144–48
Same-sex relationship, 148
Same-sex therapist, 142
Satanic ceremonies, 31
Saying no. *See* Boundaries.
Screaming, 95, 100, 101, 109, 116, 119, 120, 121
Secondary consequences, of child sexual abuse, 56–72, 87
    attention span, shortened, 56, 60
    body memories, 56, 64
    body objectification, 57, 65–66
    compulsive-addictive diseases, 57, 67
    confused thinking, 56, 61
    emotional experiences, narrow range of, 56, 58
    emotional flooding, 56, 58–59
    fatigue, chronic, 57, 66–67
    flashbacks, 56, 63–64
    helplessness, 56, 61–62
    hopelessness, 56, 61–62
    intimacy dysfunction, 57, 70–71
    minor illnesses, chronic, 57, 68–69
    multiple personality disorder (MPD), 57, 67–68
    nightmares, 56, 62–63
    numbness, emotional, 56, 59–60
    offender behavior, 57, 71–72
    panic attacks, 57, 65
    sexual dysfunction, 57, 69–70
Secrets, 43–44, 122
    and seductive physical abuse, 37
Seductive emotional sexual abuse, 24, 40–42, 50, 52
Seductive incest, 17
Seductive physical abuse, 34–38
    case of, 34–35
    survivors of, 35–38
Self concept, 197
Self-description, 197–99, 203–4
Self-destructive behavior, 113–15
Self-Discovery section, in Healing Journal, 167, 197–204
    feelings responses, 199–201
    feelings statements, 200–203
    and others, 199
    self-description, 197–99, 203–4
Self-image, 196, 219. *See also* Sexual self-image.
Self-nurturance, 79, 83
Self-worth, 88
Sex, 3

information about, 7, 186
Sexual abuse, violent, 29–33
Sexual abuse incident
    emotional, 189–90
    physical, 188–89
    writing about, 187–90
Sexual beating, 30. *See also*
    Beating.
Sexual behavior, compulsive, 67
Sexual center, 126
Sexual dysfunction, 42, 57, 69–
    70, 86
Sexual energy, 3
Sexual energy center, and held
    pain, 117–18
Sexual history, questions on,
    186–87
Sexual identity, 3, 69
"Sexualized," 37, 38
Sexual preference, 148
Sexual relationships, 148–51
    outside support for, 150
    and recovery, 149–51, 235
Sexual self, 69
Sexual self-image, 40
Sexual self-portrait, 195
Sexual stimulation, and seductive
    physical abuse, 36, 37–38
Sexual threats, 50
Sexual "toy," 26
Sexual trauma, 46
Sexual traumatization, 44–45,
    45
Shaking, 119, 121, 124
Shame, 122, 201
    and seductive physical abuse,
    34
    and violent emotional sexual
    abuse, 39–40

Shock state, in traumatization
    process, 46–47
Shouting, 31, 32, 119
Siblings, 173
    birth order of, 177
    questions on, 177
Sickness, 193. *See also* Minor
    illnesses, chronic.
Sighing, 121
Single-event sexual abuse, 19
Single parent, 154
Sisters, 10, 14, 189
Slapping, 30
Sleep, 63, 66, 147
Smoking, 114–15
Sobbing, 95, 101, 109, 119, 121,
    124, 136, 137
"Special status," and seductive
    physical abuse, 36–37
Spirit, 84, 90–91
    and magical inner child, 107
Spiritual activities, 81
Spiritual exploration, 224–25
"Spiritual Reflections" section,
    in Healing Journal, 167,
    223–26
    letter writing, 224
    spiritual exploration, 224–25
"Splitting off," 51
Spontaneous memories, 63
Stepbrother, 10, 87
Stepfamily, 175, 177
Stepfather, 10, 15, 34–35, 69, 81,
    82, 217
Stepmother, 10
Stepsister, 10
Strangers, 19–21, 52
Stress, 201, 235. *See also* Tension.

and multiple personality dis-
    order, 68
Support person, 119
Suppositories, 29
"Surrogate spouse" scenario, 41
"Survival alert," 54
Survival living, 72
    and tension, 54–56
Survivors, 54
    of child sexual abuse, 4–5, 15–
        16, 19–20
    of seductive physical abuse,
        35–38
Survivors' support groups, 148,
        232, 233
    and Healing Journal, 163–64
    and healing techniques, 76–77
    and therapist, finding, 140
Swinger magazines, 69
"Switching off" feelings, 46, 51
Symptoms. See Secondary conse-
    quences.

T
Tape-recording, for meditations,
    126, 128, 158
Teacher, 16
Temple of the Heart meditation,
    158–59
Tension, 93, 200. See also Stress.
    and survival living, 54–56
Terror, 32, 122. See also Fear.
    and torture, 31
Therapeutic environment, 120
Therapist, 96, 150
    female, 142
    finding good, 140–44, 233–34
    male, 142
    massage, 142–43

opposite-sex, 142
personal referral to, 140
questions for, 140–41
relationship to, 142
same-sex, 142
test of, 142
Therapy group, and Healing
    Journal, 163–64. See also
    Group therapy.
Throat, physical trauma in,
    132–34
Time, 120, 164
Tiredness. See Fatigue, chronic.
Toilet, going to, 27, 189
Toilet training, 6
Torture, 30–31, 50, 68
Total denial, 53
Touch, healing, 101, 134–38
    in group setting, 136–38
Touching or rubbing, inappro-
    priate, 25, 27
Toxic energy, 121–22
Toys, 205
    sexual, 26
Trauma
    inability to resolve, 47–48
    reexperiencing, 92, 95, 100
    sexual, 46
Traumatization process, 44–54
    and child, 45–46
    core defenses, 48–54
    inability to resolve trauma,
        47–48
    sexual trauma, 46
    sexual traumatization, 44–45,
        45
    shock state, 46–47
Treatment options, 144–48
    group therapy, 144

individual therapy, 144
intensive treatment programs,
    146–47
psychiatric drugs, 147
support groups, 148
treatment programs, 145–46
Treatment programs, 145–46
    inpatient, 145–46
    intensive, 146–47
    outpatient, 146
Trembling, 121
Trust, and inner child, 112
Twelve Steps of Alcoholics
    Anonymous (AA), 148
Twelve-step support group, 82,
    135, 148
Tying, 30

U
Uncle, 9, 10, 23, 53, 89, 97–98,
    100, 171, 177
"Unconscious" abuse, 6
Unconscious mind, 48, 63, 212,
    219
"Unfelt" feelings, 72
"Unsent" letters, 178–79

V
Vaginal douches, 29
Validation, 79, 164
Violent abusive incident, one-
    time, 20
Violent emotional sexual abuse,
    39–40
Violent sexual abuse, 50
    and dissociation, 51
Vision, inner, 110
Visualization, 114, 125, 130
Vomiting, 123

Vulnerability, 101

W
Walking, 193
"Walling off" feelings, 70
Washing, 6
Watching or hearing someone
    else being sexually abused,
    25, 28
Weekend retreat, 146
"Welcoming Inner Child" sec-
    tion, in Healing Journal,
    167, 205–11
    dialoguing with inner child,
    208–11
    letter writing, 206–8
Whole person, 84–91,
    body, 84, 85–86
    emotions, 84, 86–88
    mind, 84, 88–90
    spirit, 84, 90–91
"Why me?" question, 223, 224
Women, 14, 96, 142, 172
    Earth Healing meditation for,
    125, 126–28, 132
    questions on sexual history,
    186–87
Workaholism, 67
Wound, 3–4
    exposing, 92, 93–95, 99–
    100
    guiding healing energy into,
    after emotional release
    work, 116–25,
    healing, 92, 96–97, 101
Wounded heart, and Blue Sphere
    meditation, 130–32
Wounded inner child, 104–7,
    109, 205

parenting, 113–15
Writing, 95. *See also* Letter writing.
  affirmations, 220
  as cleansing, 218

Writing exercises, in Healing Journal, 164–65

Y
Yelling, 121

ABOUT THE AUTHOR

Wayne Kritsberg is internationally recognized for his pioneering work with adult survivors of childhood sexual trauma and Adult Children of Alcoholics. Wayne also leads counselor training and personal recovery workshops throughout the international community and maintains a private practice in Olympia, Washington, where he lives with his family.

TO THE READER

It is not always possible for me to answer the mail I receive from readers. However, I greatly appreciate learning about your experiences in working with this material. If you would like to share your experience, please write to: Wayne Kritsberg, 2103 Harrison NW, Suite 2163, Olympia, WA 98502.

The *Healing Journal* described in Part Three of this book is available by mail order. This journal is completely assembled with printed dividers and can be purchased either singly or in quantity. To order the *Healing Journal* and Wayne Kritsberg's audiotapes, or to receive information about workshops and intensives, please call 1-800-452-5362 or write to: The Address above.